Forthcoming
in the same
SCREEN SERIES
edited by Peter Cowie
produced by The Tantivy Press

GERMANY
by Felix Bucher

SWEDEN
by Peter Cowie

JAPAN
by Arne Svensson

ITALY
by Felix Bucher & Hanspeter Manz

AMERICAN COMEDY
Since Sound
by Allen Eyles

Reference volumes
published in
**THE INTERNATIONAL
FILM GUIDE SERIES**

A DICTIONARY
OF THE CINEMA
by Peter Graham

THE WESTERN
by Allen Eyles

BRITISH CINEMA
by Denis Gifford

screen
SERIES

EASTERN EUROPE

AN ILLUSTRATED GUIDE
BY NINA HIBBIN

A. ZWEMMER LTD., LONDON
A. S. BARNES & CO., NEW YORK

Acknowledgments

I WOULD LIKE TO THANK the following organisations and their staffs for supply of information, photographs, etc.: British-Albanian Friendship Society, Cinémathéque Nationale Bulgare, Czechoslovak Film Institute, Ceskoslovensky Filmexport, Institut für Filmwissenschaft (Berlin), Staatliches Filmarchiv der D.D.R., Hungarofilm, Film Polski (Warsaw), Film Polski (London), Romania Film, The Association of Filmworkers of the U.S.S.R., Sovexport (Moscow), Sovexport (London), The Editorial Board of *Kino Slovar* (Moscow), Zagreb-Film, Institut za Film (Belgrade), Hungarian News Agency (London), British Film Institute, Gala Films.

And warm individual thanks to: W. B. Bland, G. Stoyanov-Bigor, Mercia Mac-Dermott, N. Bistrov, Dr. S. Zvonícek, Eckart Janke, Dr. Freyer, Dr. Krautz, Stanley Forman, Irina Fick, Claire Kristóf, E. Gavai, W. K. Grabowski, Boleslaw Sulik, Mrs. Vilk, Ion Mihaileanu, Viorica Munteanu, A. Karaganov, A. Novogrudsky, E. Dobin, Y. Khodjaev, N. Steklov, N. Ogneev, Prof. Manevitch, Prof. Galperin, Peter Cowie, Z. Matko, M. Ilić, Sally Hibbin, Eric Hibbin.

TO ERIC AND SALLY
for their massive help and tolerance

COVER STILLS
Front: Bondarchuk's WAR AND PEACE
Back: Forman's THE FIREMEN'S BALL (top)
Tatiana Samoilova in Zarkhi's ANNA KARENINA (below)

Library of Congress Catalog Card No.: 69-14898

SBN Number: 498 07421 8 (U.S.)

302 02006 3 (U.K.)

Printed in the United States of America

Contents

GERMANY (EAST) 47

POLAND 86

U.S.S.R. 132

CZECHO-SLOVAKIA 25

HUNGARY 62

ROMANIA 116

YUGO-SLAVIA 170

BULGARIA 11

ALBANIA 8

INDEX TO FILM TITLES 193

Choice of Entries

THE CINEMA OF EASTERN EUROPE is arousing an increasing amount of interest as first one country, then another, bursts forth with fresh creative achievements. National film weeks, the work of specialised cinemas and small distributing companies and international cinema series on television are helping to keep the public abreast of developments.

This guide has been designed to help filmgoers and televiewers to get to know more about the films they have enjoyed and the film-makers they admire, and at the same time to provide students of cinema with a compact source of information, most of which has not been previously collated in English, about filming in Eastern Europe.

In deciding whose biographies to include and whose to omit I have borne both these interests in mind.

The main basis of selection of directors has been their contribution to postwar cinema, especially in the past decade, with distribution or knowledge of their films in the West as an important factor. I have also tried to reflect the special features of each country's film-making by including, for instance, a high proportion of animators in the Yugoslav section and of documentarists in the German section.

These factors apply even more strongly to the selection of actors, actresses, cameramen, scriptwriters and composers, which has necessarily had to be more restricted.

The process of selection and elimination has been particularly difficult in the U.S.S.R. section, from which I have reluctantly had to omit some of the "greats" of world cinema where it appeared that their major contribution was made before the war. In taking this decision I was partly influenced by the fact that information about them is fairly readily available elsewhere (e.g. Peter Graham's A *Dictionary of the Cinema*, in a parallel series to that of the present volume).

N.H.

How To Use the Guide

THERE ARE two main starting-points from which you can track down information. You can look up names in the national sections, each of which has biographies of leading film personalities, in alphabetical order. Or you can look up film titles in the title index, which lists all the films mentioned in the biographies.

If you look up a film title, the reference numbers beside it will lead you to the relevant biographies. Production dates normally appear in the directors' biographies, and are not repeated in the other biographies. They are also given in the title index in brackets (together with the director's name, when the director himself has no biographical entry).

The title index includes the original title of every feature film listed. Simplified phonetic systems have been used for the transliteration of Russian and Bulgarian titles. These systems do not necessarily apply to name entries, because they would cause confusion over familiar spellings (e.g. Heifitz would become Kheifits).

Each national section is prefaced by a brief survey of postwar production. Bold type has been used in the prefaces for the names of directors whose biographies are included. The name of the director and the date of production is given, in the preface, along with the film title, when the director has no biographical entry. Films mentioned by name only also appear in the biographies; you can therefore trace information about them through the title index.

In order to bring the biographies as up-to-date as possible, films which were under production when this book went to press have been included. The titles of films dated 1969 should therefore be treated as provisional.

To avoid a proliferation of initials, film schools are referred to by the name of the city in which they are situated (e.g. Graduated Budapest 1958).

Abbreviations have been kept to the minimum:

> asst. — assistant.
> asst. dir. — assistant director.
> co-prod. — co-production.
> doc. — documentary.

Dates are given in full except in the filmography part of the biographical entries where, for space reasons, the last two digits only are given (e.g. 68 instead of 1968).

ALBANIA

ALBANIA

Pop. 1,394,000. Mainly agricultural country with a very young, small but developing film industry.

Production:

Documentaries—about 12 a year. Feature films: 1957 to 1965—one a year; 1966—2; 1967—3; 1968—4 (planned)

Cinemas:

1938—17; 1964—76 (7 in Tirana). In addition to permanent cinemas, mobile cinemas carry films to the villages, even to the remotest mountain areas. (In the first three months of 1968, over 1,000 filmshows were given in the district of Saranda alone.)

Studios

"Shaipëria e re"—New Albanian Studios.

Albania is by far the youngest and smallest film-making country in Eastern Europe. Before the war there was no film industry at all.

The first film was a newsreel of President Hoxha's visit to Southern Albania in 1947. It was shot by Hamdiu, one of the founders of documentary production. Until 1957 production was confined to documentaries and newsreels, with the single exception of the feature film *The Great Warrior Skanderbeg*, made in Albania by the Soviet director **Yutkevitch** in 1954. It told the epic story of a national hero (played by the Georgian actor Georgi Khavara) who fought against the Turkish oppressors in the Fifteenth century.

Regular feature production started in 1957, four years after the opening of the modern studios "Shaipëria e re," under the auspices of the Albanian State Film Enterprise. Up to 1966 feature film output was at the rate of one a year. The majority of films were based on war, resistance and historical themes. A notable exception was *Tana*, made by the talented young director Dhamo in 1958, which dealt with contemporary life in the countryside.

In 1966 the tiny industry took a leap forward by producing two full-length features, *The Commissar of Light* and *Echoes on the Shore*. The second of these, an anti-Fascist drama based on the play *The Fisherman's Family* by Sulejman Pitarka, aroused some controversy but was generally considered to be the most mature artistic achievement to date. In particular, it succeeded in breaking away from the theatricality of some of the previous productions by using a sprinkling of new actors and actresses who were beginning to develop a genuine screen style.

In 1967 the Albanian State Enterprise proudly announced a plan for three feature films, although in the event the most important of them, *Broad Horizons*, was complete in 1968. Set among the workers of a dockyard, this was the first film to deal with contemporary problems in industry.

Over 200 people are now working in the industry, which planned to complete 4 features in 1968.

Documentary production includes films depicting social change in the countryside ,and in industry, films about national figures of history, literature and art, and popular

THE GREAT WARRIOR SKANDERBEG

science films. Important documentaries of the mid-Sixties include, *Vangjush Mio—People's Painter*, made in 1966 to commemorate the artist's Seventy-fifth anniversary, *The Victors* (both in colour) and *In the Flames of the Revolution* (full-length), 1967.

Among the leading film-makers are:

Dhimitër Anagosti—Shot: *Our Soil, Discussion* (with Gjika). Directed: *The Commissar of Light* (with Gjika) 66; *Silent Duel* 67.

Kristaq Dhamo—Directed: *Tana* 58; *Storm* 59; *The First Years; Special Duty.*

Gësim Erebara—Directed: *Vangjush Mio, Victory Over Death* (with Milkani).

Viktor Gjika—Shot: *Discussion* (with Anagosti), *Special Duty* (with Milkani). Directed and shot: *Commissar of Light* (with Anagosti), *Broad Horizons* 67-8; *The Victors* 68.

Hysen Hakani—Directed: *The Discussion, Our Soil, Echoes on the Shore.*

Piro Milkani—Shot: *Special Duty, Vangjush Mio, The First Years.* Directed: *Victory over Death* (with Erebara) 67; *The Victors* (with Gjika) 68.

Endri Keko—Documentary director. Films include: *Letter from a Kuci Doctor, Mountain Village School, The First Shock Brigade, They Carve a New Way Forward, In the Flames of the Revolution* 67.

Marianthi Xhako—Documentary director. Films include: *Report from Kurnesh, George Kastriot—Skanderbeg, In the Current of Life.*

Other documentary directors: M. Kochi, S. Musha, I. Nani, X. Firzati, D. Lala.

Note:—   The original titles of the feature films mentioned in this section can be found in the title index at the back.

BULGARIA

BULGARIA

Pop. 8,206,000. Small, mainly agrarian country with a small but steadily growing film industry.

Production:

	Features	Documentaries	Popular Science	Cartoon	Puppet
1952	2	37	18	1	1
	increasing by average of one a year to				
1960	10	52	48	4	4
1967	10	86	100	8	4

Cinemas:

Prewar 165 (37 of them rural)
1967—2,957 (2,597 rural. 43 in Sofia).

Studios:

Film Centre halfway up Vitosha mountain, 12 km south of Sofia. **Feature Studio** produces feature and cartoon films and dubs foreign films. **Documentary Studio** produces documentaries, newsreels and satirical screen magazine Focus. **Popular Science Studio** produces popular science, educational and publicity films and film strips.

Training:

No film school. Actors and actresses can train at Sofia Institute of Theatrical Arts. Film-makers usually train at Moscow, Lódź or Prague; some at Budapest, Potsdam and Paris.

The general backwardness of the Balkan countries made them all comparatively late entrants into the field of film-making. Although Bulgaria was the first Balkan country to produce films, it is one of the youngest film-making countries in Eastern Europe.

Its first feature *Bulgarians Are Gentlemen (The Gallant Bulgarian)* was made in 1910 by Vassil Gendov, a film pioneer who battled for thirty years for national film-making. The early pioneers had no resources and worked under very primitive conditions; they raised what money they could on their own account, using whatever they could gather in the way of technical help. Up to the Second World War, the total feature production was about 50 films, of which only a few—*Under the Old Sky* (N. Larin 1922), *Graves Without Crosses* (Boris Greshov 1931); *The Cairn* (Alexander Zazov 1936); *Voevoda Strahil* (Yosip Novak 1938)—remain noteworthy. In the Thirties, with the advent of sound, a few intensely nationalistic films were produced by commercial interests.

The first documentary was made in 1912 during the Balkan war. Total prewar production of documentaries was about 200, plus a solitary cartoon film.

It was not until towards the end of the war (1944) that the basis of a national film industry was laid, with the establishment of the first Bulgarian Film Foundation (Bulgarsko Delo). The nationalised industry was established in 1948; first feature after nationalisation was *Kalin the Eagle* (Borozanov 1950).

After the War: With little experience or tradition behind them, the new post-war directors had to carve their own way forward, often using Soviet production of that period as their pattern. Early postwar productions like *Dawn Over the Homeland, Danka, Under the Yoke, Song of Man* and *People of Dimitrovgrad* were based on strong, patriotic anti-Fascist themes, sometimes forceful and moving, but inclined to simple heroics and a black-and-white approach. It was in this period that **Zhandov**, **Marinovich** and **Sharaliev** began their careers as directors. Towards the end of the Fifties a new generation of directors, representative of the post-war youth, began to emerge. In the struggle against the older, more dogmatic approach, directors like **Vulchanov** and **Radev** were well to the fore. Others to emerge in this period were **Zheljazkova, Kovachev, Mundrov, Korabov, Piskov, Yanchev, Petrov, Sharland-giev** and **Heskia**. At first, anti-Fascism and the struggle for national independence remained popular themes. But with the end of the decade the approach became more complex and human. The Bulgarian-G.D.R. co-production *Stars* (1959), a notable attempt at finding a personalised retrospective evaluation of Nazism, was a turning-point. Others that followed include *Poor Man's Street, The First Lesson, We Were Young, The Captured Squadron, The King and the General* and *The Longest Night.*

It was not until the mid-Sixties that contemporary themes began to be successfully developed, with films like *The She-Wolf, The Troubled Road* (Yakim Yakimov, 1965), *Hot Noon* (Zacco Heskia, 1966), *Knight Without Armour, Men* (Vassil Mirchev 1966) and *The Attached Balloon. Sidetrack* struck a new contemporary note both in content and style.

In the past decade there has been a small but sustained output of detective and spy stories and thrillers.

Cartoons and documentaries: Bulgarian cartoons leapt into the world class largely through the work of the brilliant animator, **Todor Dinov**, pioneer of animation within his own country. Other gifted cartoonists include **Donju Donev, Stoyan Dokov, Hristo Topousanov, Stefan Topaldgikov**, Radka Buchvarova and Zdeba Doicheva.

Documentary and popular science films range over a wide field, sometimes simply informative, sometimes arguing for the acceptance of new ideas. Among the sources of information for popular dissemination is Bulgaria's rich and constantly developing store of archaeological treasures. Leading documentarists include Yuri Arnaudov, Numa Belogorski, **Roumen Grigorov, Hristo Kovachev, Yuli Stoyanov, Nevena Tosheva** and **Lada Boyadgieva**.

1 Andonov, Ivan (1934-   ). Popular actor of stage and screen. Graduated Sofia Theatre Institute, 1956. Started acting career in provinces. Member of National Youth Theatre and of Satirical Theatre. Films include: *Too Late for Love, On the Little Island, On the Eve of the 13th, The Golden Tooth, On the Pavement, Sidetrack.*

2 Boyadgieva, Lada (1927-   ). Leading documentarist with over 40 films to her credit. Graduated in journalism, Paris, and in cinematography, Prague, 1953. At Documentary Studio until 1960, when she transferred to Popular Science Studios. Directed feature *Return*, 1967. Documentaries and popular science films include: *How Tales Come to Life* 56; *Songs and Dances by the River Mesta* 58; *Story Books* 63; *Palmira* 63; *A Trip* 63; *Return of the Ikons* 65.

3 Bratanov, Ivan (1920-1968). Screen actor who was much in demand for tense and troubled roles. After release from concentration camp, 1944, worked as drama teacher and stage actor. Joined Feature Film Studio in 1950 and has since taken part in a score of films including: *Septembrists, Song for Man, Troubled Road, People of Dimitrovgrad, First Lesson, The Stoublen Lindens, The Longest Night.*

4 Buchvarova, Radka (1918-   ). Prize-winning woman cartoon and popular science director. Graduated Institute of Pictorial Art, Sofia. Began film career 1948. Films: *The Mouse and the Pencil* (co-dir. Zdenka Doicheva) 58; *The Snowman* 60; *Long-Ears* 61; *Deceitful Gosho* 63; *Fable, The Proud Bulb* 64; *The Star* 65; *A House on Wheels, What Shall I Be?* 66; *The Balloons* 67.

5 Dakovski, Dako (1919-1962). Director best known for films dealing with peasant life. Wide experience as stage actor before graduating Moscow, 1952. General Secretary of the Film Union for many years. Final film *Kaloyan* was unfinished. Other films: *Under the Yoke* 52; *The Troubled Road* 55; *The Secret Supper of the Sedmatsi* 57; *The Stoublen Lindens* 60.

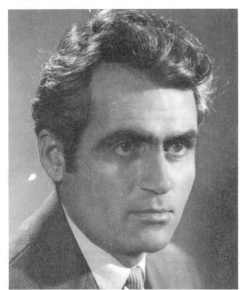

14 BULGARIA

6   Dinov, Todor (1919-   ). Gifted animator of international repute. Artistic manager of Cartoon Department at Sofia Feature Film Studios and Secretary of Union of Film-makers. Films: *Brave Marco* 55; *The Careful Little Angel* 56; *The Outwitted Fox* 57; *Little Ann, In the Country of the Cannibals* 58; *Prometheus, The Secret of the Golden Shoes* 59; *Tale of the Pine Bough* 60; *Lightning Road, Little Grey Thing* 62; *The Apple* (co-dir. Doukov), *Jealousy* 63; *Adventures, The Daisy* 65; *Expelled from Paradise* 67.

7   Donev, Donyu (1929-   ). Caricaturist and cartoon director. Graduated Institute of Pictorial Art, Sofia 1954. Newspaper cartoonist 1954-6. Joined Cartoon Film Dept. 1956, first as asst. dir. then as director. Soyuzmultfilm, Moscow 1959-60. Films: *Duet* 61; *The Queue* 63; *The Second I* 64; *A Tale for Everyone* 65; *The Second Bottle* 65; *Spring* 66; *Marksmen, A Joke* 67; *The Friends of Gosho the Elephant* 67; *The Cow Who . . .* (co-dir. Topouzanov) 68.

8   Doukov, Stoyan (1931-   ). Director, producer and scriptwriter of cartoon films. Graduated Higher Institute of Pictorial Art, Sofia. Worked as artist 1958-62. Films directed: *The Apple* (co-dir. Dinov) 63; *The Golden Treasure, Beginning* 64; *Adventure* 65; *Journey in the Cosmos* (co-dir. Anton Trayanov), *There Was a Man Roaming* 66; *Home-Castles* 67.

9   Ganev, Hristo (1924-   ). Prize-winning scriptwriter. Graduated Moscow (under Arnshtam) 1950. Directed prize-winning full-length documentary *Holiday of Hope*, 1962. Films scripted include: *Song for Man, Two Victories, We Were Young, Parade of Disgrace*.

10   Georgiev, Georgi (1926-   ). Distinguished stage and screen actor. Graduated Institute of Theatrical Art Sofia 1953. Member of National Theatre, Sofia. Films include: *A Land of Ours, Troubled Road, First Lesson, On the Eve of the 13th, The Steep Path, We Were Young, The Black River, The King*

and the General, The Longest Night, Scent of Almonds.

11 Grigorov, Roumen (1921-   ). Leading documentarist and newsreel director. Appointed Director of Documentary Film Studio 1951. Films include full-length documentary on Georgi Dimitrov *He Lives On* 1949. Also: *New Initiatives, Struggle for Peace, Struggle for Bread* 50; *Story of the Homeland* 55; *Dawn Over the Danube* 56; *At Wembley Stadium* 57; *On the Will of Man* 59; *Songs of Motors* 61; *Eyes of the Sea* 63; *Shores and People* 64; *Bulgarian Summer, Visas for London, Science Workers* 66.

12 Haliolchev, Vassil (1908-   ). Veteran cameraman of documentaries and features. Graduated in cinematography in Paris where he was prewar political refugee. Returned to Bulgaria 1940. Began work as cameraman 1942, after release from concentration camp. Cameraman at the front. Shot first feature film *Redemption* in 1947. Cameraman of first film after nationalisation, *Kalin the Eagle.* Also shot: *Septembrists, First Point, Beyond the Horizon, We Were Young, Thirteen Days.*

13 Karamitev, Apostol (1923-   ). Prominent stage actor and member of National Theatre. Has appeared in many films, including: *Dawn Over the Homeland, Under the Yoke, Land of Ours, Song for Man, The Heroes of Shipka, It Happened in the Street, Legend of Love* (Czechoslovakian), *Favourite No. 13, Two under the Sky, Knight without Armour.*

14 Kokanova, Nevena (1938-   ). Very popular actress who rose rapidly to the top. Left school 1956 and made

film début in *Too Late for Love?* same year. Subsequent films include: *On a Quiet Evening, The Steep Path, Be Happy, Ann!, Tobacco, The Inspector and the Night, The Peach Thief, Carambol, The Longest Night, Sidetrack, The Scent of Almonds.*

15 Kolarov, Dimo (1924-   ). Outstanding cameraman who works in close collaboration with Vulchanov. Graduated Moscow. Began work at Sofia Feature Film Studios 1960. Films include: *On the Little Island, The Commander of the Detachment, First Lesson, Sun and Shadow, The Inspector and the Night, The She-Wolf.*

16 Korabov, Nicolai (1929-   ). Feature director of generation that emerged in late Fifties. Graduated Moscow 1952. Worked in collaboration with Mundrov (q.v.). Feature films: *People of Dimitrovgrad* (with Mundrov) 56; *The Little Girl* 59; *Tobacco* 62; *Voula* 65.

17 Kovachev, Hristo (1929-   ). Prize-winning documentary film-maker.

Left: Nevena Kokanova in Radev's THE LONGEST NIGHT

Began career as cameraman at Documentary Studios 1950. Films include: *Steel Made in Bulgaria* 54; *Lights and People* 60; *People and Storms* 63; *Lime* 65; *From One to Eight, A Parade of Disgrace* 66; *Day without Land, Threads of the Rainbow, A Thousand Cranes* (full-length) 68.

ending. Graduated Moscow 1950. Collaborated with Korabov on documentary about the poet Nicola Vaptzarov and on feature *People cf Dimitrovgrad* 1956. Then directed: *The Commander of the Detachment* 59; *Captured Squadron* 62; *The End of the Summer* 67.

18   Marinovich, Anton (1907-   ). Prolific veteran director with wide experience in film journalism and distribution. Made several thrillers. Films: *New Days Will Come* 45; *Ivan Sussanin, Dawn Over the Homeland* 51; *A Land of Ours* 53; *Daughter-in-Law* 54; *Adam's Rib* 56; *The Geraks, Poor Man's Joy* 58; *The Other Happiness* 60; *On the Eve of the 13th* 61; *The Golden Tooth* 62; *Midnight Adventure* 64; *On the Pavement* 67.

19   Mundrov, Dutcho (1920-   ). Feature director of generation that emerged in late Fifties. Actor in semi-professional theatre before war. Imprisoned by Fascists in wartime and sentenced to death but saved by war's

20   Peichev, Stefan (1905-   ). Veteran actor specialising in strong character roles. Wide prewar stage experience. Film *début* 1936. Postwar roles include: *Under the Yoke, Septembrists, Heroes of Shipka, It Happened in the Street, The Geraks, On the Little Island, Stars, The Steep Path, Tobacco, The Golden Tooth, Thirteen Days.*

21   Petrov, Valeri (1920-   ). Eminent poet and author who has scripted several films. Works in close association with Vulchanov (q.v.). Scenarios include: *On the Little Island, First Lesson, Sun and Shadow, Knight without Armour.*

22   Pironkov, Simeon (1927-   ). Composer, violinist and conductor. Composed the music for many of the best-

Two films by Radev: THE KING AND THE GENERAL with Peter Slabakov (above) and THE PEACH THIEF (with Rade Markovic) (below)

known films including: *On the Little Island, Stars, First Lesson, We Were Young, Sun and Shadow, The Inspector and the Night, The Peach Thief, The King and the General, The Longest Night, The Attached Balloon.*

23 Piskov, Hristo (1927-   ). Director of anti-Fascist and resistance films. Graduated Moscow 1954. Films: *A Lesson in History* (Soviet-Bulgarian co-prod.) 57; *Poor Man's Street, There Is No Death* 63.

24 Radev, Vulo (1923-   ). Distinguished director with richly human and poetic style. Graduated Moscow 1953. Worked as documentary director and cameraman until very striking *début* as feature director in 1964. Feature films: *The Peach Thief* 64; *The King and the General* 66; *The Longest Night* 67.

25 Shariliev, Borislav (1922-   ). Feature director of significance in early period of nationalisation. Early films have strong anti-Fascist themes. Actor in semi-

professional theatre before graduating in Romm's class, Moscow 1950. Films: *Song for Man* 54; *Two Victories* 56; *On a Quiet Evening* 60; *Two Under the Sky* 62; *Vaskata* (T.V. feature) 64; *Knight without Armour* 66.

26 Sharlandgiev, Ljubomir (1931-   ).Distinguished director with strong feeling for character conflict. Graduated Theatre Institute, Sofia, and at Moscow. Films: *A Chronicle of Sentiments* 62; *The Chain* 64; *Carambol* 66; *The Scent of Almonds* 67; *The Prosecutor* 68.

27 Slabakov, Peter (1923-   ). Outstanding stage and screen actor. Member of National Theatre, Sofia. Graduated Institute of Economics. Tried various jobs before starting as actor, 1953. Has played at National Theatres in Varna, Bourgass and Plovdiv. Film roles include: *There Is No Death, The Captured Squadron, Tobacco, The Intransigents, The King and the General, The End of the Summer, Shibil.*

28 Stoupel, Peter (1923-   ). Popular light composer who specialises in theatre and film music. Wrote music for many features, documentaries and cartoon shorts, including: *Two Victories, Favourite No. 13, Be Happy, Ann!, An Incredible Story, The Ancient Coin.*

29 Stoyanov, Todor (1930-   ). Talented cameraman who made a notable *début* as director with *Sidetrack* (1967) in collaboration with Grisha Ostrovski. Cameraman for: *Poor Man's Street, Two under the Sky, There Is No Death, The Peach Thief.*

30 Stoyanov, Yuli (1930-   ). Documentary director. Graduated Prague, 1956. Films: *A Hundred Days with the*

Right: Sharlandgiev's THE SCENT OF ALMONDS

Nevena Kokanova in Stoyanov's S₁. ΓTRACK

Ship "Bulgaria", For the Flourish of the Homeland 55; The Blue Stadium 57; To Distant Shores, In the Foothills of the Pirin Mountain 58; They Sang in Sofia 61; The Harbour 63; Days 64; Meeting of Friendship 65; Pages of a Culture's History 66; The Variety and Poetry Theatre 67.

31 Topaldgikov, Stefan (1909-   ). Director of puppet and popular science films. Graduated in law 1934. Worked as lawyer and sculptor. Popular Science films (1950-57) include: Radiography, In Our Caves, Koprivshtitsa, Nessebur, In the Shadow of the Ages. Puppet films include: Drake, Mirco the Invisible, The Match Box 58; Hats Down!, The Magic Hoe 60; Tourists, The Happy Man 61; The Naughty Chicken 62; The Three Heroes 64; Swan Lake 65.

32 Topouzanov, Hristo (1930-   ). Prize-winning puppet film directc Graduated at short-lived Three-Year Cinema School, Sofia 1954. Director at Popular Science Studio until 1959, where he made The Boyana Master, 1956. Joined Cartoon Film Department 1959. Puppet and animated films include: Nightingale's Tail 59; Parade 60; Easy-Breezy Seeks the Easy Way 61; Silence 62; Pictures from an Exhibition 63; Concert 64; Masquerade, The Scissors and the Little Boy 65; The Scissors and the Little Girl 66; I'm Five 67; The Cow Who . . . (co-dir. Donev) 68.

33 Tosheva, Nevena (1922-   ). Outstanding woman documentarist, with special interest in child and educational themes. Wide journalistic experience. Graduate in Bulgarian philology. Began film career 1951. Films include: Three

Teachers 62; *A Sketch* 63; *International Ballet Competition—Varna* 64; *The Village of Yastrebino* 65; *Bulgaria, Land, People, Sun, A Man for Man* 66; *Our Holiday, Am I So Bad?* 67.

34 Vagensetine, Anzhel (1922-   ). Eminent scriptwriter. Graduated Moscow, 1950. Films include: *Alarm, A Land of Ours, Septembrists, Adam's Rib, Two Victories, Stars, Two under the Sky, The Chain.*

35 Vulchanov, Rangel (1928-   ). Outstanding director with highly individual and imaginative style. First film was turning-point in struggle against screen dogmatism. Early work closely associated with the distinguished author Valeri Petrov. On leaving high school, tried various jobs. Graduated Sofia Institute of Theatrical Art, 1952. Films: *On the Little Island* 58; *First Lesson* 60; *Sun and Shadow* 62; *The Inspector and the Night* 63; *The She-Wolf* 65; *Between Two Worlds* (full-length documentary) 68; *Aesop* (Bulgarian-Czechoslovakian coprod.) 69.

36 Yanchev, Vladimir (1930-   ). Director with a special interest in comedy. Born in Moscow. Parents Bulgarian political emigrants. Graduated Moscow 1955; began work in Sofia Studios the same year. Films: *Favourite No. 13* 58; *Be Happy, Ann!* (co-prod. with Soviet Union) 61; *An Incredible Story* 64; *The Ancient Coin* 65; *The First Courier* (coprod. with U.S.S.R.) 68.

37 Yankov, Yanko (1924-   ). Feature director. Graduated Moscow (under Gerasimov) 1952. Made *début* as director with *On Holiday* (short) 1950. Feature films: *It Happened in the Street* 56; *Too Late for Love?* 57; *The Steep Path* 61; *The Intransigents* 64.

38 Zhandov, Zahari (1911-   ). Veteran director of popular anti-Fascist films. Began filming as an amateur before war. Directed several shorts during war and helped lay foundation of postwar Bulgarian cinema with a number of documentaries in immediate postwar period. Filmed Bulgarian part of Joris

Ivens's *First Days* 1949. Feature films: *Alarm* 51; *Septembrists* 54; *Land* 57; *Beyond the Horizon* 60; *The Black River* 64; *Shibil* 68.

39 Zheljazkova, Binka (1923-   ). Feature director best known for her prize-winning *We Were Young* 1961 which she followed with *The Attached Balloon* 1967. Graduated Sofia Theatre Institute 1958. Asst. dir. at Sofia Studio for many years.

Below: Zhandov's LAND

CZECHOSLOVAKIA

CZECHOSLOVAKIA

Pop. 14,272,000. A strong, expanding cinema with a long history of film-making.

Production:

	Full-length:			
	Features		Documentaries	
	Czech	Slovak	Czech	Slovak
1945	3	—	2	—
1950	21	3	5	2
1955	14	2	4	2
1960	27	4	1	—
1965	32	7	2	1
1967	33	7	—	—

Shorts:			
Documentaries		Cartoons	
Czech	Slovak	Czech	Slovak
38	23	35	—
49	24	46	2
51	20	60	8

Cinemas:

1939—1,254; 1945—1,656; 1966—3,584 (including large proportion of 16 mm theatres, about 130 open-air and about 12 mobile).

Studios:

Barrandov Studios, Prague—features
Koliba Studios, Bratislava—features, documentaries
Cartoon and Puppet Studios, Prague
Kudlov Studios, Gottwaldov (Moravia)—mainly documentaries

Training:

F.A.M.U.—Film and Television Faculty of the Academy of Performing Arts, Prague (referred to in biographies as "Prague"). Four-year and five-year courses in writing, direction, camera, documentary work, editing, production and theory.

When Czechoslovak cinema was nationalised in 1945 it already had forty-seven years of film-making behind it. The first films, made by Jan Křížnecký, were shown in 1898 and regular feature production began in 1908.

Although most of the 700 feature films made before 1945 were of a routine order, there was an impressive minority of lasting and worthwhile productions. The foundations of a national film tradition were laid in the last years of the silent era with films like Lamač's *Schweik*, Machatý's *Ecstasy* and *Erotikon*, Pražský's *The Amazing Battalion* and Junghan's *Such is Life*. Other significant directors were Anton, Slavinský, Krnaňský, Kubásek and **Frič**. **Frič**, whose *Jánošik* and *Revisor* were valuable contributions to the Thirties, and **Vávra**, who also made a number of outstanding films at that time, became leading forces in postwar cinema. A key film of the Thirties was Rovenský's *The River*. By the end of the decade the Barrandov Studios were working at full swing.

Thus, although Czech cinema was cut off from the rest of the world during the six years of Nazi occupation, it had plenty of experience to draw upon, and reasonable film-making facilities, in the early postwar days. Documentaries, cartoons and puppet films gained the first international successes, and these have remained a vital part of national film-making. Landmarks in the immediate postwar period were *Strike, Moon over the River, Kidnap* and the full-length puppet film *The Czech Year*. At first, feature production was undertaken by experienced film-makers like **Frič**, **Vávra**, **Weiss**, **Steklý** and **Krška**, but with the establishment of the Film Faculty, a new generation including **Krejčik**, **Kachyňa**, **Jasný**, **Lipský** and **Vláčil** achieved some distinguished successes in the Fifties. This was not a happy period for cinema in any of the Eastern European countries however, and feature production declined both in output and standard.

The situation was transformed in the early Sixties by the emergence of a very talented and forward-looking group of film-makers from the Film Faculty, who, with widely different styles and approaches, created the internationally-acclaimed Czech "new wave." They fell, very roughly, into two groups. **Chytilová**, **Schorm**, **Němec**, **Juráček**, **Jireš** were concerned mainly with the realm of ideas (although **Schorm**, in particular, expressed them in deeply personalised ways); while **Forman**, **Passe**, and **Menzel** were interested in observation of human character and frailty.

Vávra, **Kadár** and **Klos** were among the established directors closely associated with the "new wave." For a time, in the mid-Sixties, the movement was damped down by official pressures, but the sweeping changes in early 1968 were directed towards wide and free expansion of creativity, and despite the political upheavals of August that year, the situation in the film industry appeared reasonably stable. It was feared, however that censorship in the arts could become more severe.

Slovak Cinema: Film-making in Slovakia was almost non-existent until after the war although several Czech directors (including Machaty for *Ecstasy*) had used Slovak locations. **Frič**'s *Jánosik*, based on the legendary exploits of a Slovak folk hero, (played by **Bielik**) broke new ground. After the war, **Bielik** collaborated with **Frič** on *The Warning* and then made *The Wolves' Lair*, the first wholly Slovak feature film, at the newly-established Koliba Studios. Like many of the films that followed, it was about the Slovak national uprising of 1944. **Kadár's** comedy *Katya* was a further milestone.

Slovak cinema, like the Czech, leapt into life in the early Sixties, with directors **Uher**, **Solan** and **Barabáš** well to the fore. Uher's *Sunshine in a Net* was made in the same year as Chytiľová's *The Ceiling* (Czech) and these two films are considered to represent the beginning of the "new wave." Other Slovak directors who helped to bring Slovak cinema forward were Martin Hollý, Eduard Grečner and Juraj Herz. Newest "new wave" directors on the scene include **Jakubisko**.

Cartoon and Puppet Films: Fantasy film-making has been a consistent and very high-level aspect of postwar cinema, with **Trnka** whose *The Hands* is considered by many to be "the perfect film") as the indisputable artistic leader. Other important puppet and cartoon film-makers, all of whom are his pupils, are **Pojar**, **Brdečka**, Zdenek Miller, Zdenek Smetana, Vladimir Lehky, František Vystrčil and Pavel Prochazka. **Týrlová** specialises in films for young audiences and **Zeman** combines live action with animation in a highly individualised style. Among the up-and-coming animators, **Švankmajer** is outstanding.

40 Barabáš, Stanislav (1924-   ). Important Slovak director. Graduated at Prague. Made many documentaries. Feature films: *Song of the Grey Dove* 61; *Trio Angelos* 63; *Knell for the Barefooted* 65; *Tango for a Bear* 66; *The Gentle One* (TV) 68.

41 Bielik, Pal'o (1901-   ). A leading figure in Slovak cinema—as director, screenwriter and actor. Went into amateur theatricals after leaving business college: then acted in various Martin Frič films, including *Jánošík* 1936 (based on the life of a Slovak highwayman and folk hero). Spent several months in Nazi prison during war. Made documentary *Far Freedom* 1945 compiled from own camera records of wartime Slovak rising. Worked with Frič (q.v.) on first true Slovak feature *The Warning*. Acting role in *Tales by Čapek*. His films, all with Slovak themes, include a second version of *Jánošík* (parts 1 and 2). Films: *Fox Holes* 48; *The Dam* 50; *The Mountains Are Stirring* 52; *Friday the Thirteenth* 53; *Forty-four* 57; *Captain Dabač* 59; *Jánošík* 62-63; *The Hangman* 65; *The Three* 69.

42 Bočan, Hynek (1938-   ). One of the youngest new wave directors. Graduated Prague 1961. Assistant to Kachyňa, Němec and Weiss (all q.v.) before becoming director. Documentary: *Black Dolphin Camp* 66. Feature films:

Nobody Gets the Last Laugh 65; *Private Gale* 67; *Honour and Glory* 68.

43 Brdečka, Jiři (1917-   ). Director and screenwriter of fantasy and trick films: writer and journalist. Studied art history at Charles University until it was closed by the Nazis. Wrote Wild West parody *Lemonade Joe* 1940 (later filmed by Lipsky). Began film work as animator, 1943. Scenarios include: *The Springer and the S.S. Men*, *The Emperor's Baker*, *That Cat*, *Lemonade Joe*, *The Emperor and the Nightingale*, *Old Czech Legends*, *A Midsummer Night's Dream*. Films: *The Zeppelin and Love* 47; *A Comic History of Aviation* 58; *Look Out!* 59; *Our Red Riding Hood* 60;

Man under Water, The Television Fan 61; *Reason and Emotion* 62; *The Grotesque Chicken* 63; *Minstrel's Song, Letter M* 64; *The Deserter* 65; *Why Is Mona Lisa Smiling?* 66; *Forester's Song, Power of Destiny; Revenge* (one episode); *Prague Nights* (one episode) 68.

44 Brejchová, Jana (1940-   ). Most popular and best-known screen actress. Made her *début* as thirteen-year-old girl in *Red Whitsun*. Has since played in over thirty Czech films and in three West German productions. Czech roles include: *Wolf Trap, A Local Romance, Desire, Talent Competition, A Higher Principle, Baron Munchausen, The Labyrinth of the Heart, Sunshine in a Net, If a thousand Clarinets, Wandering, Courage for Everyday Life, Pipes, Return of the Prodigal Son, The Night of the Bride, Marathon.*

45 Brodský, Vlastimil (1920-   ). Distinguished stage and screen actor. Studied at E. F. Burian School for Actors. Member of Na Vinohradech Theatre, Prague. Has appeared in scores of films including: *The Stolen Frontier; The Mystery of Blood; September Nights; Five out of a Million; Tales from the First Republic; That Cat; Courage for Everyday Life; Closely Observed Trains; Capricious Summer.*

46 Brynych, Zbyněk (1927-   ). Middle generation director and screenwriter: started film work after winning screen-story competition. Head of Short Film Studios at Prague and Gottwaldov for three years. During army service, wrote and directed shorts for Czechoslovak Army School. Assistant to Weiss and others before directing own films. Several of his films have strong anti-Nazi themes: others are about emotional problems of young people. Films: *A Local Romance* 58; *Five out of a Million* 59; *Skid* 60; *Every Penny Counts* 61; *Don't Take Shelter from the Rain,* 62; *Transport from Paradise* 63; *A Place in the Crowd* (one episode), *The Fifth Horseman Is Fear* 64; *Transit Carlsbad* 66; *Constellation Virgo* 66; *I, Justice* 67; *Dialogue* (one episode) 68.

Two films by Forman: above, PETER AND PAVLA;
below, THE FIREMEN'S BALL

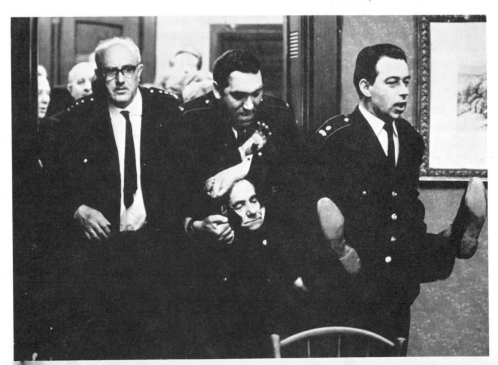

47 Chytilová, Věra (1929-   ). A leading director of "new wave": expresses her ideas mainly through female characterisations. Married to Kučera, the cameraman (q.v.), also seen in photo above. Worked as model, continuity girl and asst. dir. before studying at Prague. Graduated 1953. Graduation film: *The Ceiling* 62. Documentary: *A Bag of Fleas* 62. Feature films: *Another Way of Life* 63; *Pearls of the Deep* (one episode) 65; *Daisies* 66; *We May Eat of the Fruit of the Trees of the Garden* (co-prod. with Belgium) 69.

48 Čuřík, Jan (1924-   ). Cameraman of the "new wave." Started film work as cameraman for shorts, at Czechoslovak Army Film Studio, 1951. Director of photography for: *The Tank Brigade, A Local Romance, Five out of a Million, White Dove, Don't Take Shelter from the Rain, Transport from Paradise, Another Way of Life, Josef Kilián, A Place in the Crowd, Courage for Everyday Life, Wandering* (also co-dir.) 65; *The Unfortunate Bridegroom, Five Girls like a Millstone round One's Neck.*

49 Forman, Miloš (1932-   ). Highly successful comedy-maker of "new wave," with flair for candid camera observation of ordinary life. Graduated drama department Prague. Assisted with screenplay for *Leave It to Me;* co-writer and asst. dir. for *Puppies;* asst. dir. to Radok (q.v.) for *Old Man Motor-Car* and directed under Radok's guidance some early *Magic Lantern* presentations. Returned to cinema proper 1962. Works in close co-operation with scriptwriter Ivan Passer (q.v.). In 1968 went to U.S.A. to set up film about modern youth. Medium length features: *If There Were No Music, Talent Competition* 63. Full-length: *Peter and Pavla* 63; *A Blonde in Love* 65; *The Firemen's Ball* 67.

50 Frič, Martin (1902-1968). Director, screenwriter and actor. Made over a hundred films. Taught and encouraged many gifted newcomers. Became actor at sixteen; worked as laboratory assistant, cameraman and screenwriter in Twenties; directed four films before introduction of sound. Although Czech,

52 Jakubisko, Juraj (1938-   ). Slovak director—one of the newest of the "new wave." Graduated Prague, 1964. First two features were shown at International Festivals. Diploma film: *Waiting for Godot* 64. Shorts: *The Emigrant, Rain* 65. Feature Films: *The Crucial Years* 67; *Deserters and Pilgrims* 68.

played key role in developing Slovak cinema, with *Jánošik* 1936 and *Warning* 1947, in collaboration with Pal'o Bielik (q.v.). Films include: *Tales by Čapek* 47; *The Steel Town, The Trap* 50, *The Emperor's Baker, The Baker's Emperor* 51; *The Mystery of Blood* 53; *Leave It to Me* 55; *King of Kings* 63; *A Star Named Wormwood* 64; *People on Wheels* 66; *The Best Woman in My Life* 67.

51 Goldberger, Kurt (1919-   ). Leading director of popular science films. Studied natural science and physics in London prewar; started film career as sound editor in British studios. Made British instructional films during war. Then joined Prague Studio of Popular Science and Educational Films. Directed many documentaries on transport and public health with special emphasis on children. Films include: *The Valley of Health and Quiet* 49; *Retarded Life* 60; *Surgery of Mitral Stenosis; Resection of the Lungs; I'm NOT Going to Eat* 61; *Unloved Children* 64;

53 Jasný, Vojtěch (1925-   ). Feature director with lyrical and frequently experimental style. Foremost of first generation to emerge from Prague film school, early Fifties. In forced labour camp during war. Studied philosophy, 1945, then entered film faculty in camera department: later switched to direction class. Worked with fellow-student Kachyňa (q.v.) on graduation film *The Clouds Will Roll Away* 1950. Continued partnership for several documentaries and a feature *Everything Ends Tonight* 1954. Then: *September Nights* 57; *Desire* 58; *I Survived Certain Death* 60; *Pil-*

grimage to the Virgin Mary 61; *That Cat* 63; *Pipes* 65; *All Good Citizens* 68.

Prague. Experimented with polyscreen, Magic Lantern and puppet films. Feature films: *The First Cry* 63; *Pearls of the Deep* (one episode) 65; *Bitter Almonds* (unfinished) 66; *The Joke* 69.

54 Jireš, Jaromil (1935-   ). "New wave" director with romantic style. Trained for work in film administration at technical school. Directed short feature *Footprints* 1960 while student at

Krejcik's THE UNFORTUNATE BRIDEGROOM

55 Juráček, Pavel (1935-   ). Young director and scriptwriter. Graduated

Prague 1963; first worked as screen-writer mainly with older generation directors. Scenarios include: *The Ceiling, Icarus XB-1, A Jester's Tale, Nobody Gets the Last Laugh, End of August at Hotel Ozone, Daisies* (co-writer). Directed: *Josef Kilián* (co-dir. Schmidt) 63; *Every Young Man* (two episodes) 65.

56 Kačer, Jan (1936-   ). Outstanding actor of contemporary screen. Graduated as director at Faculty of Dramatic Arts, Prague. Actor and director in The Drama Club, Prague. Film roles include: *Death Is Called Engelchen; Courage for Everyday Life; Nobody Gets the Last Laugh; The Return of the Prodigal Son; Pipes; Wandering; The End of Agent W4C.*

57 Kachyňa, Karel (1924-   ). Feature director. One of first Prague graduates; made graduation film jointly with Jasný (q.v.): continued to collaborate with him on documentaries and one feature. First used army themes: then turned to psychological themes especially about

young people. Feature films: *Everything Ends Tonight* (with Jasný) 54; *The Lost Trail* 56; *That Christmas* 58; *Smugglers of Death* 59; *The Slinger* 60; *Fetters, Stress of Youth* 61; *Vertigo* 62; *Hope* 63; *The High Wall* 64; *Long Live the Republic!* 65; *Coach to Vienna* 66; *The Night of the Bride* 67; *Christmas with Elizabeth* 68; *Our Foolish Family* 69.

58 Kadár, Ján (1918-   ). Feature director from Slovakia; younger half of Kadár-Klos team. Gave up law studies to join Bratislava Film School 1938. In Nazi labour camp during war. Then asst. dir. and producer at Bratislava Short Film Studio. Made outstanding documentary short *Life Is Rising from the Ruins* 1945. Joined Barrandov Studios as scenario-writer and asst. dir. 1947. Met Klos (q.v.) while working on *Dead among the Living* 1947. Made one independent film, *Katya* 1950, a comedy important to Slovak film history, before joining with Klos in 1952. Kadár-Klos documentaries, etc.: *Young Days* 56; *The Spartakiade, The Magic Lantern II, Youth* (polyscreen) 60. Kadár-Klos features: *Kidnapped* 52; *Music from Mars* 54; *House at the Terminus* 57; *Three Wishes* 58; *Death Is Called Engelchen* 63; *The Defendant* 64; *Shop on the High Street* 65; *Something Is Drifting on the Water* (co-prod. with U.S.A.) 69.

59 Klos, Elmar (1910-   ). Feature director from Moravia: older half of Kadár-Klos team. Started film work as sixteen-year-old schoolboy, helping his scriptwriter uncle during early days of sound. Played one minor acting role. Founded film studio of Bata Shoe Company. Helped prepare postwar structure of film industry while member of illegal wartime filmworkers' organisation. Directed documentaries and held various administrative posts from 1945

Above: THE SHOP ON THE HIGH STREET, directed by Kadar
(right, below), and Klos (at left)

until he joined forces with Kadár, 1952. Films: see **Kadár, Ján.**

60 Krejčík, Jiří. (1918-   ). Middle generation director whose work may be seen as link between classics and "new wave." Forced to abandon studies at beginning of war when Prague Technical University was closed by Nazis. Took occasional jobs as extra at Barrandov studios. Made several wartime documentaries at Shorts Film Studio. Feature films: *A Week in a Quiet House* 47; *The Village on the Frontier* 48; *Conscience* 49; *Dawn above Us* 52; *The Sisters* 54; *Mrs. Dulská's Morals, On Miraculous Happenings* (one episode) 58; *Awakening* 59; *A Higher Principle* 60; *The Labyrinth of the Heart* 61; *Midnight Mass* 62; *Tales from the First Republic* (incorporating *The Oriental Carpet* and *Chintamans*) 65; *The Unfortunate Bridegroom* (*Wedding under Supervision*), *Boarding House for Bachelors* 67.

61 Krška, Václav (1900-   ). Poet and author; veteran scriptwriter and director with lyrical style. Early films were biographical, historical, or adaptations of literary works and opera. Turned to contemporary subjects in 1958. Postwar films include: *The Violin and the Dream* 47; *The Revolutionary Year* 49; *Mikoláš Aleš, Messenger of Dawn* 51; *Youthful Years* 52; *Moon over the River* 53; *The Silvery Wind* 54; *From My Life* 55; *Dalibor* 56; *A Legend of Love* 57; *Hic Sunt Leones* 58; *The Day the Tree Will Bloom* 61; *A Place in the Crowd* (one episode), *Comedy around a Door Handle* 64; *The Last Rose from Casanova* 66; *A Girl with Three Camels* 67; *Spring Waters* 68.

62 Krumbachová, Ester (1923-   ). Costume designer, artist and "new wave" screenwriter. Co-writer (with directors) of screenplays of: *The Party and the Guests, Martyrs of Love, Daisies, We May Eat of the Fruit of the Trees of the Garden.* In 1968 she wrote two screenplays with a view to directing them herself: *The Murder of Engineer Devil* and *A Man with a Dog.* Other scripts completed in 1968: *Valeria and the Week of Miracles* (for Jireš), *The Three Brothers and the Miraculous Spring* (for Němec).

63 Kučera, Jaroslav (1929-   ). Outstanding cameraman associated at first with Jasny and later with "new wave." Husband of Chytilová (q.v.). Graduated as cameraman, Prague. Director of photography for: *Everything Ends Tonight, The Lost Trail, September Nights, Desire, I Survived Certain Death, Pilgrimage to the Virgin Mary, That Cat, The First Cry, Diamonds of the Night, Pearls of the Deep, A Boring Afternoon, Daisies, Dita Saxova.*

64 Lipský, Oldřich (1924-   ). Comedy director best known for Wild West satire, *Lemonade Joe.* Began film career as actor; then asst. dir. and scenarist. Films include: *The Show Is On* 54; *Hašek's Exemplary Cinematography* 55; *The Star Goes South* (co-prod. with Yugoslavia) 57; *The Circus Is Coming* (full-length doc.) 60; *The Man from the First Century* 61; *Lemonade Joe* 64; *Happy End* 66.

65 Máša, Antonín (1935-   ). Screenwriter and director with a penchant for black humour. Graduated in drama dept. at Prague. Screenplays: *A Place in the Crowd, Courage for Everyday Life, People on Wheels.* Directed: *Wandering* (co-dir.: Čuřík) 65; *Hotel for Strangers* 66; *Looking Back* 69.

66 Menzel, Jiří (1938-   ). Wry humorist of the "new wave"; film director who enjoys acting; has appeared as actor in "new wave" films including his own, and continues to work as director and actor at Prague Theatre Club. Graduated Prague 1963. Graduation film: *The Death of Mr. Foerster.* Acted in: *The Defendant, The Ceiling, If a Thousand Clarinets, Courage for Everyday Life, Nobody Gets the Last Laugh, Return of the Prodigal Son, Hotel for Strangers.* Directed: *Pearls of the Deep* (one episode), *Crime at the Girls' School* (one episode) 65; *Closely Observed Trains* (also acted) 66; *Capricious Summer* 68; *Crime at the Night Club, Larks on a Thread* (projected) 69.

67 Müller, Vlado (1936-   ). Important screen actor. Graduated at College of Music and Dramatic Arts, Bratislava. Member of Bratislava theatre The New Scene. Films include: *Death Is Called Engelchen; The Defendant, On a Tightrope, Tales from the First Republic, Knell for the Barefooted, The Hangman, The Crucial Years.*

Jana Drchalova
in Menzel's CAPRICIOUS SUMMER

68 Neckář, Václav (1943-   ). Actor and pop-singer who made striking film *début* in Menzel's *Closely Observed Trains*. Began career in Workers' Theatre at Most. Gained third place in pop-singer popularity poll run by a Czech youth magazine 1966. Subsequent roles: *That Czech Song of Ours*, *The Lame Devil*.

69 Němec, Jan (1936-   ). Controversial "new wave" director with experimental style, fascinated by psychology of persecution and oppression. Graduated Prague, 1960. Graduation film: *A Bite to Eat*. Short films: *Memory of Our Day* 63; *Life After Ninety Minutes* (co-dir.: Schmidt) 65, *Mother and Son* (in Neths.) 67. Feature films: *Diamonds of the Night* 64; *Pearls of the Deep* (one episode) 65; *The Party and the Guests* (also acted), *Martyrs of Love* 66.

70 Ondříček, Miroslav (1933-   ). "New wave" cameraman closely associated with Forman (q.v.). Began film career at Documentary Film Studios. Director of photography for: *Talent Competition*, *If There Were No Music*, *A Blonde in Love*, *Intimate Lighting*, *The White Bus* (in Engl.), *Martyrs of Love*, *The Fireman's Ball*, *If* (in Engl.).

71 Passer, Ivan (1933-   ). Young comedy screenwriter and director with sharp eye for absurdities of petit bourgeois life. Graduated Prague. Collaborated with Miloš Forman (q.v.) on screenplays of all Forman's films. Co-wrote the scenarios for his own films: *A Boring Afternoon* (short), *Intimate Lighting* 65.

72 Pojar, Břetislav (1923-   ). A leading animator. Runs his own studio. Films include: *A Drop Too Much* 56; *The Little Umbrella* 58; *A Midnight Incident* 60; *The Lion and the Ditty* 62; *A Cat's Word of Honour*, *Drawing for Cats*, *School for Cats* 63; *Billiards*, *The Introductory Speech Is By* . . . . 64; *Romance*, *Ideal* 65; *Come and Play*, *Sir* (series of three) 65-67; *Hold on to Your Hats* 67.

73 Pucholt, Vladimír (1942-   ). Popular and talented young actor with unusual screen personality. Was telephone engineer apprentice before graduating in Drama at Prague Academy of Arts. Left cinema in 1967 to study medicine in England. Film roles include: *Hašek's Exemplary Cinema*, *The Goalkeeper Lives in Our Street*, *Tell-tales*, *Little Bobes*, *Talent Competition*, *Chance Meeting*, *Peter and Pavla*, *The Hoppickers*, *A Blonde in Love*, *The Constellation Virgo*, *The Unfortunate Bridegroom*.

74 Radok, Alfréd (1914-   ). Leading figure of the modern stage; creator of *Magic Lantern* (spectacle combining

Two films by Nemec: MARTYRS OF LOVE (above) and
THE PARTY AND THE GUESTS (below)

Vladimir Pucholt on the defensive in Rychmann's THE HOP-PICKERS

film, slides and live stage performances). Became drama critic after graduation at Charles University; then stage manager and producer. Began taking active interest in films in 1947 and has helped many gifted newcomers to cinema, including Forman (q.v.). Has devoted himself solely to theatre in Sixties. Films: *Distant Journey* 49; *The Magic Hat* 52; *Old Man Motor-car* 56.

75 Rychmann, Ladislav (1922-   ). Director of features, including musicals. Films: *The Case Is Not Yet Closed* 57; *The Circle* 59; *The Hop-pickers* 64; *The Lady of the Lines, Crime at the Girl's School* (one episode) 65.

76 Schmidt, Jan (1936-   ). Young director and screenwriter. Graduated Prague. Films: *Josef Kilián* (co-dir. Jurá-cek) 63; *Life After Ninety Minutes* (Doc. Co-dir. Němec) 65; *The End of August at Hotel Ozone* 66; *The Lanfieri Colony* 69.

77 Schorm, Evald (1931-   ). Leading "new wave" director, often referred to as its spokesman or "spiritual authority." Creator of Czech-style angry young man. Graduated Prague 1962. Directed several outstanding documentaries before turning to features. Graduation film: *The Tourist*. Documentary films: *Helsinki, Trees and People, The Land* 62; *Railwaymen, To Live One's Life* 63; *Why?* 64; *Reflections* 65; *Carmen* 66. Acting roles in: *The Party and the Guests, Hotel for Strangers.* Feature films: *Courage for Everyday Life* 64; *Pearls of the Deep* (one episode) 65; *The Return of the Prodigal Son* 66; *Five Girls like a Millstone round One's Neck* 67; *Re-*

Schorm's FIVE GIRLS LIKE A MILLSTONE ROUND ONE'S NECK

venge (one episode), *Prague Nights* (one episode) 68; *Pastor's End* 69.

78 Solan, Peter (1929-   ). Slovak director. Graduated Prague. Films: *The Devil Never Rests* (co-dir. Záček) 57; *The Man Who Did Not Return* 59; *The Boxer and Death* 62; *The Face at the Window* 63; *The Story of Barnabáš Kos* 64; *Before This Night Is Over* 65; *Dialogue* (one episode) 68.

79 Steklý, Karel (1903-   ). Veteran director specialising in screen versions of literary works. Went into theatre straight from school, first as actor, then as stage manager. Began film career as scriptwriter 1933. Directed first postwar Czechoslovak feature. Films include: *The Breach* 46; *The Strike* 47; *The Career* 48; *Darkness* 50; *Anna, the Proletarian* 52; *The Piper of Strakonice* 55;

The Good Soldier Schweik (Pts. 1 and 2) 57; *The Avenger* 59; *Lucy* 63.

80 Švankmajer, Jan (1934-   ). Brilliant young animator with highly individual style. Studied at Higher School of Art and in Marionette Faculty of Academy of Fine Arts. Worked as theatre director and was associated with Magic Lantern until 1962. Nearly all of his cartoon and puppet films have won international awards. Films include: *The Last Trick of Mr. Schwarzwald and Mr. Edgar* 64; *J. S. Bach—Fantasy in G Minor* 63; *Motifs with Stones* (Austrian) 65; *The Coffin Shop, Etcetera* 66; *The Garden* 67; *The Flat* (live action and animation), *Historia Naturae* 68.

81 Trnka, Jiří (1912-   ). Eminent puppet film creator and artist. During

Misfit 51; Nine Chicks 52; The Taming of the Dragon 53; The Naughty Ball, Goldilocks 56; The Swineherd 57; The Lost Doll, The Little Train 59; A Lesson 60; The Inquisitive Letter 61; The Knot in the Handkerchief 62; The Marble 63; The Woolly Tale 64; The Blue Pinafore 65; The Snowman, Boy or Girl? 66; Dog's Heaven, Christmas Tree 67.

boyhood, pupil of distinguished puppeteer Professor Skupa. Studied at Arts and Crafts School, Prague 1929-35. On leaving, founded own puppet theatre. During war, illustrated children's books and designed stage sets. Began directing 1945 at Prague Cartoon and Puppet Studio. Films: Grandpa Planted a Beet (cartoon) 45; The Animals and the Brigands (cartoon), The Springer and the S.S. Men (cartoon) 46; The Czech Year 47; The Emperor and the Nightingale 48; Song of the Prairie, The Story of the Bass-Cello 49; Prince Bayaya 50; The Golden Fish (cartoon) 51; How Grandpa Changed till Nothing Was Left (cartoon), Old Czech Legends 53; The Good Soldier Schweik 54; A Midsummer Night's Dream 59; Obsession 61; Cybernetic Grandma 62; The Archangel Gabriel and Mrs. Goose 64; The Hand 65.

82 Týrlová, Hermína (1900-   ). Director of children's puppet films. Began career in Twenties with trick and experimental publicity cartoons. Postwar films: The Revolt of Toys 47; Lullaby 48; The

83 Uher, Štefan (1930-   ). Feature director of Slovakian "new wave;" poetic, intellectual style. First feature helped to raise reputation of Slovak cinema to level of the Czech. Graduated Prague 1955. Director at Bratislava Documentary Studio 1955-61, then at Bratislava Feature Studio. Graduation film: Above the Clouds. Shorts and documentaries include: The Teacher 55; People of the Vihorlat Mountains 56; Here Walks Tragedy 57; Sailors without a Sea 58; Through the Eyes of a Camera, Marked by Darkness 59. Feature films: Form 9A 61; Sunshine in a Net 62; The Organ 64; The Miraculous Virgin 66; Three Daughters 67.

ROMANCE FOR TRUMPET, directed by Vavra (portrait below)

84 Vávra, Otakar (1911-). Scenario-writer and feature director, mainly of screen adaptations of literary works. As lecturer at Prague, helped forward many "new wave" directors. After studying architecture, became publicist with special interest in films. Shot several experimental films and worked as scriptwriter and asst. dir. before becoming independent director in late Thirties. Postwar feature films: *Rosina the Foundling* 45; *The Mischievous Tutor* 46; *Presentiment* 47; *Krakatit* 48; *The Silent Barricade* 49; *Fall In!* 52; *Jan Hus* 55; *Jan Zizka* 56; *All Our Enemies* 57; *Citizen Brych* 58; *The First Rescue Party* 59; *The Closing Hour, A Sunday in August* 60; *A Guest in the Night* 61; *The Ardent Heart* 62; *The Golden Rennet* 65; *Romance for Trumpet* 66; *The Thirteenth Room* 69.

Jan Werich in Jasny's THAT CAT

85 Vláčil, František (1924-   ).
Middle-generation documentary direc-
tor: turned to features in late Fifties.
Gifts as artist and painter apparent in
his films. Studied aesthetics and art his-
tory at Brno after the war. Then worked
with cartoon and puppet group at Brno
Popular Science studios. Made dozens
of popular science shorts at Brno and at
Czechoslovak Army Studio, in Fifties.
Feature films: *The White Dove* 60; *The
Devil's Trap* 61; *Markéta Lazarová* 67;
Valley of the Bees 68.

film career as documentarist. Spent the war years in England, where he worked with Crown Film Unit. Feature films: *The Stolen Frontier* 47; *Wild Beasts* 48; *New Warriors Shall Arise, The Last Shot* 50; *My Friend the Gypsy* 53; *Doggie and the Four* 54; *Life Was the Stake* 56; *Wolf Trap* 57; *Appassionata* 59; *Romeo, Juliet and Darkness* 60; *The Coward* 61; *The Golden Fern* 63; *Ninety in the Shade* 64; *Murder—Czech Style* 67.

87 Werich, Jan (1905-   ). Playwright, satirist and veteran comedy actor of stage and screen. With partner Jiří Veskovec, founded Pocket Revue, late Twenties and avant-garde Emancipated Theatre, Prague in '30s. In Paris, 1930, compered *Paramount Revue*. Made several prewar films based on their stage comedies and musicals. Their final collaboration was on a polit-

86 Weiss, Jiří (1913-   ). Leading older-generation director, closely associated with British film industry. Began

Zeman's THE JESTER'S TALE

trations (*Baron Munchausen*). After leaving business college, became poster-artist and window-dresser. Began directing films 1943 at Gottwaldov studios. Created famous cartoon character Mr. *Prokouk* for publicity series in late Forties. Films include: *A Christmas Dream* 45; *King Lávra* 50; *The Treasure of Bird's Island* 52; *A Journey to the Primeval Times* 55; *An Invention for Destruction* 57; *Baron Munchausen* 61; *A Jester's Tale* 64; *The Stolen Airship* 66; *Mr. Servadac's Ark* 68.

ical satire. Since the war, Werich has appeared in many films, including: *The Emperor's Baker, The Baker's Emperor, Hašek's Exemplary Cinematograph, Baron Munchausen, That Cat.*

88 Zeman, Karel (1910-   ). Distinguished creator of fantasy films in which live action is blended with puppetry and animation. His animation material ranges widely, including glass figurines (*Inspiration*) and period illus-

GERMANY (EAST)

GERMANY (EAST)

Pop. 17,300,000. Small country with a well-organised and comparatively large film industry.

Production:
      Feature films: 2 in 1946; 8 in 1950, 13 in 1955, 27 (including 2 co-prods.) in 1960; 15 (including 1 co-prod.) in 1965; 13 in 1968 (planned).

Cinemas: About 1,300

Studios: (all owned by the state film organisation DEFA):
      Feature Studios, Potsdam
      Popular Science Studios, Potsdam
      Newsreel and Documentary Studios, Berlin
      Cartoon Studios, Dresden
      Dubbing Studios, Berlin

Training:
      Deutsche Hochschule für Filmkunst, Potsdam, (referred to in biographies as "Potsdam"). Established 1954. Departments for directing, production, scriptwriting, camera and acting.

Although several documentaries and newsreels were made in the immediate postwar months, the film industry was officially established on a state-owned basis in October 1946, when the DEFA Studios were opened on the former Althoff Studio site at Dresden, in what was then the Soviet zone of Germany.

The intellectual void created by Nazism, the wartime loss and dispersal of equipment, the shortage of trained personnel, and the dramatic postwar social changes, made production difficult at first. The Soviet Union helped not only with finance and equipment, but also with the loan of technicians. A number of established film people, including directors **Staudte**, **Maetzig**, **Dudow** and **Engel**, cameramen Baberske, Klagemann and Fiedler and the composer **Eisler**, helped to put the industry on its feet. Before the Film School was established at Potsdam, a new generation of film-makers was trained at Moscow and Prague film schools. Outstanding among the directors to emerge in the Fifties was **Wolf**, who continues to lead the field.

From its inception, cinema in East Germany has reflected the social conditions and problems of a divided country that had suffered twelve years of Nazi rule. The first feature film, *The Murderers Are among Us* 1946, was a forerunner of a whole series of productions with strong anti-Fascist themes. Two years later, *The Blum Affair* drew international acclaim. Other anti-Fascist films of the period were *Council of the Gods, Matrimony in the Shadows, Our Daily Bread* and *The Condemned Village*. They were followed in the Fifties with *The Captain of Cologne* and the polemical **Thorndike** documentaries.

Many of the films of the Fifties dealt with the struggles of the working-class movement. Among the most successful were *Sailor's Song, Stronger than the Night,*

They Called Him Amigo, The Unconquered and the Ernest Thaelmann films, (Pts. 1 and 2).

The first film to tackle a contemporary theme was *Women's Fate,* 1952. Among later films depicting family and personal problems that arise from rapid social change were *Lot's Wife* and *The Best Years.*

A notable trend in the Sixties was the emergence of a whole number of films dealing with the problems of split families in Berlin. Among the most important were *Stories of That Night, The Divided Sky* and the documentary, *Aces,* which uses on-the-spot television technique. Anti-Fascism continued to be the major theme, but the approach became more personalised. The Bulgarian-German co-production *Stars,* 1959, was an early and very successful attempt at breaking away from the old-style dogmatism. Although there has been no significant move towards "new cinema," films like *Farewells, The Divided Sky* and above all, the outstanding *I Was Nineteen* have carried the personalisation process further forward.

Films made specially for children have been a consistent feature of DEFA production; an interesting example is *Sheriff Teddy,* which tackles the "divided city" theme from a young person's point of view.

A rather unexpected development is the production of several Westerns of which *Chinachgook—the Great Snake,* 1967, (*dir:* Richard Groschopp) is a typical example.

Co-production has been undertaken on a wider scale than in most Eastern European countries; there have been collaborations not only with the U.S.S.R., Poland, Czechoslovakia and Bulgaria, but also with Sweden and France.

In the past decade many of the leading directors have given their main attention to television.

Documentaries and cartoons: The annual Festival of Documentaries and Shorts at Leipzig is an indication of the great importance which East German cinema gives to documentary production. A strong documentary tradition has been built up, considerably wider and more free-flowing than feature production. Styles range from the sharp-edged polemics of the **Thorndike** compilation films to the warm and intimate productions by **Karl Gass** and the very talented, down-beat films of **Böttcher.** Other leading documentarists are **Heynowski, Scheumann, Huisken, Junge,** Gitta Nickel, Max Jaap, Joachim Hellwig and Richard Cohn-Vossen whose *Paul Dessau,* a half-hour study of the composer, has been widely acclaimed.

Cartoon production was carried out at the Popular Science studios until the opening of the Cartoon Studios at Dresden in 1955. Among the leading animators are **Katja** and Klaus **Georgi, Günter Rätz** and Kurt Weiler. Bruno Bottge specialises in silhouette films.

89 Bergmann, Werner (1921-   ). Outstanding cameraman who works in close association with director Konrad Wolf (q.v.). Trained as photographer; was front-line cameraman during war. Joined Popular Science studios 1947. Chief cameraman of many documentary films before 1953. Feature films include: *The Little and the Big Happiness, Alarm in the Circus, One is Less than One, Recovery, The Captain of Cologne, Lissy, Stars, Men with Wings, Professor Mamlock, The Divided Sky, I Was Nineteen.*

90 Beyer, Frank (1932-   ). Film and theatre director. Studied Drama Theory in Berlin: then went to Prague Film Faculty, Graduated 1957. Asst. dir. to Maetzig (q.v.) until 1959. Appointed Director of Staatstheater, Dresden, 1966. Films: *Two Mothers* 57; *Old Love* 59; *Five Bullets* 60; *Invincible Love, Naked among the Wolves* 62; *Carbide and Sorrel* 63.

91 Böttcher, Jürgen (1931-   ). Documentary director. Studied at Academy of Fine Arts. Then worked as freelance painter in Dresden. Graduated Potsdam, 1960. Films include: *Three of Many* 61; *In the Pergamon Museum* 62; *New Year's Eve, Stars* 63; *Charlie and Co., Barefoot and Hatless* 64; *Children's Theatre, Karl Marx Street* 65; *The Secretary, Feast of Friendship* 67; *The Reliable Man* 68.

92 Carow, Heiner (1929-   ). Feature director. Qualified in directors' class at DEFA Training Studio. First worked at Popular Science Studios. Joined feature studio 1957. Films: *Sheriff Teddy* 57; *They Called Him Amigo* 58; *Life Begins* 59; *Mongolia* (co-dir.) 61; *The Länneken Wedding* 63; *Journey to Sundevit* 66.

93 Dessau, Paul (1894-   ). Distinguished composer of symphonies, opera, workers' songs and music for theatre and film. Wrote music for several Brecht plays and for a number of important documentary films. Musical director at theatres in various German cities in Twenties. Left Germany for America 1933. Returned 1948. Plays leading role in musical life of GDR. Member of Academy of Arts. In 1967, Richard Cohn-Vossen made the film *Paul Dessau* as a tribute to his work. Wrote scores for: *The German Story, Holiday on Sylt, Operation Teutonic Sword, Mother Courage and Her Children, The Russian Miracle, Four Hundred Cubic Centimetres.*

94 Dudow, Slatan (1903-1963). Feature director who played important role in early postwar cinema. Born in Bulgaria: emigrated to Germany 1922. Studied architecture; switched to acting. In production team of Lang's *Metropolis.* Worked closely with Brecht during Thirties. Made significant feature film *Kuhle*

Wampe 1932. Had to flee Germany after making film satire *Soap Bubbles*, 1933. Worked in French theatre until outbreak of war. Interned in Switzerland 1939-46. Then returned to GDR and rapidly achieved a leading position in cinema, which he retained until his death in a car accident. Films: *Our Daily Bread* 49; *The Benthin Family* (co-dir: Maetzig) 50; *Women's Fate* 52; *Stronger than the Night* 54; *The Captain of Cologne* 56; *Love's Confusion* 59; *Christine* (unfinished) 63.

95 Egel, Dr. Karl-Georg (1919-   ). Scriptwriter. Studied medicine and was assistant doctor until called up in 1944. Began to write while in English p.o.w. camp. Worked on Cologne radio after war, before settling in East Berlin. Chief scriptwriter of DEFA feature studios. Began a series of script collaborations with Paul Wiens, 1965. Since 1962, has concentrated on scripts for TV. Feature films scripted: *The Solvay Dossier*, *Dangerous Freight*, *Recovery* (co-writer: Wiens), *Sailor's Song* (co-writer: Wiens), *Men with Wings* (co-writer: Wiens), *Pro-*

fessor Mamlock, *Sunday Excursion* (co-writer: Kohlhaase).

96 Eisler, Hanns (1898-1962). Distinguished composer who has written music for many world-famous films. Studied music in Vienna under Arnold Schönberg. Met Bertholt Brecht and Slatan Dudow while a teacher at Klindworth-Scharwenka Conservatoire, Berlin, 1925-33. Wrote music for politically-significant film *Kuhle Wampe* 1932. Left Germany 1934. Settled in America 1938. Was Professor at Los Angeles University where he had a special grant for research in film music. Prewar film scores include Lang's *Hangmen also Die* and several Joris Ivens films. Wrote book *Composing for Films*. Returned to Europe 1948, first Vienna, then Berlin. Was Member of German Academy of Arts, Berlin and Professor at Music Institute, which was posthumously named after him. Postwar film scores include: *Monsieur Verdoux*, *Our Daily Bread*, *Council of the Gods*, *Wilhelm Pieck—the Life of Our President*, *Women's Fate*, *Bel Ami* (Austrian), *The Witches of Salem*, *Nuit et Brouillard* (in France), *The Fledermaus Squadron*, *Muddy Water* (co-prod. with France), *Intractable Spain*.

97 Engel, Erich (1891-1966). Theatre and cinema director whose first postwar film was of key importance. Well-known before war for classic and modern stage productions, notably first performance of Brecht's *Threepenny Opera*, 1928. Directed first film 1931. Director of State Theatre, Munich, 1945. Then artistic director of Berliner Ensemble. Worked in West German cinema, 1949-55. Films: *The Blum Affair* 48; *The Beaver Coat* 49; *Fledermaus Squadron* 58.

98 Gass, Karl (1917-   ). Documentary director. Trained as estate

Beyer's NAKED AMONG THE WOLVES (with Erwin Geschonneck)

agent: then studied economics until called up. In English p.o.w. camp, 1945. Worked on radio in his home-town, Cologne, until 1948, when he settled in E. Berlin. Appointed Director of Popular Science Studios 1954, and Director of Documentary Studios 1960. Member of the Presidium of Leipzig Festival. Vice-president of International Association of Documentary film-makers. Films include: *Factory in Germany 54; Island of Roses, Between Heaven and Earth 57; The Bulls of Hidalgo 59; Freedom, Freedom above All, Five Seasons 60; I Sing of Peace, Allons enfants . . . . pour l'Algérie, With Motorbike and Tent to Tunisia, September Thoughts 61; Look at This City 62; Time Off 64; Aces 65; At Home in May 66; Ernst Busch 67.*

99 Georgi, Katja (1928-   ). Cartoon and puppet film-maker. Studied Ceramics and Graphic Art, 1949-53. Started as free-lance artist, then as artist on cartoon films. After directing *Brave Hans*, with her husband Klaus Georgi, turned to puppet films. They include: *The Princess and the Pea, The Devil's Valley 59; The Pyramid 61; Matches 62; Musicians 63; Plastic in the Park 64; Good Day, Mr. H. (with Klaus Georgi), Concurrence 65; The Thorn 67.*

100 Günther, Egon (1927-   ). Feature director, scriptwriter and author. Studied German philology and educational theory. Teacher, publishers' reader and script adviser. Has written four novels. Wrote several scripts before becoming director. Films directed: *Lot's Wife 65; Farewell 68.*

101 Hellberg, Martin (1905-   ). Stage and film director. Actor before war. Wide experience in theatre. Ap-

Above: Günther's LOT'S WIFE (with Marita Böhme and Günther Simon). Below: Klein's BERLIN, SCHOENHAUSER CORNER (with Ekkehard Schall and Gerhard Rachold)

pointed Professor at Potsdam, and head of Theatre in Schwerin. Published book on stage and film art 1955. Occasionally takes acting roles. Usually writes his own scripts. Feature films directed: *The Condemned Village* 51; *The Solvay Dossier* 52; *The Little and the Big Happiness* 53; *The Ox of Kulm* 54; *The Judge of Salamea* 55; *Thomas Muentzer, Yvette's Millions* 56; *Wherever You Go, Emilia Galotti* 57; *Captains Do Not Leave the Ship* 58; *Senta Goes Astray, Intrigue and Love* 59; *The Black Galleon, Minna von Barnhelm* 62; *Much Ado about Nothing* 64.

102   Heynowski, Walter (1927-   ). Director of cinema and TV documentaries. Often works in collaboration with Scheumann (q.v.). Films made independently include: *Murder in Lvov* 62; *Action J, Brothers and Sisters, Globke Today* 63; *Here and There* 64; *Commando 52* 65; *Love Letters* 66. Films made in collaboration include: *O.K.* 64; *Four Hundred Cubic Centimetres, The Laughing Man, P.S. to the Laughing Man* 66; *With Special Praise, The Witness* 67; *Pilots in Pyjamas* 68.

103   Huisken, Joop (1901-   ). Veteran documentary director. Born in Amsterdam. Asst. dir. to Joris Ivens in late Twenties and early Thirties. Directed first film independently 1933. Deported to Germany 1941. Remained in Berlin after war. Professor at Potsdam 1961-63. Films include: *Potsdam Rebuilds* 46; *With Our Own Strength* 48; *Steel* 50; *Friendship Wins* (with the Thorndikes) 51; *After Nine Hundred Days* 53; *China—Between Today and Tomorrow* 56; *Living Tradition* 60; *Arnold Zweig* 62; *Free Peasants* 65; *The Creation, The Allies* 66.

104   Junge, Winfried (1935-   ). Documentary director with special interest in childhood and education. Studied educational theory at Humboldt University 1953, transferred to Potsdam 1954. Worked in script department of Popular Science studio 1958. Asst. dir. to Karl Gass 1959-60. First independent work, 1960. Films include: *Until Man Came* 60; *The Ape Terror, Wait Until I Go to School* 61; *After One Year* 62; *Holidays* 63; *Girl Students—Impressions of a Technical College* 65; *Eleven Years Old* 66; *The Brave Truants* (feature) 67; *With Both Legs in the Sky* 68.

105   Klein, Gerhard (1920-   ). Director. Son of engineering worker. Studied theatre and cinema at home. Scripted shorts and made several documentaries before joining feature studio in 1954. Feature films: *Alarm in the Circus* 54; *Berlin Romance* 56; *Berlin, Schoenhauser Corner* 57; *The Story of Poor Hassan, The Confirmation* 58; *One Summer Day Does Not Mean Love* 60; *The Gleiwitz Case* 61; *Sunday Excursion* 63; *Stories of That Night* (one episode) 67.

Above and below: Kunert's THE ADVENTURES OF WERNER HOLT

Two films by Maetzig:
above, THE GIRL ON
THE DIVING-BOARD; below,
CASTLES AND COTTAGES

played in Hamburg, Lubeck, Dresden and Berlin theatres. Began working in films 1951. Member of Deutschen Theatre Ensemble since 1967. Film roles include: *The Judge of Zalamea, Thomas Muentzer, The Captain of Cologne, The Gleiwitz Case, Much Ado about Nothing, As Long as I Live, Farewell.*

106 Kohlhaase, Wolfgang (1931-). Author and scriptwriter, often dealing with problems of youth. First worked in films as editor and adviser in script department. Has been writing scripts for cinema and TV since 1953. Scripts for: *Alarm in the Circus, Berlin Romance, Berlin, Schoenhauser Corner, The Silent Planet* (co-writers: Rücker and Reisch), *The Gleiwitz Case* (co-writer: Rücker), *Sunday Excursion* (co-writer: Egel), *I Was Nineteen.*

107 Kunert, Joachim (1929-). Feature director. Began film work as asst. dir. at feature studios. Worked as independent director at Documentary and Newsreel Film Studios until 1955. Feature films: *Special Marks—None* 55; *It Happened in Berlin* 57; *The Lottery Swede* 58; *Lorenz v. Lorenz* 59; *No. 8 Seiler Street* 60; *The Last Night* (TV film) 61; *The Second Track* 62; *The Adventures of Werner Holt* 64; *The Dead Stay Young* 68.

108 Ludwig, Rolf (1925-). Distinguished comedy actor. After war

109 Maetzig, Kurt (1911-). Feature director; key figure in early postwar cinema. Studied philosophy, psychology and law. Entered films as asst. dir. 1933. Helped to re-establish DEFA in 1946. Made first postwar newsreel and first documentary 1946. *Matrimony in the Shadows* (also scripted) was the first international success of GDR cinema. Director of Potsdam Film School and Professor of Film Direction since 1955. Films: *Matrimony in the Shadows* 47; *The Chequered Bedspread* 49; *The Benthin Family, Council of the Gods* 50; *Story of a Young Couple* 52; *Ernst Thaelmann* Pts I and II 54-55; *Castles and Cottages* 56; *Don't Forget My Traudel* 57; *Sailor's Song* (co-dir: Reisch) 58; *The Silent*

Planet 59; September Love 60; Captain Loy's Dream 61; At a French Fireside 62; Prelude Eleven 63; The Girl on the Diving-board 67; The Flag of Kriwoj Rog 67.

110 Marczinkowski, Günter (1927-   ). Cameraman for film and TV. Studied film technique. Served in forces during war. Then worked as stage-hand at Berliner Hebbel-Theatre. Technical assistant during postwar reconstruction of DEFA studios. Worked as asst. cameraman, and trained under Staudte (q.v.). Shot several TV films in Sixties including Wolf's *The Little Prince.* Feature films shot include: *Captains Do Not Leave the Ship, Old Love, Lorenz v. Lorenz, Five Bullets, Invincible Love, Naked among the Wolves, Carbide and Sorrel, Farewell.*

111 Merz, Otto (1908-   ). Cameraman. Began work as asst. cameraman at Feature Studio 1940. Chief electrician during reconstruction of DEFA studios after war. Asst. cameraman for several cartoon films before working independently. Has mainly concentrated on TV films in the Sixties. Feature films include: *Castles and Cottages, It Happened in Berlin, Two Mothers, Sailor's Song, The Lottery Swede, Maybowl, Lot's Wife.*

112 Plintzner, Karl (1911-   ). Prominent cameraman. Started work as laboratory trainee. Then asst. cameraman at Potsdam Studio. Has shot many important feature films including: *The Benthin Family, Story of a Young Couple, The Condemned Village, Ernst Thaelmann pts I and II, Stronger than the Night, Fledermaus Squadron, Senta Goes Astray, New Year Punchbowl, Captain Loy's Dream, The Black Galleon, Minna von Barnhelm, For Eyes Only.*

113 Rätz, Günter (1935-   ). Leading animator. Studied sculpture 1950-54. Then joined puppet and cartoon film team at Popular Science studios. Transferred to newly-established Cartoon Studios, Dresden 1955. Asst. dir. until 1958. Films include: *Teddy Brumm 58; The Unlucky Little Elephant 59; King of the Beasts, Song of the Dove 60; Measure for Measure 63; The Apostle, Photography, Western, Congratulation, Harmony 65; Aviation, Curiosity 66; Anton the Musician, Three Wishes 67; Stamp-collecting 68.*

114 Reisch, Günter (1927-   ). Feature director. Began career as theatre actor. Worked as assistant to Maetzig (q.v.) before directing independently. Co-writer of script for *The Silent Planet.* Feature films: *Fresh Vegetables 56; Tracks in the Night 57; Sailor's Song* (co-dir. Maetzig) *58; Maybowl 59; New Year Punchbowl 60; Merry Christmas Indeed! 62; The Thief of San Marengo 63; As Long as I Live 65; A Lord at Alexanderplatz 67.*

115 Rücker, Günther (1924-   ). Scriptwriter and director. Graduated Music Academy, Leipzig. Radio producer and playwright 1949-54. Began film work as scriptwriter for documentaries, collaborating closely with the Thorndikes (q.v.). Documentaries scripted: *The German Story, Holiday on Sylt, Operation Teutonic Sword, The Russian Miracle.* Feature films scripted: *Fresh Vegetables, The Silent Planet* (co-writers—Kohlhaase and Reisch), *The Gleiwitz Case.* Directed: *The Best Years 65.*

116 Scheumann, Gerhard (1930-   ). Cinema and TV director, often works in collaboration with Heynowski (q.v.).

117 Staudte, Wolfgang (1906-   ). Feature director whose first postwar film was of major importance. Studied at Technical Institute, Oldenburg. Acted under Max Reinhardt and Erwin Piscator. Made advertising shorts before the war. Directed and wrote scripts for three features 1946-49. Went to West Germany, 1955, where he made several important films including *Roses for the Prosecutor* 1959, *The Threepenny Opera* 1962, and *Herrenpartie* 1964. Feature films made in East Germany: *The Murderers Are among Us* 46; *The Strange Adventure of Herr Fridolin B.* 48; *Rotation* 49; *The Kaiser's Lackey* 51; *The Story of Little Mook* 53; *Beacon* 54.

118 Thate, Hilmar (1931-   ). Eminent stage, film and TV actor. At sixteen, went to State Drama School, Halle. Spent six years at Maxim Gorky Theatre, Berlin and then joined Berliner Ensemble, where he became one of the best-known actors in the country. Film roles include: *One is Less than One, Sailor's Song, Men with Wings, Mother Courage and Her Children, The Gleiwitz Case, Professor Mamlock, The Divided Sky.*

119 Thorndike, Andrew (1909-   ). Director, in collaboration with his wife Annelie (see below), of high-powered polemical documentaries. Was official of UFA advertising film department before war. Arrested 1942 on suspicion of subverting troops; sent to front as medical orderly. Four years p.o.w. in U.S.S.R. Returned 1948 and joined DEFA studio as newsreel and documentary-maker. Has had own production group at Potsdam Studio since 1967. Films: *The 13th October, From Hamburg to Stralsund* 49; *The Way Up, Wilhelm Pieck—The Life of Our President* 50; *Friendship Wins* (co-dir: Huisken) 51; *The Examination*

52; *Seven from the Rhine* 54; *The German Story* 55; *Holiday on Sylt* 57; *Operation Teutonic Sword* 58; *The Russian Miracle* 63; *Life in Germany* 65; *The Germans* 68.

120 Thorndike, Annelie (1925-   ). Documentary director: works in collaboration with her husband, Andrew (see above). Trained as teacher, and became head of a school in Penzlin which she had helped to found. Met Andrew during shooting of *The Way Up* at the school. Films: (see Andrew Thorndike 1951 onwards).

121 Wiens, Paul (1922-   ). Gifted poet and scriptwriter. Studied philosophy and political economy Switzerland 1939-42. Arrested in 1943 and sent to S.S. corrective labour camp in Vienna. Worked as teacher in Vienna for two years after war. Returned Berlin 1947 since when he has become well-known as poet, translator and scriptwriter (in association with Egel). Film scripts include: *The Little and the Big Happiness,*

Staudte's THE MURDERERS ARE AMONG US (with Hildegarde Knef and E. W. Borchert)

Recovery (co-writer: Egel), *One is Less than One*, *Sailors' Song* (co-writer: Egel), *Men with Wings* (co-writer: Egel).

122 Wolf, Konrad (1925-   ). Prize-winning feature director. Son of author Friedrich Wolf. Emigrated with parents to U.S.S.R., 1933. Officer in Red Army during war. Worked at House of Soviet Culture, Berlin until 1949 when he joined director's class at Moscow (under Gerasimov). While studying was asst. to Maetzig (q.v.) and Joris Ivens. Graduated 1955. Gained international awards for *Stars* and *Professor Mamlock*. President of German Academy of Art. Films: *One is Less than One* (graduation film), *Recovery 55; Lissy 57; Stars* (co-prod. with Bulgaria) *59; Men with Wings 60; Professor Mamlock 61; The Divided Sky 64; The Little Prince* (TV film) *66; I Was Nineteen 67.*

Two shots from Wolf's I WAS NINETEEN
(with Jaecki Schwarz)

HUNGARY

HUNGARY

Pop. 10,135,000. Small country with long film-making traditions and a lively, expanding industry.

Production:

Feature films: Prewar—30-40 annually. Postwar—5 in 1947; 4 in 1950; 10 in 1955; 14 in 1960; 20 in 1965; 23 in 1967.
Analysis: 1967—23 feature films, 44 documentaries, etc., 44 educational; 7 at Béla Balázs studios. 35 cartoons, 2 puppet films.

Cinemas:

1935: 452 (including 123 in Budapest). 1945: 972 (including 113 in Budapest). 1967: 4,248 (including 172 in Budapest). (This figure includes cinemas at clubs and local organisations).

Training:

Academy for Cinematographic Art—four-year courses for directors and cameramen (referred to in biographies as "Budapest").
Post-graduate experience at Béla Balázs studios.

Studios:

Hunnia Studios, Budapest—features (Four production groups).
Budapest Studios—newsreel, documentary and educational films.
Pannonia Studios—Cartoons, puppet films and dubbing.
Béla Balázs Studio—for young film-makers.

Hungary is one of the oldest film-making countries in Europe, with a tradition of feature production and film theory dating back to before the first world war. The first film was a newsreel shot in 1896; and after various experiments, regular feature production began in 1912. Hungary was the first country to have a nationalised film industry, beating the Soviet Union by a few months. During the short-lived Council of Republics, April to August 1919, the state-owned industry made 31 films. But with the defeat of the Council by the Horthy forces, the cinema was restored to private ownership, film-workers were singled out for special attack, and many of the leading directors, including Sándor (Alexander) Korda, were forced to flee to Britain and America. Throughout the Twenties and Thirties, production was prolific but highly commercialised, consisting in the main of poor imitations of the Hollywood style. Outstanding actor of the Thirties was Gyula Kabos; most popular and prolific directors were Steve Sekely and Béla Gaál. Among the directors of the period who have helped to found the nationalised industry and who remain active today are **Keleti** and **Gertler**. The most outstanding film to emerge in the pre-liberation period was *People of the Alps,* made by the then very young director István Szőts in 1941.

Postwar: The studios had suffered considerable wartime damage. Reconstructing and re-organising them, and gathering new equipment and staff, was no easy task. The transitional period, before nationalisation in 1948, yielded two outstanding films: *Song of the Cornfields* (Szőts) and *Somewhere in Europe* (G. Radványi) both made in 1947. The first feature film of the nationalised industry was *The Soil under Your Feet.* These films, together with *Mattie the Gooseboy,* the first colour production, were early ex-

Opposite: Zoltan Latinovits in Jancso's CANTATA

amples of a tradition for a kind of lyrical realism which became the keynote of the Fifties, after the period of stagnation which Hungary, along with most other countries, suffered. The greatest directors of the period were **Fábri** (*Merry-Go-Round, Hannibal,* etc.) and **Máriássy** (*Spring in Budapest, A Pint of Beer*). Other important directors were **Makk, Ranódy, Révész** and **Herskó. Fehér**'s *Sunday Romance* was among the most internationally successful films.

The political events of 1956 were rapidly reflected and analysed on the screen by films like *At Midnight, Yesterday, Danse Macabre, Dialogue,* and, much later, by the immensely mature and probing *Twenty Hours.* After a bad patch of administrative difficulty in the early Sixties, *Cantata* followed by *Twenty Hours* and the interview film *Difficult People* opened the door for a dynamic cinema renaissance in which traditional filming flourished alongside the emergence of a "new wave." Among the "new wave" film-makers were middle generation directors like **Kovács, Jancsó** and **Bacsó** and a new generation of directors not long out of Film School, like **Szabó, Gaál, Kardos, Kósa** and Pál Sándor. In widely differing ways they began to tackle difficult, and even touchy, contemporary themes in styles which broke away from the classicism of the past.

An important factor in the emergence of the new generation was the establishment of the Béla Balázs studios in 1957 (fully operative 1961), which were designed to give young directors and cameramen fresh from film school the opportunity to experiment and create.

Cartoons and documentaries: Cartoon production began in a modest way, under difficult conditions, at the end of the Forties. The first big international successes were achieved in 1960 with *The Pencil and the India-rubber* and *The Duel,* made by Macskássy and Várnai. Among other leading animators are **Nepp**, György Kovásznai, Péter Szoboszlay, József Gémes, Attila Dargay and the puppet film-maker Ottó Foky.

Documentaries play an important part in Hungarian cinema. An unusually large number of women directors, including **Marianne Szemes, Livia Gyarmathy,** Anna Herskó, Ilona Kolonits and Márta Mészáros have been successful in the shorts and documentary field. Among their male colleagues are **Csöke, Takács,** and **Timár.**

Veterans **Kollanyi** and **Homoki Nagy** played a big part in developing Hungary's reputation for nature films.

Tamás Banovich specialises in dance on film and Miklós Szinetár specialises in opera.

123 Bacsó, Péter (1928-). "New wave" director concerned with contemporary problems. Writes own scenarios. Graduated Budapest 1950. Screenwriter of many successful films including Fábri's *Anna* and *The Last Goal.* Directed: *No Problems in Summer* 63; *Cyclists in Love* 65; *Summer on the Hill* 67; *Shot in the Head* 68; *The Witness* (projected) 69.

124 Bálint, András (1943-). Young actor closely associated with István Szabó's films. Studied acting Budapest 1963. Then joined National Theatre Company of Pécs, playing contemporary and classic roles. Film roles in *The Age of Daydreaming, Deadlock, Father, Hallo Vera!*

125 Bán, Frigyes (1902-). Veteran director of nearly forty features including first major production of nationalised industry, *The Soil under Your Feet.* Started film career as actor. Postwar films include: *The Prophet of the Fields* 47; *The Soil under Your Feet* 48; *Gentry Skylarking* 49; *Liberated Land* 50; *Baptism by Fire* 51; *Semmelweis* 52; *Rákóczi's Lieutenant* 53; *Extinguished Flames* 56; *A Quiet Home* 57; *Fatia Negra* 59; *A Husband for Susy* 60; *The Money-maker* 63; *Car Crazy* 64; *The Healing Water* 66.

126 Bessenyei, Ferenc (1919-). Distinguished actor. Member of Budapest National Theatre. Stage successes include classic roles in Shakespeare, Chekov etc. An outstanding stage Falstaff. Started career as singer. Began acting 1945. Film roles include: *Full Steam Ahead!, The Storm, Under the City, The Day of Wrath, A Strange Mark of Identity, Fever, Extinguished Flames, Be Good until Death, A Summer Rain, The Brute, Truth Cannot Be Hidden, Hail Days, Autumn Star, Fig-Leaf, The Last of the Nabobs.*

127 Csőke, József (-). Versatile and prolific director of shorts, newsreels, travelogues, with special interest in films on sport. Qualified as teacher, 1946; began film career, 1950. Graduated as journalist while working at newsreel studios. Awarded Béla Balázs prize, 1964. Most important recent films: *Margaret, A Visit in Hungary, Hungary Today, Ten Golden Medals* 65; *European Champions, In the Traces of the Ball* 66; *Budapest—City of Sports, Hallo, Here's Mexico, Master of Gymnastics, Paddling in a Kayak* 67; *Siqueiros* 68.

128 Fábri, Zoltán (1917-). Distinguished director of world repute with highly individual style and special feeling for country life. Trained as artist, graduated Academy of Dramatic Art, Budapest 1941. Began career as actor, stage manager and set designer. Usually designs sets for his own films. Films: *The*

Above: Ban's THE SOIL UNDER YOUR FEET.
Below: Mari Torocsik in Fabri's MERRY-GO-ROUND

Storm 52; Fourteen Lives Saved 54; Merry-Go-Round 55; Professor Hannibal 56; Summer Clouds 57; Anna 58; The Brute 59; The Last Goal 61; Darkness in Daytime 63; Twenty Hours 64; A Hard Summer (TV) 65; Late Season 67; The Paul Street Boys 68; The Tót Family (projected) 69.

129 Fehér, Imre (1926-   ). Feature director who made his mark with his first film. Graduated Budapest 1950. Has worked as dramatist and director. Films: A Sunday Romance, A Bird of Heaven 57; Walking to Heaven, Sword and Dice 59; Truth Cannot Be Hidden, Woman at the Helm 62; Harlequin and His Lover 66.

130 Gaál, István (1933-   ). "New Wave" director. Special interest in peasant themes. Graduated Budapest, 1959. Also studied at Centro Sperimentale, Rome. Made several prize-winning shorts. Was cameraman for prize-winning .documentary, Gypsies 1962 (directed by Sára, with whom he worked closely until 1964). His first feature won

two international awards. Shorts: Surfacemen 57; To and Fro 62; Tisza—Autumn in Sketches 63. Feature films: Current 64; The Green Years 65; Baptism 67.

131 Gábor, Miklós (1919-   ). Popular actor of stage, cinema and TV. Graduated at Academy for Dramatic Art, 1940. Started stage career 1941. Stage roles include an internationally-acclaimed Hamlet. Film roles include: Somewhere in Europe, Spring in Budapest, At Midnight, Sword and Dice, Three Stars, The Bells Have Gone to Rome, A Certain Major Benedek, Alba Regia, Every Day—Sunday, Father, Lost Generation (Walls).

132 Gertler, Viktor (1901-   ). Veteran director. Started work as bank clerk, then studied singing and graduated in drama. Was actor, asst. dir. and cutter before becoming director in 1933. Among first to start working after war: helped establish nationalised cinema. Postwar films include: Without

Two shots from Fabri's PROFESSOR HANNIBAL

Gaal's CURRENT (with Andrea Drahota at centre front)

Lies 45; Gala-Suit 48; Honesty and Glory, Battle in Peace 51; State Department Store, The Magic Chair 52; Me and My Grandfather 54; Hit and Run 55; Fever 57; Red Ink 59; The Man with the Golden Touch 62; Lady-Killer in Trouble 64; And then the Guy 66.

133 Gyarmathy, Livia (1932-   ). Prize-winning documentary director. Started career as chemical engineer, then joined Hungarian Film School and graduated 1964. Films: Fifty-eight Seconds 64; Message 67.

134 Herskó, János (1926-   ). Distinguished director, film educationalist and leading personality in Hungarian film world. After university, graduated Budapest, 1949. Then studied at Moscow Film School. Professor of Film Directing at Budapest (Assistant Director of the School). Feature films: Under the City

53; The Iron Flower 57; A Houseful of Happiness 60; Dialogue 63; Hallo, Vera! 67.

Above and opposite: Jancso's THE ROUND-UP

135 Homoki Nagy, István (1914-). Distinguished director of nature films. Graduated in law 1934 and practised as lawyer before the war. Observed and photographed bird life and nature as hobby. Began film career 1949. Full-length films include: *A Kingdom on the Waters, From Blossom-Time to Autumn Leaves, Pals, Pals over Mounts and Dales.* Shorts include: *Silent Ruins, The Naughty Bird, The Young Eagle, An Afternoon Full of Adventures, Moments in the Forest, A Woodland Pond.*

136 Illés, György (1914-). Leading cameraman whose work spans the entire postwar period. Professor at Budapest. First worked as studio spotlight operator. Became cameraman 1948. Shot over twenty features including: *Anna Szabó, Baptism by Fire, The Storm, Spring in Budapest, Danse Macabre, The House under the Rocks, Sleepless Years, Fatia Negra, Calvary, Don't Keep Off the Grass, Test Trip, Dialogue, Skylark, Twenty Hours, Cyclists in Love, Late Season, Lost Generation, The Paul Street Boys.*

137 Jancsó, Miklós (1921-). Leading "new wave" director with strong, formal, highly individual style. Studied law, folklore and history of art at University. Graduated Budapest, 1950. Began film career as newsreel director, then made a number of shorts and documentaries. Shorts and documentaries include: *Autumn in Badacsony, 54; Colourful China 57; Derkovits*

Two films by Jancso: THE RED AND THE WHITE (above) and SILENCE AND CRY (below)

58; *Immortality* 59; *Dusks and Dawns* 61; *Living Tree* 63. Feature films: *The Bells Have Gone to Rome* 58; *Three Stars* (Part 1) 60; *Cantata* 63; *My Way Home* 64; *The Round-Up* 65; *The Red and the White* 67; *Silence and Cry*; *The Confrontation, Sirokkó* (co-prod. with France) 69.

138   Kardos, Ferenc (1937-   ). Director who made a big impact with his first feature. Graduated Budapest, 1961. Made several shorts at the Béla Balázs Studios. Feature films: *Grimace* 65 (co-director János Rózsa); *Red-Letter Days* 67.

139   Keleti, Márton (1905-   ). Director of popular features and musicals, with over forty films to his credit. First film 1937. Postwar films include: *The Schoolmistress* 45; *Mickey Magnate* 49; *Singing Makes Life Beautiful* 50; *Erkel* 52; *Two Confessions* 57; *The Lady and the Gypsy* (co-prod. with France) 58; *A Few Steps to the Frontier, Yesterday* 59; *A Rainy Sunday* 62; *Villa Negra* 64; *The Corporal and the Others* 65; *The*

Story of My Stupidity 66; *Changing Clouds,* A *Study about Women* 67.

140   Kollányi, Ágoston (1913-   ). Distinguished director of popular science and nature films. Graduated in maths and physics. Worked in films since 1946. Has made over thirty films most of which have gained international prizes. They include: *The Structure of Matter* 51; *Aquarium* 54; *Kati and the Wild Cat, The 2000-Year Anniversary of Pécs* 55; *Cradles* 57; *István Szőnyi, The Story of a Second* 59; *The Island of the Mongooses, Living Traps, Silver Threads* 61; *Like a Drop in the Sea* 62; *What You Gave is Life Itself, Jumping Legs, Swinging Wings, Song About Iron* 63; *Eternal Renaissance* (full length) 66.

141   Kósa, Ferenc (1937-   ). Director whose first feature was a key contribution to "new wave." Graduated Budapest, 1963. Asst. dir. until 1965. Shorts: *Study of a Working Day* 61; *Light, Notes on the History of a Lake* 62. Feature

Two films by Kovacs: above, Zoltan Latinovits (centre) in COLD DAYS; below, Miklos Gabor (at left) in LOST GENERATION (with Philippe March and Bernadette Lafont)

films: *Ten Thousand Suns, Suicide* (short feature) 67.

142 Kovács, András (1925-   ). Director of films with serious, searching themes. Played an important part in establishing "new wave," partly through his socially critical documentary *Difficult People*. Graduated Budapest 1950.

Head of Dramatic Department of Hunnia Studios 1951-57. Films: *A Summer Rain* 60; *On the Roofs of Budapest* 61; *Autumn Star* 62; *Difficult People* 64; *Two Portraits* (short), *Today or Tomorrow* (short) 65; *Cold Days* 66; *Lost Generation (Walls)* 67; *The Relay* (projected) 69.

143 Latinovits, Zoltán (1932-   ). Versatile actor with gift for suggesting inner tension. Despite early acting ambitions, studied architecture at University. After graduation, joined provincial theatre; soon became leading actor. First film role 1959. A leading member of Gaiety Theatre, Budapest since 1962. Closely associated with films by Kovács and Jancsó (both q.v.). Film roles include: *Walking to Heaven, Cantata, Goliath, Photo Haber, Skylark, And Then the Guy, The Round-Up, The Last of the Nabobs, Three Nights of a Love, Cold Days, Silence and Cry, Baptism, Lost Generation, House of Cards, A Study about Women.*

Above: Miklos Gabor in Mariassy's SPRING IN BUDAPEST (with Zsursa Gordon)
Opposite: Antal Pager in Fabri's LATE SEASON

144 Makk, Károly (1925-   ). One of the most important directors to

emerge in the Fifties. Started film work as asst. dir. in 1944. Second assistant on *Somewhere in Europe*. Graduated Budapest 1949. Feature films *Liliomfi* 54; *Ward No. 9* 55; *Tale on the Twelve Points* 56; *The House under the Rocks* 58; *Brigade No. 39* 59; *Don't Keep Off the Grass* 60; *The Fanatics* 61; *The Lost Paradise* 62; *The Last but One* 63; *His Majesty's Dates* 64; *Before God and Man* 68.

145 Máriássy, Félix (1919-   ). Distinguished director with a strong lyrical style. Has worked in films since 1939. Played leading part in establishing and developing nationalised cinema. Collaborated with Radványi on *Somewhere in Europe*. Professor at Budapest since 1947. His wife, Judith, writes most of his screenplays. Films: *Anna Szabó* 49; *Catherine's Marriage* 49; *Full Steam Ahead!* 51; *Relatives* 54; *A Glass of Beer,*

turned to Hungary 1956. Has played in over 120 films including: *Dani, Yesterday, Calvary, Don't Keep Off the Grass, A Summer Rain, The Lost Paradise, Villa Negra, Skylark, Twenty Hours, Sweet and Bitter, Late Season, A Study about Women, House of Cards, Something Is Drifting on the Water* (U.S.-Czech. co-prod.).

Spring in Budapest 55; Smugglers 58; Sleepless Years, A Simple Love 59; It Is a Long Way Home, Test Trip 60; Every Day—Sunday (co-prod. with Czechoslovakia) 62; *Goliath 64; Fig-leaf 66; Bondage 68.*

146   Nepp, József (1934-   ). Prize-winning cartoon director with economical style and a feeling for the grotesque. Graduated at Academy of Fine Arts. Initiated the popular "Gustavus" series. Films include: *Passion 61; Wish Whatever You Want 62; From Tomorrow On, A Tale about a Beetle 63; Five Minute Murder 66; Don't Irritate the Mouse 67.*

147   Páger, Antal (1899-   ). Very distinguished screen actor with experience ranging from comedy and operetta to classical tragedy. Wanted to become lawyer and painter but at university displayed remarkable acting talent. Started professional career at Szeged theatre 1919; entered films as soon as talkies were introduced. Spent twelve years in Argentina, earning living as painter. Re-

148   Ranódy, László (1919-   ). Middle generation feature director. Graduated Budapest and also in law. Began film career as artistic director of Hungarian Film Studios. Technical adviser on *Mattie the Goose-Boy* 1949. Films: *Love Travels By Coach 54; Abyss 55; Danse Macabre 57; For Whom the Larks Sing 59; Be Good until Death 60; Skylark 64; The Golden Kite 66.*

149   Rényi, Tamás (1929-   ). Middle generation director. Worked at textile mill before enrolling at Budapest, 1950. Joined army while student, worked as director in Army Film Institute. Asst. to Fábri (q.v.) 1956-62. Feature films: *Tales of a Long Journey 62; Two Days—*

Above: Radvanyi's SOMEWHERE IN EUROPE, co-scripted by Mariassy, with Miklos Gabor at right
Below: Ranody's SKYLARK, with Mari Torocsik and Zoltan Latinovits

Like the Others 63; *From Noon to Dawn* 64; *No Love Please* 65; *Deadlock* 66; *The Valley* 67.

150 Révész, György (1927-   ). Prize-winning director of emergent generation of Fifties. Graduated Budapest 1950. Films: *Two Times Two Are Sometimes Five* 54; *Gala Dinner* 56; *At Midnight* 57; *What a Night!* 58; *The Right Man* 59; *Four Children in the Flood* 61; *The Land of Angels, Hail Days* 62; *Well, Young Man?* 63; *Yes* 64; *No* 65; *All Beginnings Are Hard* 66; *Three Nights of a Love* 67.

151 Ruttkay, Éva (1927-   ). Attractive and gifted leading lady of stage and screen, so popular in Budapest that she is known as "The Ruttkay." First stage appearance at a children's theatre at the age of two. Stage successes include St. Joan, Juliet, and Electra in the O'Neill play. Has been in cinema since 1949. Film roles include: *Anna Szabó, Catherine's Marriage, A Strange Mark of Identity, A Glass of Beer, Tale on the Twelve Points, Extinguished Flames, At Midnight, What a Night!, Sleepless Years, Sword and Dice, Three Stars, Memories of a Strange Night, Every Day—Sunday, Woman at the Helm, Photo Haber, The Story of My Stupidity, The Last of the Nabobs, The Fake "Isabella", A Study about Women.*

152 Sára, Sándor (1933-   ). Gifted cameraman, closely associated with "new wave." Graduated Budapest 1957. Won international award for diploma work *Surfacemen* (directed by Gaál). Helped found Béla Balázs Studio. Has shot over thirty shorts and directed several. Worked closely with Gaál (q.v.) until 1964. Directed prize-winning short *Gypsies*, 1962 for which Gaál was cam-

eraman. Directed first feature (also cameraman and scriptwriter) 1968. Feature films shot: *Current, Grimace, Father, Ten Thousand Suns, Red Letter Days, Suicide.* Feature film directed: *The Thrown-up Stone* 68.

153 Somló, Tamás (1929-   ). Prize-winning cameraman best known for work on Jancsó's films. Graduated at Camera Faculty, Budapest 1949. Has worked on over sixty shorts at Newsreel and Documentary studio. Shorts shot and directed: *Cybernetics* 64; *Music and Computer* 65; *Chapters about the Human Brain, One Lamp—Many Lamps* 66. Films shot include: *Derkovits, The Bells Have Gone to Rome, Song about Iron, My Way Home, The Round-up, Three Nights of a Love, The Red and the White, The Girl.*

154 Szabó, István (1938-   ). One of youngest and most significant "new wave" directors. Graduated Budapest 1961. Diploma work *Concert* won him immediate acclaim. All his films have gained international awards. Shorts (at

Above: Mari Torocsik (with Gabor Koncz) in Renyi's DEADLOCK.
Below: Miklos Gabor (at left) and Andras Balint in Szabo's THE AGE OF DAYDREAMING

village. Started film work as laboratory assistant. Became asst. cameraman, working with Fábri (q.v.) who took him under his wing and gave him first opportunity as director of photography. Films include: *Professor Hannibal, The Iron Flower, Anna, Land of Angels, The Lost Paradise, Well, Young Man?, Yes, Cold Days.*

156 Szemes, Marianne (1924-   ). Screenwriter and documentary director. Deals with social problems in *cinéma vérité* style. Started career as photographer. Graduated Budapest 1949. Wrote screenplays for *The Sledge* and feature film *Dani*, both directed by her husband, Mihály (q.v. below). Co-writer of *Photo Haber*. Documentaries include: *Divorce in Budapest* 64; *I'm Angry for Your Sake* 67; *It's So Simple* 68.

Béla Balázs studios): *Variations upon a Theme* 61; *You* 63. Feature films: *The Age of Daydreaming* 64; *Father* 66.

155 Szécsény, Ferenc (1922-   ). Prize-winning cameraman. Born in small

157 Szemes, Mihály (1920-   ). Feature director. Started film career 1942 at newsreel studios. Made several short

Miklos Gabor in Szabo's FATHER

features, including the award-winning *The Sledge* 1955, scripted by his wife Marianne (q.v. above). Feature films: *Dani* 57; *Our Kid* 59; *A Certain Major Benedek* 60; *Alba Regia* 61; *New Gilgames* 63; *Sweet and Bitter* 66.

158 Szirtes, Ádám (1925-   ). Leading actor. Son of poor peasants, left school early. Worked as agricultural labourer, then as harness-maker. Seized new opportunities opened up by post-war government to study at Academy of Dramatic Art. Chosen while still a student to play lead in *The Soil under Your Feet*. Subsequent roles include: *Anna Szabó*, *Catherine's Marriage*, *Liberated Land*, *Battle in Peace*, *Merry-Go-Round*, *Bird of Heaven*, *A Few Steps to the Frontier*, *It Is a Long Way Home*, *The Fanatics*, *Villa Negra*, *The Girl*.

159 Takács, Gábor (1928-   ). Scientific and education film-maker with special interest in art. Graduated Budapest 1951. Asst. dir. on several feature films. Has worked as newsreel director. Films include: *Béla Bartók* 55; *Joseph Haydn* 59; *The Children Are Singing* 60; *Composition in Painting* 61; *The Golden Section* 62; *Colours in Painting, Space and Perspective in Painting* 64; *Mikrokosmos* 66.

160 Timár, István (1926-   ). Documentary director dealing mainly with social problems. Graduated Budapest 1960. Has won many international prizes. Films include: *Mosaic* 62; *Visit* 63; *Crime* 64.

161 Tolnay, Klári (1914-   ). First lady of stage and screen. Played *ingénue* roles in the Thirties but rapidly broadened her range after the war. Her theatrical successes include leading roles in Shakespeare, Ibsen, Chekhov, Tennes-

see Williams and Arthur Miller; equally at home in comedy and tragedy. Outstanding roles include: *Mrs. Déry*, *Relatives*, *Dani*, *For Whom the Larks Sing*, *Don't Keep Off the Grass*, *The Land of Angels*, *Hail Days*, *Skylark*, *Father*, *Late Season*, *The Widow and the Police Officer*.

162 Törőcsik, Mari (1935-   ). Popular actress of stage and screen. Graduated Budapest 1957. First role in *Merry-Go-Round*, while still a student. Member of Budapest National Theatre. Film roles include: *Merry-Go-Round*, *Two Confessions*, *The Iron Flower*, *Anna*, *Sword and Dice*, *Our Kid*, *Walking to Heaven*, *Three Stars*, *A Houseful of Happiness*, *Be Good until Death*, *The Lost Paradise*, *Autumn Star*, *Skylark*, *No, And Then the Guy . . .* , *Deadlock*, *Silence and Cry*, *A House of Cards*.

163 Várkonyi, Zoltán (1912-   ). Director of popular features. Long association with theatre as actor and director. Graduated at Academy for

Above: Mari Torocsik (with Imre Soos) in Fabri's MERRY-GO-ROUND
Below: Varkonyi's THE LAST OF THE NABOBS

Dramatic Art and joined National Theatre. Started film career prewar as actor. Became director in 1953, but continues to take film roles. Latest film, a Sixteenth-century historical epic, is most ambitious project yet undertaken by Budapest Studios. Films directed: *The Day of Wrath* 53; *West Zone, The Birth of Menyhert Simon* 54; *A Strange Mark of Identity, Georges Dandin* 55; *Pillar of Salt* 56; *Crime at Dawn* 58; *Three Stars* (third episode), *Csutak and the Grey Horse* 60; *Memories of a Strange Night* 61; *Photo Haber* 63; *Men and Banners* 65; *The Last of the Nabobs* 66; *The Stars of Eger* 69.

164 Vas, Judit (1932-   ). Director of educational films. Graduated Budapest 1954. Later graduated in psychology at Budapest University. Films include: *Polarised Light* 60; *Who Can Carry On Longer?* 62; *Circadian Rhythms, Bobe* 65; *Where Are You Going?* 66; *Who Is Your Friend?, Trio* 67.

Varkonyi as actor in Hersko's THE IRON FLOWER

POLAND

POLAND

Pop. 35,000,000. Flourishing film industry.

Production:

> Features—prewar: 15-25 a year. 2 in 1947; 4 in 1950; 9 in 1955; 21 in 1960; 32 in 1965; 26 in 1967.

Cinemas:

> Prewar: 700-800. 1968: About 4,000 (About 1,400 35mm; the rest 16mm. Over 100 have panoramic screens).

Training:

> Leon Schiller State Theatre and Film School at Lódź, (referred to in biographies as "Lodz"): for directors, actors and cameramen.
> Film acting courses at Theatre Schools in Warsaw and Cracow.

Studios:

> Feature film studios at Warsaw and Wroclaw.
> Documentary Studios at Warsaw (documentaries and newsreels).
> Educational Film Studio at Lódź.
> Se-ma-for Studio (puppet and featurette) at Tuszyn, nr. Lódź.
> Minature Film Studio (cartoons) at Warsaw.
> Cartoon Film Studio, Bielsko-Biala.

Although Poland can boast some important film pioneers and a long history of theory and production, its postwar cinema had a rather meagre inheritance to draw upon. Several short comedies were produced in 1902; regular production developed from 1908 onwards. The first studio was established in 1920, two years after the restoration of the independent Polish State. Between the wars, film production was a matter for small-time speculation; companies making only two or three films each would mushroom and disappear. Of about 146 companies, only six made more than ten films each. Among the best-known names of commercial cinema were directors Aleksander Hertz, Wiktor Bieganski and Józef Lejtes, cameraman Ryszard Boleslawski, and actresses Jadwiga Smosarska and Pola Negri. Three film-makers who made their *débuts* in the Twenties— **Ford, Buczkowski** and Eugeniusz Cekalsi—helped to establish postwar cinema. **Ford's** *Legion of the Street* was the most popular film of 1932.

The *avant-garde* film society START (Society of the Devotees of the Artistic Film), established in 1929 by a group of students including **Jakubowska,** Cekalski and Stanislaw Wohl, and later joined by **Bossak, Ford,** Ludwik Perski and Jerzy Toeplitz, although unable to exert much direct influence at the time, helped to lay the theoretical basis for postwar cinema. The practical basis was laid during the war through the film units that were organised in Polish military detachments in Britain, France, the Near East and the U.S.S.R.

Postwar: Because of wartime occupation and devastation, the newly-nationalised industry had virtually to start from scratch. But it had the experiences of the wartime directors and cameramen to draw upon. The early productions were largely documentary in character and the first feature, *Forbidden Songs* (1947) had no personalised hero.

Opposite: Munk's EROICA

In the following three years only seven films were made, but of these, three—*The Last Stage, Border Street* and *The Treasure*—proved to be of lasting artistic value. Production increased in the Fifties, but in the atmosphere of dogmatism, which affected film-making throughout Eastern Europe at the beginning of the decade, the results were mainly undistinguished. **Ford** emerged as the dominant director of the period with *Youth of Chopin* and *Five Boys from Barska Street;* Jerzy Zarzycki's *Unvanquished City* was another notable film: **Rybkowski** made several worthwhile contributions to feature film development.

The first big step forward came with the emergence of **Kawalerowicz** and **Wajda,** followed by **Munk.** The establishment of decentralised, self-supporting production groups in 1955 resulted in a new burst of creative initiative, and the term "Polish film school" began to be applied to the directors of the very talented and highly individual films that emerged. Films by **Wajda, Munk** and **Kawalerowicz,** and then by **Has, Kutz, Różewicz, Lesiewicz, Passendorfer, Chmielewski,** the husband-and-wife team the **Petelskis,** and the scripts by **Stawiński,** displayed a wide variety of styles. At first they tended to concentrate on problems of wartime and the immediate postwar period (*A Generation, Kanal, Cross of Valour, Panic on a Train* etc.), but later, they began to tackle contemporary themes (*Innocent Sorcerers, Bad Luck* etc.) in highly personalised ways. Many of the films, notably those of **Munk,** were fraught with the special kind of irony which is inherent in Polish literary traditions. The death of **Munk** in 1961 was a sad blow to Polish film art. Among the outstanding historical films of the period were *Knights of the Teutonic Order* and the psychologically complex *Mother Joan and the Angels.* The ambitious colour spectacle *Pharaoh* was completed in 1965.

In the early Sixties, the vitality of the "Polish film school" abated and production in general was less interesting, apart from the emergence of two outstanding directors, **Skolimowski** and **Polański,** both of whom preferred to work abroad. **Skolimowski** returned to Poland to make *Hands Up!* in 1968. Among the newer directors **Leszcyzyński** and **Kluba,** both of whom had worked closely with "Polish film school" directors, showed great promise. During the political turbulence of 1968, the production teams were disbanded and re-organised on a non-self-supporting basis, and by the end of the year the future remained uncertain.

Cartoons, documentaries and shorts: Poland has a world-wide reputation for its documentaries and cartoons; the Cracow Festival of Short Films is an important annual international event. Many well-known feature directors, including **Wajda, Munk, Passendorfer, Hoffman, Lesiewicz** and **Lomnicki,** made their names at first in the documentary field. Among the leading documentarists are **Bossak, Jaworski, Karabasz, Kidawa, Majewski, Makarczyński** and **Ślesicki.** Outstanding nature-film directors are Karol Marczak, Wlodzimierz Puchalski and Józef Arkusz.

Animated production falls into two main categories—films for children and films for adults. Big successes have been achieved in the first category by Zenon Wasilewski (who died in 1966), Wladyslaw Nehrebecki, Lechoslaw Marszalek, Wacklaw Wajser, Teresa Badzian, Edward Sturlis, Lida Hornicka, **Haupe** and Halina Bielinska.

The number of satirical or sophisticated cartoons for adults is growing annually; leading directors in this category are **Szczechura**, Miroslaw Kijowicz, **Giersz**, Jerzy Zitzman, **Lenica** and **Borowczyk**, (the last two have been working abroad). Films in both categories are usually without dialogue, and among the eminent composers who have written scores for animated films are **Penderecki**, Zbigniew Turski, Jerzy Abratowski, Wlodzimierz Kotoński, Jerzy Maturskiewics and Waldemar Kazanecki.

165　Baird, Tadeusz (1928-　). Outstanding contemporary composer of orchestral works, vocal-instrumental compositions, chamber music, music drama etc. Has written or arranged music for over thirty films, including *The Noose, Lotna, The Sky is Our Roof, Year One, Panic on a Train, The Last Battle, Samson, Between Two Shores, The Broken Bridge, The Passenger, Everyday, The Wooden Rosary, Room for One.*

166　Batory, Jan (1921-　). Feature director. Graduated Lódź. Worked as asst. dir. until 1954. Films include: *Podhale on Fire* (co-dir. and co-writer: Henryk Hechtkopf) 56; *The President's Visit* 61; *Death of a Taxi-driver* 63; *Farewell to a Spy* 64; *Moon Thieves, A Cure for Love* 65; *Dancing at Hitler's Headquarters* 68.

167　Borowczyk, Walerian (1923-　). Artist and animated film-maker. Individual, *avant-garde* style. Painter. Studied Cracow Academy of Fine Arts, 1946-51. Lithographic work, cinema posters, 1951-56. Made several films in collaboration with Lenica (q.v.) 1957-58. Then went to France, where he made a large number of films including: *Astronauts* (with Chris Marker) 60; *Les Jeux des Anges* 64; *Renaissance, Grandmother's Encyclopaedia* 65, full-length cartoon *Théâtre de Monsieur et Madame Kabal,* and live-action feature, *Goto, l'Ile d'amour.* Returned to Poland 1968 to make full-length live-action film, *Mazepa.* Films made in Poland with

Lenica: *Once upon a Time, Rewarded Feelings 57; The House 58.* Independently, *The School 58.*

168　Bossak, Jerzy (1910-　). Born Rostov-on-Don. Outstanding documentary director; a leading force in postwar documentary production. Artistic Manager of Warsaw Documentary Studio which he helped to found. Professor at Lódź. Studied law and history Warsaw University. One of the organisers of START (see Preface). Together with Ford, organised Film Unit of Polish Army in U.S.S.R. during war. After war became Editor of Polish Newsreels. Has made over forty documentaries and special newsreels; began first feature 1968. Films include: *Battle of Kolobrzeg, The*

Buczkowski's FORBIDDEN SONGS

Fall of Berlin 45; 600 Years of Bydgoszcz 46; The Flood 47; Peace Conquers the World (co-dir: Joris Ivens. Full-length) 51; Our Oath 52; Bicycle Race 54; Meeting in Warsaw (with three co-directors. Polish-U.S.S.R. co-production) 55; Songs of the Vistula 56; Mister Dodek (feature) 69. Films made in collaboration with Waclaw Kazimierczak include: Return to the Old City 52; Warsaw 1956 56; September 1956 (full-length) 61; Requiem for 500,000 (full-length) 63; Documents of Fight 68.

169 Bratny, Roman (1921-   ). Distinguished poet and author who has adapted many of his own novels for the cinema and television and has written several original scripts. First works pub-lished 1946. First contact with cinema 1951. Scripted important TV series, based on own novel 1968. Scripts: The Difficult Love; Return to the Past; The Broken Bridge; The Beater; Life Once More; No Justice on Sunday; Contribution.

170 Buczkowski, Leonard (1900-66). Veteran director of popular features. A founder of nationalised feature production. Began film career as asst. dir. 1923. Directed many shorts and documentaries. First feature 1928. Made first full-length postwar feature Forbidden Songs, 1947. Other postwar features: The Treasure 49; The First Start 51; The Marienstadt Adventure 54; The Case of Pilot Maresz 56; A Rainy July, Orzel, 58; Time Past 61; Teenager 62; The Inter-

Zbigniew Cybulski in Has's THE SARAGOSSA MANUSCRIPT

rupted Flight 64; *Maria and Napoleon* 66.

171 Chmielewski, Tadeusz (1927-). Feature director with swift, tense style. Made big impact with first film. Graduated Lódz; worked as asst. dir. while studying. Films include: *Eve Wants to Sleep* 58; *Jack of Spades* 60; *Two Mysterious Men* 62; *Where is the General?* 64; *Two Times a Dream* 68; *How I Unleashed the Second World War— How I Finished the Second World War* 69.

172 Cybulski, Zbigniew (1927-1967). Born in Ukraine, U.S.S.R. Very popular actor of international fame, associated with "Polish school." His celebrated dark glasses symbolised contemporary hero at odds with reality. Studied at Academy of Commerce and Journalism, at Cracow Jagiellonian University and in actors' class at Theatre School, Cracow. First stage appearances at Cracow, 1953. In 1954 went to Gdańsk, where, with Bogumil Kobiela, he established student satirical theatre "Bim-Bom." Was artistic manager, director, co-author and actor at the theatre. In 1956 established "Theatre of Talks," also with Kobiela. Many stage successes in Gdansk and Warsaw as actor and director. First film role, 1954. Was about to start directing a film based on his own script when he

Above: Ford's FIVE BOYS FROM BARSKA STREET, with Tadeusz Janczar (and Aleksandra Slaska)
Opposite: Ford's KNIGHTS OF THE TEUTONIC ORDER

was killed in a railway accident, Wroclaw, 8th Jan. 1967. Film roles in thirty-seven films, including: *A Generation, Shipwrecks, Ashes and Diamonds, The*

Eighth Day of the Week (West German-Polish co-production), *The Cross of Valour, Baltic Express, Parting, Passengers Who Are Late, See You Tomorrow* (also co-scripted), *Innocent Sorcerers, He, She or It* (in France), *L'amour a vingt ans* (Wajda episode), *How To Be Loved, Everyday, The Murderer and the Girl, Silence, No More Divorces, The Saragossa Manuscript, To Love* (in Sweden), *Salto, Penguin, Mexico To-morrow, Christmas Eve, The Code, Full Steam Ahead, Jowita, The Murderer Leaves a Clue.*

173 Ford, Aleksander (1908-). Leading feature and documentary director of older generation, bridging gap between prewar and postwar. Studied art at Warsaw University in Twenties. Active member of START (see preface). Started directing 1928. First feature 1930. Outstanding films of the Thirties: *Legion of the Streets, People of the Vistula* (co-

dir: Jerzy Zarzycki), *Awakening*. During war, worked in Soviet Film Studios and with Bossak (q.v.), organised Polish Army Film Unit, which laid basis for nationalised cinema. Was artistic manager of "Studio" unit. Postwar feature films: *Border Street* 48; *The Youth of Chopin* 52; *Five Boys from Barska Street* 53; *The Eighth Day of the Week* (co-prod. with West Germany) 58; *Knights of the Teutonic Order* 60; *The First Day of Freedom* 64; *Der Arzt stellt fest* (Swiss-West German co-prod.) 66; *Good morning, Poland* (projected full-length documentary) 69.

174 Giersz, Witold (1927-). Prize-winning director and designer of animated films. Graduated Academy of Fine Arts. Began work at Cartoon Studios, Mielsko-Biala, 1956. Moved to Warsaw when Miniature Film Studio was established there. Directed, designed and scripted nearly fifty films between 1956 and 1969. Most important films: *The Little Western* 60; *Dinosaura* 62;

175 Has, Wojciech Jerzy (1925-). Feature director and scriptwriter of "Polish film school" with subtle, melancholy style. Graduated Film Institute, Cracow, 1946. Later studied painting at Academy of Fine Arts. Directed a number of important shorts at Documentary Studio 1948-51 and at Educational Film Studio, Lódz, 1951-56. His first feature was an immediate success. Feature films: *The Noose* 57; *Farewells* 58; *One-Room Tenants* 59; *Parting (Goodbye to the Past)* 60; *Gold* 61 (also acted); *How To Be Loved* 62; *The Saragossa Manuscript* 64; *The Code* 66; *The Doll* 68.

176 Haupe, Wlodzimierz (1924-). Director of animated and live-action films. Studied at Technical College in Warsaw. Started film career as director of puppet films 1951. Then turned to feature films. Puppet films include: *The Rascal Snail* 51; *Lawrence's Orchard* 52; *Janosik* (full-length), *The Circus* 54; *A Moon's Tale* 55; *Changing*

Two films by Has: above, HOW TO BE LOVED;
below, THE SARAGOSSA MANUSCRIPT

of the Guard 59. Feature films include: Lucky Tony (co-dir: Bielinska) 61; The Suit Almost New 64; The Counsel for the Prosecution Has the Floor 65; Matrimonial Advice Column 68.

177 Hoffman, Jerzy (1932-   ). Director of prize-winning documentaries and several features. Graduated Moscow 1955. In collaboration with Skórzewski 1955-65, made many outstanding documentaries dealing with contemporary social problems. They made several films in Cuba, 1961. Documentaries made in collaboration with Skórzewski include: Are You Among Them? 54; Attention Holligans 55; A Souvenir from Calvary, The Carousel of Lowicz 58; Gaudeamus, The Rail, Tips for Today 59; Postcards from Zakopane, Two Faces of God 60; They Met in Havana, Patria o muerte (full-length) 61; Visitez Zakopane 63. Feature films made in collaboration: Gangsters and Philanthropists 62; The Law and the Fist 64; Three Steps in Life 65. Films made by Hoffman alone: Mar-

ket of Miracles (doc.) 66; Colonel Wolodyjowski 67-69.

178 Holoubek, Gustaw (1923-   ). Prominent actor with a reflective, introverted style; very popular on stage, screen and T.V. Studied acting at Theatre School, Cracow. Began stage career in Cracow. Actor, manager and director in Silesia theatre 1949-56. Drama Theatre, Warsaw, 1958. One of his biggest stage successes was in Oedipus Rex. First film role 1953. Has played in nearly thirty films, including: Soldier of Victory, The Noose, Farewells, One-Room Tenants, Time Past, Gangsters and Philanthropists, Café from the Past, Yesterday in Fact, The Law and the Fist, The Saragossa Manuscript, Salto, Maria and Napoleon, The Game. Directed: Those Who Are Late (one episode) 62.

179 Jahoda, Mieczyslaw (1924-   ). Outstanding cameraman closely associated with films of Has (q.v.). Studied simultaneously at Film Institute, Cracow, and at Architecture Faculty, Jagiellonian University. Then in camera class, Lódź. Started work at Documentary and Educational Film Studios. Director of photography for many important feature films including: The Noose, Winter Dusk, Farewells, Knights of the Teutonic Order, Mountains on Fire, Those Who Are Late (also acted), Café from the Past, The Saragossa Manuscript, Mexico Tomorrow, Visit at Twilight, The Code, Gates to Paradise.

180 Jakubowska, Wanda (1907   ). Distinguished woman director of key importance in development of early postwar feature production. Was production manager of "Start" Production Group. Studied History of Fine Arts, Warsaw University in Twenties. A founder member of START (see preface). Made docu-

Jakubowska's THE LAST STAGE

mentaries in the Thirties and collaborated with Ford on *Awakening*, 1934. Her full-length feature *On the Niemen River* was destroyed during the war. Her wartime sufferings in Auschwitz and Ravensbrück are reflected in several of her films, notably in prize-winning feature *The Last Stage*. Feature films: *The Last Stage* 48; *Soldier of Victory* 53; *An Atlantic Story* 54; *Farewell to the Devil* 56; *King Math I* 57; *Encounters in the Dark* (co-production with East Germany), *It Happened Yesterday* 60; *The End of Our World* 64; *The Hot Line* 65.

181 Janczar, Tadeusz (1926-   ). Very popular stage and screen actor. Graduated Theatre School, Warsaw 1947. Was already well-known in theatre when he made screen début 1953. Film roles include: *The Crew, The Soldier of Victory, The Career, Five Boys from Barska Street, A Generation, Kanal, Farewells, Bad Luck.*

182 Jaworski, Tadeusz (1926-   ). Prize-winning director of documentary and educational films. Started as asst. dir. of feature films, then as director at Educational Film Studio. Joined Warsaw Documentary Studio, 1958. Began directing television features 1966. Made several films for W.H.O. in the Sixties. Has made over forty documentaries including: *Strzelno; The Gniezno Portal* 57; *The War* 58; *The Lazienki Park in Warsaw* 59; *Bassari, N 'Fuma, The Ferrymen from Accra* 60; *The Source* 62; *I Was Kapo, A Place for the School* 63; *Decline of the Wizards* 65; *The Secretary* 66; *Manufactures, Okudżawa* 67.

183 Karabasz, Kazimierz (1930-   ). Leading documentarist. Graduated Lódź. Made his early films in collaboration with Ślesicki. His intensely personal style was first revealed in *Musicians*. Films include: *Where the Devil*

Two films by Kawalerowicz:
above, MOTHER JOAN OF THE ANGELS; below, PHARAOH

Says Goodnight (with Ślesicki) 56; *People from the Empty Area* (with Ślesicki, q.v.) 57; *A Slightly Different World, A Day without Sun* (with Ślesicki) 59; *Musicians* 60; *People on the Road, Railway Junction, Where Do You Go?* 61; *Jubilee, The First Steps* 62; *The Birds, In the Club* 63; *Born 1944, On the Threshold* 65; *A Year in Frank's Life* (co-dir: Niedbalski) 67.

est in Silesian themes. Graduated Łódź 1956. Made newsreels and TV films in Silesia 1957-60. Joined Documentary Studio, Warsaw 1961. Has made over a score of films including: *Roll Call for the Insurgents* 61; *Coal Piles, The First Shift* 62; *Competition, Salt and Sweet* 63; *The Heart* (co-dir: Florkowski) 64; *Evidence, In Silence* 65; *One of 6000, The Horizon* 66; *Chopin's Birth Place, Anatomy of a Town, A Walk in the Clouds, Sand and Stone* 67; *The Just* 69.

184 Kawalerowicz, Jerzy (1922-). Born in Ukraine. Feature director, scriptwriter, artistic manager of "Kadr" Production Group. Took film course organised by Cracow Film Institute immediately after war. Also studied fine arts. Worked as asst. dir. and scriptwriter before becoming director. Films: *The Village Mill* (co-dir: Sumerski) 50; *A Night of Remembrance* 53; *Under the Phrygian Star* 54; *The Shadow* 56; *The Real End of the Great War* 57; *Baltic Express* 59; *Mother Joan of the Angels* 61; *Pharaoh* 65; *The Game* 69.

185 Kidawa, Janusz (1931-). Documentary director with special inter-

186 Kluba, Henryk (1931-). Scriptwriter, actor and up-and-coming feature director. Studied at Wroclaw University, then worked as journalist. Graduated as director, Łódź 1959. During studies, acted in several student films, including three Polański shorts. After graduation worked as asst. dir. to Jakubowska, Skolimowski and others, and took small roles in their films. Acting roles include: *Two Men and a Wardrobe, When Angels Fall, Mr. Anatol's Inspection, Mammals, Walkover.* Films directed: *Salvation* (school film) 59; *Slim*

and the Others 66; *The Sun Rises Once a Day* (also acts) 69.

187 Komeda, T. Krzysztof (-   ). (Also known as Christopher Komeda.) Leading jazz pianist and composer. Has composed for films since 1958. Formed popular jazz groups "Trio" and "Komeda Quintet." Wrote scores for most of Polański's films at home and abroad, and for several other foreign films. Has written music for about sixty features and shorts, including: *Two Men and a Wardrobe, Innocent Sorcerers, See You Tomorrow, The Glass Mountain, Le Gros et le Maigre, Knife in the Water, Mammals, Barrier, Cul de Sac, Le Départ, Hands Up!, The Dance of the Vampires* (orig. *The Fearless Vampire Killers*), *People Meet, Rosemary's Baby.*

188 Konwicki, Tadeusz (1926-   ). Born in Lithuania. Prominent author and journalist; also director and scriptwriter. Graduated in literature, Warsaw University. Started work in cinema 1949, first as critic, then as scriptwriter. Scripted: *The Career, Winter Dusk, Mother Joan of the Angels; Pharaoh; Jowita.* Scripted and directed: *Last Day of Summer* (co-dir. and co-writer: Laskowski) 58; *Hallowe'en* 61; *Salto; A Moment of Peace* (French-West German-Polish co-prod. One episode) 65.

189 Kostenko, Andrzej (1936-   ). Versatile, up-and-coming cameraman and scriptwriter. While at Lódź, cameraman for Leszczyński's school films and played a main role in *Answer to Violence.* After graduating worked closely with Polański (q.v.) as cameraman for shorts 1958-62 and asst. dir. on *Knife in the Water.* Second cameraman to Lipman 1962-3. First cameraman for several documentaries and TV shorts, 1965-6. Worked with Skolimowski (q.v.) 1966-8 on *Barrier* (co-writer and co-cameraman), *Le Départ* (co-writer) and *Dialogue* (one episode); with Wajda on *Everything for Sale* (asst. dir. and actor). First feature film as dir. of photography: *The Life of Matthew.*

190 Krafft, Barbara (1928-   ). Sometimes known under married name Kraftówna. Character and comedy actress; popular star of film, stage and TV. Studied at Ivo Gall's Drama Studio, Cracow. Began acting career in Gdańsk and Wroclaw. Went to Warsaw 1953. Now member of National Theatre. First film role 1953. Film roles include: *Rainy July, Ashes and Diamonds, No-One Calling, Jack of Spades, A Town Will Die Tonight, Gold, How To Be Loved, Everyday, The Heat, The Saragossa Manuscript, Don Gabriel, The Code.*

Kraftówna, Barbara, see **Krafft.**

191 Kutz, Kazimierz (1929-   ). Feature director. Graduated Lódź and

State Theatre Institute, Cracow. Asst. dir. on *A Generation, Kanal, Answer to Violence*. Films include: *The Cross of Valour* 59; *No-One Calling* 60; *Panic on a Train* 61; *Wild Horses* 62; *Silence* 63; *The Heat* 64; *Whoever May Know* 66; *The Leap* 68; *Salt of the Black Country* 69.

192 Lapicki, Andrzej (1924-   ). Born Riga. Popular stage, screen and TV actor; theatre, radio and TV director; was newsreel commentator for many years. Graduated at clandestine State Institute of Theatre Art, Warsaw during war. First stage performance at Polish Army Theatre, Lódź, 1945. Member of Contemporary Theatre, Warsaw since 1949. Top of several popularity polls in newspapers. Directed one episode of *Those Who Are Late*. Started in films with small part in first postwar feature *Forbidden Songs*; has had important roles in about thirty films, including: *Soldier of Victory, Return to the Past, A Town Will Die Tonight, Café from the Past, Yesterday in Fact, Salto, Frame of Mind, Matrimonial Advice Column,*

Chess Club, *Everything For Sale, The Doll*.

193 Lenica, Jan (1928-   ). Artist and cartoon director. Son of Alfred Lenica, noted painter. Studied music and architecture. Turned to film animation 1957, when he worked in collaboration with Borowczyk (q.v.). Made prize-winning *Monsieur Tête*, in France 1958. Back in Poland, gained awards for *Johnny the Musician* 1960 and *Labyrinth* 1962. Since then has worked mainly abroad.

Barbara Krafft in Has's HOW TO BE LOVED

194 Lesiewicz, Witold (1922-   ). Documentary and feature director. Graduated Lódz. Began film career Documentary Studios 1951. Collaborated with Munk (q.v.), who was a close friend, on full-length semi-documentary *Stars Must Shine* 1954. Completed *Passenger* after Munk's death. Shorts include: *Szczecin—My Town; Silesia in Black and Green* (first panoramic and stereophonic film); *A Summer Day.* Feature films: *The Deserter* 58; *Year One* 60; *The Last Battle* (co-dir: Josef Hen) 61; *Between Two Shores* 62; *Room for One, The Unknown* 65; *Chess Club* 67.

195 Leszczyński, Witold (1933-   ). Director, scriptwriter and cameraman of younger generation. Studied electro-acoustics and worked as sound engineer at Lódz studio. Graduated in photography, Lódz 1962. His school films won him international acclaim. Worked as cameraman and asst. dir. in Greenland. Returned to Poland to shoot diploma work 1967. In 1968 began planning co-production with U.S.S.R., Norway and Ceylon. School films: *Rondo* (camera and editing), *Portrait of a Man with a Medallion* 59; *A Game* 60. Graduation feature: *The Life of Matthew* (also acted) 67.

196 Lipman, Jerzy (1922-   ). Cameraman with individual style. Graduated as cameraman, Lódz, 1952. Asst. cameraman on *Five Boys from Barska Street.* Director of photography for: *A Generation, The Shadow, Kanal, Real End of the Great War, The Eighth Day of the Week, Answer to Violence, Lotna, Bad Luck, Knife in the Water, L'Amour à Vingt Ans* (Wajda episode), *Gangsters and Philanthropists, Les Plus Belles Escroqueries du Monde* (Polanski episode), *The Murderer and the Girl* 63, *The Law and the Fist, Frame of Mind, Ashes,*

Zozya (U.S.S.R.), *Colonel Wolodyjowsky.*

197 Lomnicki, Jan (1930-   ). Leading documentarist with wide range of styles and themes: turned to features in the Sixties. Graduated Lódz: member of Documentary Studio and "Syrena" Unit. Won awards for: *Master Nikifor* 56; *The End of the Road* 58; *Birth of a Town, Steel* 59; *Wawel Concert* 60; *A Ship Is Born* 61; *Polish Suite* 62; *Meetings with Warsaw* (full-length) 65; *Ad Urbe Condita* 66. Feature films: *The Dowry* 63; *Contribution* 66; *Compact of Maturity* (TV) 67.

198 Lomnicki, Tadeusz (1925-   ). Popular and versatile actor of cinema, theatre and TV; style contemporary and sensitive. Stage *début* 1945 while studying acting and directing at Cracow Theatre School. Warsaw stage successes include leading role in *Inadmissable Evidence*, under Lindsay Anderson's direction. Film *début* 1946. Film roles include: *Five Boys from Barska Street, Sol-*

dier of Victory, A Generation, Eroica, Answer to Violence, The Eighth Day of the Week, The Damned Roads, Innocent Sorcerers, Time Past, The Broken Bridge, The Dowry, The First Day of Freedom, Counsel for the Prosecution Has the Floor, Barrier, Contribution, A Stable in Salvator, Hands Up!, Colonel Wolody-jowski.

1956. Has made over two dozen documentaries, many with music or art themes. Films include: A Child's Hands 45; Warsaw Suite 46; Chopin Recital at the Duszniki Festival 47; Everyday, Chopin Mazurkas 49; New Art 50; The Sin 51; The Mazowsze Ensemble 52; Medical Care 53; Living Stones 57; Singing Wood 58; The Dog's Newsreel 59; The Night 61; Magician 62; Vivat 68.

199 Majewski, Janusz (1931-   ). Prize-winning director of documentaries, features, TV films and featurettes. Graduated Lódź. School film Rondo (co-dir: Mrożek) 1958, acclaimed by critics. Documentaries include: Hospital, The Rose, Fleischer's Album 62; Opus Jazz 63; The Duel, Jazz in Poland 64; The Blue Room 65. Feature films: The Lodger 66; I Am on Fire 67.

200 Makarczyński, Tadeusz (1918-   ). Distinguished documentary director. Film adviser to W.H.O. in Geneva for several years. Studied law in Warsaw; worked as coal-miner during war. Directed feature The Warsaw Mermaid

201 Munk, Andrzej (1921-1961). Eminent director of "Polish film school." Probing style spliced with bitter irony. Gave up studying architecture for the cinema. Graduated as director and cameraman, Lódź 1952. Made several outstanding documentaries before turning to features. Was working on Passenger when he was killed in car crash. Film was completed by Lesiewicz (q.v.) as tribute to his work. Graduation work: Art of the Young 49. Documentaries: It Began in Spain 50; Direction Nowa Huta, Science Closer to Life 51; The Tale at Ursus 52; Diaries of the Peasants, A Railwayman's Word 53; Stars Must Shine (co-dir: Lesiewicz) 54; On a Sun-

Two stills from Munk's PASSENGER
(below, with Aleksandra Slaska and Marek Walczewski)

Munk's MAN ON THE TRACK

day Morning, *The Men of the Blue Cross* 55; *A Walk in the Old City* 59. Feature films: *Man on the Track, Eroica* 57; *Bad Luck* 60; *Passenger* 63.

202   Olbrychski, Daniel (1945-   ). Young actor who shot into fame in mid-Sixties. Topped newspaper popularity poll in 1967 (with Pola Raksa). Versatile amateur sportsman (judo, boxing, fencing, riding); undertakes all stunts without a double. Started as actor in Youth TV Studio. Gained international acclaim for role in *Ashes*. Frequently appears on TV, as actor and singer. Film roles in: *Wounded in the Forest, Ashes, And All Will Be Quiet, The Boxer, Jowita, Everything for Sale, Colonel Wolodyjowski, The Leap, Countess Cosel*.

203   Passendorfer, Jerzy (1923-   ). Feature director often dealing with war, occupation and resistance themes. Worked with clandestine theatre, Cracow, during war. After liberation went to Cracow Theatre School. Has worked as manipulator in touring puppet theatre, comedy-singer at night clubs, actor at Student Theatre, Cracow, and photographer-reporter for Polish Red Cross. Started studying at Łódź 1947. Scholarship to Prague 1948. Directed and scripted many educational films in Czechoslovakia 1950-51 and in Poland

1951-2. Feature films: *Captain Marten's Treasure* 57; *Answer to Violence* 58; *Signals* 59; *Return to the Past* 60; *The Sentence* (co-dir: Przezdźicki) 61; *The Broken Bridge* 62; *Christened by Fire* 63; *Scenes of Battle, No Justice on Sunday* 65; *Big Beat* 66; *Direction—Berlin* 69.

204 Penderecki, Krzysztof (-   ). *Avant-garde* composer of younger generation, internationally acclaimed. Graduated with special distinction at State Music Academy, Cracow, 1958. Lecturer there since 1959. Has written music for nearly forty stage plays, for over forty documentary and animated films, and for several features, including: *The Saragossa Manuscript, The Code, The Doll, Je t'aime, Je t'aime* (in France).

205 Petelska, Ewa (1920-   ). Feature director, usually works in collaboration with her husband, Czeslaw. She and her husband have made about 15 TV films. Studied Plastic Arts before graduating as director at Lódź. Films

made independently: *Three Stories* (one episode) 53; *Three Starts* (one episode) 55. See **Petelski, Czeslaw** for films made in collaboration.

206 Petelski, Czeslaw (1922-   ). Feature director and director of TV films. Works in collaboration with his wife, Ewa (see above). Graduated as actor, Theatre Institute, Lódź, 1952. Worked as asst. dir. to Kawalerowicz (q.v.). Films made independently: *Three Stories* (one episode) 53; *Three Starts* (one episode) 55; *The Damned Roads* 58. Films in collaboration with Ewa: *Shipwrecks* 57; *The Sky Is Our Roof* 59; *Mountains on Fire* 61; *Black Wings* 62; *The Beater* 63; *The Wooden Rosary* 65; *Don Gabriel* 66; *A Matter of Conscience* 67; *Empty Eyes* 69.

207 Polański, Roman (1933-   ). Born Paris. Director who combines feeling for "the absurd" with bitter sense of irony. One of the most important talents to emerge in Sixties. Also scriptwriter and actor. Graduated as director, Lódź,

1959. While student took part in several stage plays and films. His school works *Two Men and a Wardrobe* and *Mammals* won him international acclaim. Went to France in 1963, where he scripted *Aimez-vous les Femmes?*, scripted and directed *Le Gros et le Maigre* (short) and directed Dutch story in *Les Plus Belles Escroqueries du Monde*. In Britain 1964-68, made *Repulsion, Cul-de-Sac, Dance of the Vampires* and (in U.S.A.) *Rosemary's Baby*. Film roles include: *A Generation, Three Starts, Shipwrecks, Call My Wife* (Polish-Czechoslovak co-prod.), *When Angels Fall, Lotna, Innocent Sorcerers, See You Tomorrow, Le Gros et le Maigre, Dance of the Vampires*. Films made at Lódź Film School: *The Bicycle* 55; *Breaking the Party* 57; *Two Men and a Wardrobe* 58; *When Angels Fall, The Lamp* 59. Polish films directed: *Knife in the Water* 61; *Mammals* 62.

208 Różewicz, Stanislaw (1924-). Feature director with quiet, serious style. Gained international recognition in Sixties. Professor at Lódź. Began career early postwar as scriptwriter and asst. dir. Writes own screenplays in collaboration with his poet and playwright brother, Tadeusz. Made many documentaries. Feature films (all co-scripted by Tadeusz, except *Difficult Love, Free City* and *Westerplatte*): *Difficult Love* 53; *Three Women* 56; *Free City* 58; *No Place on Earth* 60; *Birth Certificate* 61; *Voice from Beyond* 62; *Echo* 64; *Heaven and Hell* 65; *Westerplatte* 67; *The Two Were Lonely* 69.

209 Różewicz, Tadeusz (1921-   ). Writer, poet and scriptwriter. Writes scripts for films directed by his brother, Stanislaw, often in collaboration with Kornel Filipowicz. First poems published in youth magazines, 1938. Worked in the underground movement during war. Began writing for films, 1956. For films scripted see **Stanislaw Różewicz.**

210 Rybkowski, Jan (1912-   ). Popular and prolific director with wide range of genres. Studied art; worked in theatre as designer and producer. Imprisoned by Nazis during war. Created popular "Mr. Anatol" series, about a low-grade clerk. Although very active in cinema, continues to design for stage. Feature films include: *House on the Wastelands* 49; *The Warsaw Début, First Days* 51; *Unfinished Business* 54; *The Bus Leaves at 6.20* 55; *Hours of Hope* 56; *Nikodem Dyzma* 57; *Mr. Anatol's Hat, The Last Shot* 58; *Mr. Anatol Seeks a Million, Mr. Anatol's Inspection, A Town Will Die Tonight* 61; *Yesterday in Fact, Café from the Past* 63; *Frame of Mind* 65; *Visit at Twilight* 66; *When Love Was a Crime* 67.

211 Ščibor-Rylski, Aleksander (1928-   ). Novelist, playwright, designer, photographer and film-maker. Began working in cinema as scriptwriter, 1955, often adapting own novels. Director since 1963. Was literary manager of "Rhythm" Production Group. Scripts include: *The Shadow, Pills for Aurelia, The Last Shot, Year One, Black Wings, Ashes*. Directed: *Everyday* 63; *Late Afternoon* 64; *Mexico Tomorrow* 65; *The Murderer Leaves a Clue* 67; *Wolves' Echoes* 68; *The Neighbours* 69.

212 Skolimowski, Jerzy (Yurek) (1936-   ). One of the most significant directors to emerge in Sixties. Also poet, playwright, scriptwriter, actor. Was boxer in his 'teens. Then studied ethnography, Warsaw University. Graduated as director, Lódź, 1964. Directed and co-scripted: *Boxing* (documentary)

Two stills from Polanski's KNIFE IN THE WATER with Zygmunt Malanowicz (above), and with Jolanta Umecka and Leon Niemczyk (below)

61; *Identification Marks—None* (also lead role) 64; *Walkover* (also lead role) 65; *Barrier* 66. Scripted: *Innocent Sorcerers* (co-writer Jerzy Andrzejewski. Also acted); *Knife in the Water* (co-writers: Polański and Goldberg). Acting roles in: *A Voice from Beyond, Passenger, New Year's Eve, Frame of Mind.* Left Poland to make: *Le Départ* (Belgian), *Dialogue* (one episode: Czech) 67. Returned to Poland to make *Hands Up!* Then made *Adventures of Gerard* (in Italy) 68.

213   Ślesicki, Wladyslaw (1927-   ). Eminent documentary director with personal, poetic style. Graduated Lódź. Started at Documentary Studio, Warsaw, 1956. Collaborated with Karabasz (q.v.) on three early films. Films include: *A Walk in the Bieszczady Mountains, Story about the Road* 58; *Among People* 60; *Portrait of a Small Town* 61; *The Boy and the Waves* 62; *Gypsies* 63; *The Mountain* 64; *Summer on the Baltic* 65; *The Family of Man* 66; *Energy* 67; *Father's Name* (feature) 69.

214   Stawiński, Jerzy Stefan (1921-   ). Popular novelist and short-story writer closely associated with "Polish film school." Studied law, Warsaw University 1947-51. First writings published 1953. First script, 1956. Literary manager of "Kamera" Production Group for many years. As scriptwriter, noted for socially committed approach blended with irony. As director, writes own scripts. Scripts include: *Man on the Track, Kanal, Eroica, The Deserter, Answer to Violence, Signals* (co-writer Skowroński), *Bad Luck, Knights of the Teutonic Order, It Happened Yesterday, In Pursuit of Adam, How To Be Loved.* Directed: *No More Divorces* 63; *The Penguin* 64; *Christmas Eve* (co-dir: Helena Amiradżibi) 66.

215   Szczechura, Daniel (1930-   ). Prize-winning cartoon director with highly original style. Studied History of Fine Arts, Warsaw University. Won international awards for amateur films mid-Fifties. Graduated Lódź, 1961. While student, worked as set designer at Student Satirical Theatre, Warsaw.

Above: Skolimowski in his own WALKOVER
Below: Beata Tyszkiewicz in Wajda's EVERYTHING FOR SALE

Joined SE-MA-FOR studio immediately after graduation. Made series of TV commercials 1967. Films: *Conflicts* (diploma work) 60; *The Machine* 61; *The Letter* 62; *The Seat* 63; *Duet, One, Two, Three, On the Road* 64; *Karol, The Diagram* 66; *Hobby* 67.

216   Tyszkiewicz, Beata (1938-   ). Very popular actress, much in demand by directors at home and abroad. Screen ambitions since childhood. Stage *début* at 17. Member of Contemporary Theatre, Warsaw. Film *début*, 1955, prior to studying at State Higher School of Drama. Married to Wajda (q.v.). Film roles include: *One Room Tenants, The President's Visit, A Town Will Die Tonight, Samson, Hallowe'en, Those Who Are Late, Black Wings, Yesterday In Fact, Christened by Fire, The First Day of Freedom, The Saragossa Manuscript, Ashes, The Man Who Had His Hair Cut Short* (in Belgium), *Maria and Napoleon, The Doll, Everything for Sale, A Nest of the Gentry* (in U.S.S.R.).

217   Wajda, Andrzej (1926-   ). Film, stage and TV director of key importance in "Polish film school." Much concerned with relationship between individual and world events. Involved in resistance movement as a boy. After war, studied at Academy of Fine Arts at Cracow, then film-directing, Lódź. While student, was asst. dir. on *Five Boys from Barska Street.* Co-writer of script for *Three Stories.* Several of his films have gained many international awards. Feature films: *A Generation* 54; *Kanal* 56; *Ashes and Diamonds* 58; *Lotna, Innocent Sorcerers* 59; *Samson* 61; *L'Amour à Vingt Ans* (Polish episode), *Siberian Lady Macbeth* (in Yugoslavia) 62; *Ashes* 65; *Gates to Paradise* (in Engl.) 67; *Everything for Sale* 68; *Flies Hunting* 69.

218   Winnicka, Lucyna (1928-   ). Popular actress of stage, film and TV. Went to Warsaw Theatre Academy after studying law at Warsaw University. Gained state prize for first film role. Has achieved important screen successes in films made by her husband,

Two films by Wajda: above, KANAL;
below, Zbigniew Cybulski in ASHES AND DIAMONDS (with Ewa Krzyzewska)

Two films by Wajda: above, Tadeusz Lomnicki in
INNOCENT SORCERERS (with Kryzystina Stypulkowska); below, ASHES

Kawalerowicz (q.v.). Roles include: *Under the Phrygian Star, The Real End of the Great War, Baltic Express, The Silent Planet* (in G.D.R.), *Knights of the Teutonic Order, Mother Joan of the Angels, The Suit Almost New, Frame of Mind, The Game.*

·219 Wójcik, Jerzy (1930-). Gifted cameraman, closely associated with "Polish film school." Graduated Lódź. Second cameraman on *Kanal* and *The Real End of the Great War.* Director of photography for some of the most significant films, including: *Eroica, Ashes and Diamonds, Cross of Valour, Mother Joan of the Angels, No-one Calling, Samson, Time Past, Echo, Life Once More, Pharaoh, Westerplatte, Don't Mention the Cause of Death* (in Yugoslavia).

220 Zdort, Wieslaw (1931-). Cameraman of growing importance in contemporary cinema. Graduated Lódź, 1956. Asst. cameraman on several films by Wajda, Munk and others. First cameraman for: *Wild Horses, Silence, The Heat, Room for One, Slim and the Others, A Stable in Salvator, The Sun Rises Once a Day.*

Lucyna Winnicka in Kawalerowicz's THE GAME

ROMANIA

ROMANIA

Pop. 9,105,000. Small but rapidly-expanding industry that virtually started from scratch after the war.

Production:

Features—Annual production steadily increasing from 1 in 1949 to 16 in 1967.

Documentaries—25 in 1950; 100 in 1967.

Cartoons—8 in 1964; 24 in 1967.

Cinemas:

1948—383; 1966—6,360 and 41 mobile. Films are shown in outlying areas by mobile cinemas in the summer and at schools and government buildings in the winter.

Studios:

Bucureşti Studios, at the well-equipped "film city" at Buftea, near Bucharest—Features. The Alexandru Sahia Studios—Documentaries. The Animafilm Studios—cartoons and puppet films.

Training:

Higher Education Institute of Cinematography. Courses for directors, scriptwriters, cameramen and artistic directors. (Referred to in biographies as "Bucharest").

When the Romanian film industry was established as an integrated part of cultural life, in 1945, it had very little experience or tradition behind it. The first films —a programme of Romanian landscapes—had been shown as early as 1893, but film pioneers were handicapped by lack of resources and although features were produced sporadically from 1911 onwards, the general level was low. Organised production began on a limited scale when the National Tourist Office set up a Cinematography Department, which became the National Cinematograph Office in 1936. The department produced regular newsreels and documentaries, some of which, like Călinescu's *The Country of Motzi*, were acclaimed abroad. Of the fifty full-length films made before 1945 only a handful have proved to be of lasting value. These include *War of Independence* (Grigore Brezeaunu, 1912), *Manasse* (Jean Mihail, 1925) and *A Stormy Night* (Jean Georgescu, 1942).

Film production was nationalised in 1948. Because of lack of facilities and trained personnel, a long-term plan was drawn up and put into operation, which included the building of a film city outside Bucharest, a big increase in the number of cinemas, and the establishment of the Film School.

Production in the immediate postwar years was limited in range, technique and quantity. First feature, *The Valley Resounds* 1949, was about young volunteers at a building-site. Feature production increased slowly but steadily and the newly-built Bucureşti studios achieved more-or-less full working capacity in 1957. Films in the early Fifties were mainly screen adaptations of widely-read novels depicting the social changes that were taking place in national life, especially in the countryside. Two important films of the period were *Mitrea Cocor* and *In a Village*. Until the emergence

Cocea's THE RAPE OF THE MAIDENS

of a generation of players trained for, or accustomed to the screen, acting tended to be over-theatrical. There was something of a breakthrough for acting technique in Jean Georgescu's *Our Manager,* 1955.

The second half of the Fifties saw some interesting all-round developments. A turning-point was *The Mill of Luck and Plenty,* a psychological drama set in a Transylvanian village in 1870. Liviu Ciulei came on to the scene (from considerable experience in the theatre) with *Eruption* and *The Danube Waves.* Other significant films were *The Mist Is Lifting,* a personal drama of the First World War and *The Secret Code,* a wartime adventure film. By the end of the decade, a national film tradition was beginning to take shape.

Feature production can be seen to fall roughly into two categories. On the one hand, there are the big, dramatic spectacles—some, like *Tudor* and *The Dacians,* based on historical themes and others, like *Lupeni '29,* depicting aspects of working-class struggle. Leading directors in this category are **Drăgan, Bratu, Cocea** and **Nicolescu.** On the other hand, there are personal and psychological dramas, which are becoming increasingly important. Directors in this category include **Muresan, Mihu, Pintile, Blaier, Stiopul** and **Saizescu.** Both these trends come together in the films of **Ciulei,** who combines dramatic visual qualities with deep human insight.

Films with topical themes have gained ground in the past decade. Among them were *Sentimental Story, He Was My Friend* and *A Midsummer Day's Smile.* Important "new cinema" breakaways from classical style have been achieved by *The White Trail, Sunday at Six O'Clock* and *The Mornings of a Sensible Youth.*

Cartoons: Animated films production, which is deeply rooted in national folk traditions, developed very rapidly after its inception 1950-51. Leading personality is the brilliant award-winning animator **Popescu-Gopo** who also makes full-length live-action fantasies, and whose "little man" hero has become something of a household word.

Aerial view of the Buchuresti Studios

Other important animators are **Stefan Munteanu**, Sabin Balasa, Julian Hermeneaunu, Constantin Mustefea, Virgil Mocanu, Liviu Ghigort, and Matty Aslan.

The outstanding puppet-maker is **Bob Călinescu**, who achieves amazing effects by using all kinds of traditional folk materials. **Georghe Sibianu** makes puppet and cartoon films. Olimp Vărăşteanu works with cut-outs and Sabin Bălaşa's technique involves painting in front of the camera. The importance of the Romanian contribution in the field of animation is apparent from the fact that, since 1966, the International Festival of Animated Film takes place every second year at Mamaia (alternating with Annecy).

Documentaries and Shorts: As in many of the newer film-making countries, documentaries were at first the spearhead of production and were able to develop much more rapidly than the feature films. Documentaries are made at the rate of about 100 a year, and among the leading directors are **Ion Bostan**, **Titus Mesaros**, Eric Nussbaum, Mirel Ilieşu, **Savel Stiopul, Gheorghe Vitandis**, Jean Petrovici, Gabriel Barta and Ion Moscu. **Elizabeta Bostan** specialises in shorts for children.

221 Blaier, Andrei (1933-   ). Feature director with a special interest in problems of childhood and adolescence. Graduated Bucharest. Made several films in collaboration with Sinişa Ivetici before working independently. Films made independently: *He Was My Friend* 61; *The Unfinished House* 64; *The Mornings of a Sensible Youth* 66; *The Legend* 68.

222 Bostan, Elisabeta (1931-   ). Director best-known for her sensitive evocation of childhood in a series of shorts about the little boy Năică. Graduated Bucharest 1955. Shorts: *The Brood Hen and Her Golden Chicks; Three Romanian Dances; The Hora-Dance; Năică and the Little Fish; Năică and the Stork; Năică and the Squirrels; Năică Leaves for*

Irina Petrescu and Dan Nutu in Blair's THE MORNINGS OF A SENSIBLE YOUTH

Bucharest. Feature films: *The Kid* 62; *Recollections from Childhood* 64; *Youth without Old Age* 68.

223   Bostan, Ion (1914-   ). One of the founders of Romanian documentary. Asst. dir. 1945-9. Made many art and folk-lore films 1950-5. Films include: *The City of Histros* 56; *The Murder of the Innocents* 57; *Voronet* 62; *Under the Wing of the Eagle* 63. *Winter Guests, The Heron—a Reptile Bird?, On the Traces of a Lost Film, Histria, Heraclea and Swans* 68.

224   Bratu, Lucian (1924-   ). Director of historical and contemporary features. Graduated Moscow. Initiated a series of films about Nineteenth-century revolutionary hero Tudor Vladimirescu. Feature films: *The Secret Code* 59; *Tudor* 64; *The Kiss* 65; *A Charming Girl* 66.

225   Călinescu, Bob (1926-   ). Leading director of puppet films. Amateur sculptor during his teens. Studied acting at Conservatoire. Acted in National Theatre, Bucharest and in first Romanian film, *The Valley Resounds*. Went to Czechoslovakia to work with Trnka 1948. Made the first puppet film *The Deceived Fox* 1952. Uses a wide variety of natural materials for animation, including river stones, maize stalks and, in *Rhapsody in Wood* 1960, sculptured tree roots. Themes range from traditional fairy-tale to modern parables and abstracts. Among his other films are: *The Ballad of the Maestros; The Nail; Master Goe; The Sorcerer's Apprentice; Chit in Danger; Michaela's Morning; A New Joke with Scrap Iron; Metamorphosis; Rhythm; Fantasies; Romeo and Juliet; The Axe and the Forest.*

226   Călinescu, Paul (1902-   ). Veteran director and pioneer of national cinema. Made art and tourist shorts prewar. Directed first postwar feature. Best-known film: *In a Village*. Feature films:

The Valley Resounds 49; *In a Village* 54; *On My Responsibility* 56; *Porto Franco* 61; *Titanic Waltz* 64.

227 Calotescu, Virgil (1928-   ). Leading director of documentaries. Has applied documentary approach to two features. Graduated in history. Joined Alexandru Sahia studios 1952. Written and directed over sixty shorts including: *Gifts Snatched from Nature* 52; *Tracing Back 1907, Notes from Portul Rosu* 57; *The Shells Have Never Spoken* 62; *The Testimony of a Table in a Restaurant, The Eyes of My City* 63; *Various Images* 64; *Rhythms and Images* 66. Feature films: *The White Room* 64; *The Subterranean* 67; *All Souls' Day* 68.

228 Ciobotărașu, Stefan (1910-   ). Distinguished actor of stage and screen. Graduated Conservatoire of Iassay. Many outstanding stage successes before film *début* in 1954. Film roles include: *In a Village, The Eruption, The Danube Waves, Thirst, Porto Franco, Lupeni' 29, He Was My Friend, The Sky Has No Bars, The Hawks, The Mornings of a Sensible Youth, The Column, All Souls' Day, The Legend.*

229 Ciulei, Liviu (1923-   ). Outstanding director who is also an actor: sometimes takes roles in his own films. Graduated at Faculty of Architecture and Conservatoire of Dramatic Arts. After theatre successs as set designer, actor and director, made film acting *début* in *In a Village.* Asst. dir. to Victor Illiu 1956. Directed: *The Eruption* 59; *The Danube Waves* 63; *The Forest of the Hanged* (also acted) 65. Ciulei won Best Direction Prize at Cannes for this last film.

230 Cocea, Dinu-Constantin (1929-   ). Director of historical epics. Grad-

uated Bucharest 1953. Asst. dir. until 1962. Films: *The Outlaws* 65; *The Rape of the Maidens, The Revenge of the Outlaws* 67-8.

231 Drăgan, Mircea (1932-   ). Younger generation director of historical epics, with spectacular style and flair

Above: Liviu Ciulei, at left, in his own THE FOREST OF THE HANGED (with Victor Rebengiuc)
Below: Dragan's GOLGOTHA (with Iona Dragan and Sebastian Papaiani)

for crowd scenes. Critic before becoming director. Graduated Bucharest 1955. Professor of Film Direction. Head of Direction department at Bucharest. Director of National Film Centre. Films: *Beyond the Fir-Trees* 57; *Thirst* 60; *Lupeni '29* 61; *The Hawks* 65; *Golgotha* 66; *The Column* 68.

232 Gologan, Ovidiu (1912-   ). Prize-winning director of photography with strong feeling for beauty of the countryside. One of the first newsreel cameramen; front-line reporter and cameraman during the war. Shot many documentaries before turning to features. Director of photography for: *The Mill of Luck and Plenty, The Forest of the Hanged, The Death of Joe the Indian, The Adventures of Tom Sawyer.*

233   Iacob, Mihai (1933-   ). Director of young generation. Graduated Bucharest 1955. Asst. dir. to Drăgan (q.v.) before directing independently. Lecturer in drama at Bucharest. Feature films: *Blanca* (short) 55; *Darclée* 60; *The Famous 702* 62; *The Stranger* 64; *The*

Adventures of Tom Sawyer 67; *The Death of Joe the Indian* 68.

234   Iliesu, Mirel (1923-   ). Documentary director with wide range of approach. Films include: *The Snow Storm* 53; *Winter in the Delta* 57; *Bicaz, the 563 Level* 59; *Light and Stone* 60; *The Tanners* 62; *Roots, Rhythms* 63; *Roads, Concerto Grosso* 64; *The Road* 65; *The Portrait of Cowardice, Dyestuffs, A Plot of Road* 68.

235   Iliu, Victor (1912-1968). One of the best-known directors, with special feeling for village life. Considerably influenced national film-making style, notably with *Mitrea Cocor* and *Mill of Luck and Plenty.* Films include: *Ion Marin's Letter to Scinteia* (doc.) 49; *Our Village* (in collab. with Jean Georgescu) 51; *Mitrea Cocor* 52; *A Lost Letter* (in collab. with Sică Alexandrescu); *The Mill of Luck and Plenty* 56; *The Treasure at Vadul Vechi* 63.

236   Întorsureanu, Alexandru (1932-   ). Younger generation director of photography. Graduated Bucharest 1956. Films: *When the Mist Is Lifting* (together with George Cornea and Gheorghe Fischer), *I Don't Want to Get Married, A Sentimental Story, He Was My Friend, The District of Gaiety, Virgo, Shots on the Stave, All Alone.*

237   Marcus, Manole (1928-   ). Feature director and film teacher. Graduated Bucharest 1955. His graduation film *Pinching Apples* won him early acclaim, along with co-director Iulian Mihu (q.v.). Lecturer in Directors' Section, Bucharest. Films: *When The Mist Is Lifting* (co-dir: Mihu) 57; *One Morning; I Don't Want to Get Married* 60; *The*

Streets Remember 62; *The District of Gaiety* 64; *Virgo* 66; *All Alone* 68.

238 Mesaros, Titus (1925-). Gifted younger generation documentary director. Graduated Institute of Literature 1950. Started work in cinema as documentary scriptwriter. Films: *Four Thousand Steps to the Sky, Our People* 63; *Beyond Hills and Mountains* 64; *To the Sky* 65; *Reed* 66; *Crude Oil* 67; *Metamorphosis* 68.

feature. As director, writes his own scripts. Best-known film: *Four Steps to the Infinite*. Scenarios include: *The Danube Waves* (co-writer Titus Popovici), *You Are Guilty Too* (co-writer Petre Salcudeanu). Directed: *Soldiers without Uniform* 60; *The Sky Has No Bars* 62; *At the Age of Love* 63; *Four Steps to the Infinite* 64; *Beyond the Railway Gate* 65; *The Tunnel* 66; *The Sky Begins on the Third Floor* 67.

239 Mihu, Iulian (1926-). Feature director with experimental approach. Graduated Bucharest 1953. Made an immediate mark with his graduation film *Pinching Apples* (co-dir: Marcus). Films: *When the Mist Is Lifting* (co-dir: Marcus) 57; *Sentimental Story* 61; *The White Trial* 65.

240 Munteanu, Francisc (1924-). Director with vivid, direct style; scenarist and writer. Began writing 1950. Wrote first scenario 1958. Asst. dir. to Ciulei (q.v.) 1960, then directed his first

241 Munteanu, Stefan (1926-). Director of animated films, with imaginative use of colour, humour and fantasy. Also cartoonist and book illustrator. Studied art before entering Animation Department at Bucharest. Joined Bucureşti Studio as artist 1956. Began directing, writing and drawing his own films 1959. Films include: *Hidden Little Houses; Shiver-Fever; Electronicus; Petrică and Somebody Else; Dimensions; Terra; The Little Boy and the Charcoal; Medieval; Interior; Adventure in Blue.*

242 Mureşan, Mircea (1930-). Director with wide variety of styles. Be-

gan career as actor. Graduated Bucharest 1956. While asst. dir. to Victor Iliu (q.v.) made shorts and wrote scripts. Now a lecturer in the Direction Faculty at Bucharest. Shorts: *The Pedestrian; Silence; The Cities of Chemistry.* Short and medium-length features: *Autumn* 61; *You Are Guilty Too* 63. Full-length features: *Blazing Winter* 65; *Knock-Out* 67.

243 Nicolaescu, Sergiu. (1930-   ). Director of historical spectacles. Left school at sixteen, worked as sailor, painter, engineer, cameraman, deep-sea diver. A versatile sportsman. Directed three prize-winning shorts before turning to features. Shorts: *A Habitual Spring; The Memories of a Rose; A Lesson to the Infinite.* Feature films: *The Dacians (The Immortals:* Romanian-French co-production) 66; *Michael the Brave* 69.

244 Nuţu, Dan (1944-   ). Actor associated with contemporary style cinema and theatre. Member of National Theatre of Iassy. Graduated Bucharest. Achieved acting success while still a student. Film roles in: *Sunday at Six*

Muresan's BLAZING WINTER
(with Ilarian Ciobanu)

include: *Darclée, Thirst, The Famous 702, Tudor, The White Room, Blazing Winter, The Outlaws, The Hawks, The Dacians, The Column, All Souls' Day.*

246   Petrescu, Irina (1941-   ). Versatile and sensitive actress much in demand by directors. After being "discovered" by Ciulei (q.v.) she left University to study dramatic art at Bucharest 1959. Roles in: *I Don't Want to Get Married, Sentimental Story, Steps to the Moon, White Moor, The Stranger, Sunday at Six O'Clock, The Story of My Stupidity* (in Hungary), *The Mornings of a Sensible Youth, The Malicious Adolescent.*

O'Clock, The Mornings of a Sensible Youth, Meanders, The Legend.

245   Pellea, Amza (1931-   ). Actor of stage and screen often chosen for epic film roles. Member of Theatre of Comedy, Bucharest. Graduated Bucharest 1955. Film *début* 1960. Film roles

247   Petruţ, Emanoil (1932-   ). One of the most gifted and popular younger generation actors at Bucharest National Theatre. Made film *début* while studying at Bucharest; specialises in dashing, adventurous roles. Films: *The Secret Code, Tudor, The Kiss, The Rape of the Maidens, The Revenge of the Outlaws, Youth without Old Age.*

Irina Petrescu in (above) Pintilie's SUNDAY AT SIX O'CLOCK, with Dan Nutu,
and (below) in Popescu-Gopo's WHITE MOOR (with Florin Piersic).

many international prizes and made a major contribution to national cinema. Also: *The Reconstitution* 68.

249 Pîslaru, Margareta (1943-   ). Award-winning young actress, pop-

248 Pintilie, Lucian (1933-   ). Film, stage and television director. Graduated as director at Bucharest. Now a director at the Lucia Sturdza Bulandra Theatre, Bucharest. His first feature film *Sunday at Six O'Clock* 1965 gained

Saizescu's THE SATURDAY NIGHT DANCE (with Mariella Petrescu and Sebastian Papaiani)

singer and folk singer. Popular radio, TV and recording personality. Usually composes her own songs. *Début* as singer on TV at age of fifteen. Stage *début* as Polly in *The Beggar's Opera* 1963. Screen roles in *The Tunnel, A Charming Girl, Shots on the Stave.*

250   Popescu-Gopo, Ion (1923-   ). Brilliant animator; also directs live-action features. Graduated Academy of Fine Arts. Cartoonist and director of advertising films for many years. Established first animation studio 1950. Made prizewinning "little man" trilogy 1956-8. Directed live-action science fiction and fairy-tale films in early Sixties, then returned to animation to develop "little man" theme. Animated films include: *Short History* 56; *Seven Arts* 58; *Homo Sapiens* 60. Feature films: *The Little Liar* 53; *A Fly with Money* 54; *A Bomb Was Stolen* 61; *Steps to the Moon* 63; *White Moor* 65; *Faustus XX* 66; *My City* (also acted) 67; *Sancta Simplicitas* 68.

251   Popovici, Titus (1930-   ). Popular novelist and prolific screenwriter.

Adapted his own novels *Thirst* and *The Stranger* for the screen. Other screenplays: *The Mill of Luck and Plenty, The Danube Waves* (with Francisc Munteanu), *The Forest of the Hanged, The Dacians, The Column, Michael the Brave.*

252   Rebengiuc, Victor (1933-   ). Stage and screen actor. After graduating Bucharest, made his name on the stage. Film roles: *Darclée, A Sentimental Story, He Was My Friend, The Forest of the Hanged.´*

253   Saizescu, Geo (1932-   ), Versatile younger generation feature director and actor. His performance in his own short *The Adventure of the Good Soldier Schweik* won him a state scholarship. Entered direction department, Bucharest 1953. Has directed comedy, musicals and contemporary dramas. Helped establish the first film societies and continues to take active leading part in amateur film movement. Appointed Chairman of National Committee of Film Societies 1964. Acted in: *A Bomb Was*

Above and opposite: Stiopul's THE LAST NIGHT OF CHILDHOOD

Stolen; You Are Guilty Too; The Famous 702. Directed: Two Neighbours 58; A Midsummer Day's Smile 63; Love at Freezing Point (in collab. with George Grigoriu) 64; At the Gates of the Earth 66; The Saturday Night Dance 68.

254 Sǎucan, Mircea (1928-   ). Director with poetic style. Graduated Moscow 1956. Made several documentaries and medium-length films including Pages of Bravery 1959, a prize-winning compilation film. Feature films: When Spring Is Hot 61; The Endless Shore 62; Meanders 66.

255 Sibianu, Gheorghe (1927-   ). Director of puppet and animated films. Graduated at Institute of Fine Arts and as set-designer at Bucharest. Worked at first under Bob Cǎlinescu. Films mainly for children, but Mimesis is satire for adults. Films: Negrita's Island (puppet), The Bear Taken In by The Fox (animation), The Telephone 57; The Empire of the Lazy 61; Dream sequence in

Under the Blue Cupola 62; The Lake of the Fairies (puppet) 63; Snowdrops (animation) 64; The Paper Cockerel (animation) 65; Mimesis 66; Human Folly, The Ox and the Calf 68.

256 Stan, Nicu (1931-   ). Younger generation cameraman. Also talented portrait painter. Graduated Bucharest. Films include: You Are Guilty Too, Blazing Winter, The Mornings of a Sensible Youth, The Legend.

257 Stiopul, Savel (1926-   ). Outstanding documentary and feature director. Graduated Bucharest 1950. Spent ten years making documentaries and short features, among which Counterpoint in White gained many international prizes. Documentaries: The Women Fight for Peace 49; Spring 53; Bucharest, the City in Blossom 55; The International Festival in Edinburgh 56; The Memories of an Actress 57; The School of Work 59; Beauty is with Us; A Journey to Strange Lands 60; With Needle and Thread 66. Short feature films: Facing

with Irina Gardescu (seen opposite with Liviu Tudan)

the Audience 54; *The Lad and the Fire* 62; *Counterpoint in White* 64. Feature films: *Close to the Sun* 60; *Seasons* 63; *The Last Night of Childhood* 66.

258 Tincu, Giulio (1913-   ). Outstanding artistic director of stage and screen. Has designed settings for: *A Lost Letter, On My Responsibility, Two Neighbours, The Danube Waves, Soldiers without Uniform, Porto Franco, The Sky Has No Bars, At the Age of Love, The Forest of the Hanged, Four Steps to the Infinite, Beyond the Railway Gate, A Charming Girl.*

259 Vitandis, Gheorghe (1929-   ). Prize-winning director and film theoretician. Graduated as director, Bucharest 1953. Lecturer there since 1963. Made newsreels and shorts at Alexandru Sahia studios during student years. Director for Romanian side of three co-productions with France: *The Broken Citadel* (co-dir: Marc Maurette) 56; *The Baragan Thistles* (co-dir: Louis Daquin) 58; *Les Fêtes Galantes* (co-dir: René Clair) 65. Documentaries include: *Our Lads* 59; *Poste Restante* 61; *Gaudeamus Igitur* 64; Feature films: *The Chief of the Souls' Department* 67; *The Malicious Adolescent* 68.

U.S.S.R.

U.S.S.R.

Pop. 235,000,000. A Union of fifteen republics with a very large, strong and long-established film industry.

Production:

120-140 features; 20-25 full-length documentaries, 300 shorts, 500 popular science films, 1,500 film journals and about 30 cartoons.

Cinemas:

About 34,000. *Annual admissions: 4½ billion.*

Training:

1) The All-Union State Institute of Cinematography (VGIK), Moscow (referred to in biographies as "Moscow"). Founded 1919.
2) Directors' Workshop at Leningrad Studios.
3) Cinema faculty at Kiev Institute of Theatrical Art.
4) Union of Film-makers and Committee for Cinematography—two-year courses for directors and scriptwriters in Moscow.
5) Leningrad Institute for Cinema Engineers.

Studios:

For feature films (annual production in brackets):

Mosfilm, Moscow (about 30)

Maxim Gorky Studios for Films for Children and Young People, Moscow (10-15)

Lenfilm, Leningrad. Oldest in the country: modernisation and extension began 1968 (12-13)

Dovzhenko Feature Studios at Kiev, Ukraine (12-13)

Odessa Feature Studios (7-8)

Byelarusfilm Studios, Byelorussia (7-9)

Gruziafilm Studios, Georgia (5-6, to be increased to 8-10 a year on completion of reconstruction)

Amo Bek-Nazarov Studios, Armenia (2-4)

Djafar Djabarly Studios, Azerbaidjan (2)

Kazakhfilm Studios, Kazakhstan (2)

Uzbekfilm Studio, Uzbekistan (5-6)

Turkmenfilm Studio, Turkmenia, first feature 1966 (Plan to develop facilities to produce 3-4 films a year)

Lithuanian Film Studio, Vilnius (3-4)

Latvian Film Studio, Riga (7-9)

Kirghizfilm Studio, Kirghizia (1)

Moldafilm Studio, Moldavia (1-2)

Tallinfilm Studio, Estonia. First feature 1945 (2-3)

Tajikfilm Studio, Tadjikstan. Founded 1929 (2-3)

Documentary production: Central Studio of Documentary Films, Moscow; Central Leningrad Studio of Popular Science Films; documentary and/or popular science studios at Sverdlovks (also occasional feature production), the Ukraine (two), Minsk,

Opposite: Chukhrai's THE FORTY-FIRST

Tashkent, Yerevan, Georgia; local branches of the Russian Federation studios at Leningrad, Kuibyshev, Novosobirsk, Irkutsk, North Caucasas, Lower Volga Region, Kazan and the Far East.

Documentary films are also produced in the feature studios of some of the Union republics.

Cartoon and puppet production: Soyuzmultfilm, Moscow (about 25 cartoon and puppet), and production at several studios in the republics.

Early production: Soviet cinema was, of course, firmly established long before the Second World War. The film industry, which had produced some 2,000, mainly low-level, full-length films between 1907 and 1917, achieved a dazzling standard soon after its nationalisation in 1919. The early works of the giants of Soviet cinema— Eisenstein and cameraman Tissé (*Battleship Potemkin*, *Strike*, etc.), Pudovkin (*Mother*, *The End of St. Petersburg* etc.) and Dovzhenko (*Earth*, *Shors* etc.) are too well-known to need elaboration. Among the directors who gained international fame in the Twenties were Barnet, Ermler, **Kosintsev**, Kuleshov, Perestiani, Protozanov, **Raizman**, Roshal, Schub, Trauberg, Turin and Vertov. With the coming of sound these were joined by, among others, Alexandrov, Arnshtam, Digzan, **Gerasimov, Heifitz, Kalatosov, Pyriev, Romm,** Savchenko, **Yutkevitch** and **Zarkhi.** In 1934, the Vasilyev brothers made *Chapayev* and in 1938 **Donskoy** completed the first film in his Gorky Trilogy.

During the War and After: Wartime cinema was notable for its courageous front-line reportage, including outstanding documentaries by **Karmen, Kopalin,** Vasily Belyayev and **Raizman.** In the later part of the war a great many popular features, dealing with war and revolutionary themes, were produced. It was in this period that Eisenstein created his celebrated *Ivan the Terrible*, the second part of which was sharply criticised by the authorities and not released until 1958.

The trend for films with heroic themes continued into the immediate postwar period; among the best and most significant were *The Young Guard* and *The Story of a Real Man*. Contemporary themes were tackled in *The Village Doctor* and *The Village Schoolteacher* (both scripted by M. Smirnova) and in *The Return of Vasily Bortnikov*. But official pressures and restrictions made it increasingly difficult to deal realistically with contemporary problems, and for a time film biographies became the main fashion.

By 1953, the restrictive official policy for "quality, not quantity" had stultified creativity and feature production had fallen from over 100 annually to under ten. But because scripts were still being written and young film-makers were continuing to emerge from Film School, the wheels were able to start turning again fairly quickly after the death of Stalin and the revelations of the "cult of the personality." The mid-Fifties can be seen as a kind of transitional period, with films like *The Big Family*, *The Rumiantsev Case*, *The Heights*, *Spring in Zarechnaya Street* and satirical comedies by **Kalatozov** and **Ryasanov** paving the way for a burst of creativity at the end of the decade. This period saw the emergence of **Chukhrai** (*The Forty-first*, *Ballad of a Soldier*) and **Bondarchuk** (*Destiny of a Man*) as important new forces in the cinema. These films, together with *The Cranes Are Flying*, represented a breakaway from simple heroics and the establishment of a more complex and personalised approach to wartime themes. A whole number of new directors, including **Derbenev, Karasik, Kalik, Daneliya** and **Shukshin** emerged at this time and continued to flourish in the Sixties.

The social problems and personal tragedies that arose from the "cult of the personality" period became an important trend in the Sixties with films like *The Battle on the Road* and *Clear Skies*. The trend was carried forward with increasing candour and clarity by *The Chairman*, which was a kind of turning-point, and afterwards by *Nobody Wanted to Die* and *Bitter Grain* (Gazui and Lysenko).

Peace to the Newcomer was one of the first attempts to make a retrospective evaluation of Nazism in personalised terms. Present-day problems of conscience, freedom and responsibility began to be tackled in new and interesting ways by older generation directors in films like *Nine Days of One Year* and *Your Contemporary*, and **Khutsiev** emerged as a significant director of films dealing with alienation. *Ivan's Childhood* was an early indication of the present trend for a kind of harsh-eyed lyricism and gradually, throughout the Sixties, an important minority of new generation directors and scriptwriters, including **Tarkovsky, Konchalovsky** and several film-makers from the Union republics have been able, amid considerable public controversy, to represent the past and the present on the screen in a mood of cool, contemporary re-appraisal.

A consistent feature of Soviet cinema, throughout its history, has been its high-level production of screen versions of the classics—novels, opera and ballet. Outstanding examples of the Sixties are *Lady with a Little Dog, War and Peace, Anna Karenina, The Brothers Karamazov* and *Katerina Ismailova*. There is also a staple output of full-length films for children and young people, mainly from the Gorki studios.

A multi-national cinema: Soviet cinema has been multi-national from the beginning of its history; there are studios in all fifteen republics. Dovzhenko produced his masterpieces in the Ukrainian studios at Kiev, which have since been named after him. The Odessa and Georgian studios were established soon after the revolution. Pioneers of Georgian cinema include Perestiani, Nikolai Shengalaya, Chiarelli, Dolidze and Shanavili. Modern Georgian films, especially the lively and warm-hearted comedies, are popular all over the Union. Leading figures in Georgian cinema today are **Abuladze, Chkeidze, Eldar Shengalaya** and his brother Georgi, and among the up-and-coming film-makers are Gogoberidze, Kobakhidze and **Yoseliani**. In neighboring Armenia, the studios have been named after the pioneer Amo Bek-Nazarov, who established them in the late Twenties. **Paradjanov** returned there in 1968 after working at the Dovzhenko studios, and among the younger generation directors are Dovlatyan (*Hallo, It's Me*) and Malyan (*The Triangle*). Armenia also has an impressive output of documentaries.

Lithuanian film-making has made rapid strides in the past decade. Despite a production of only two or three feature films a year, its small but lively group of film-makers, headed by director **Žalakevičius** and cameraman **Gricius**, achieve a remarkably high standard. Other important Lithuanian directors are Žebriuñas, Vabalas and the talented cameraman-turned-director Araminas. Latvia has achieved some outstanding successes in the documentary field, notably *Report of One Year*, directed by Freimanis. Among the leading Latvian directors are Leimanis, Armand and Brenčs. Estonia is especially noted for its puppet films. At the Moldavian studios, newest in the country, all the directors including cameraman-director **Derbenev**, Gazhui and Lysenko are young.

Directors **Aimanov**, Begalin and Hojikov in Kazakhstan, and **Yarmatov**, Ganiyev, Faiziyev and Abbasov in Uzbekistan have played leading roles in the development of their national film production and the two young directors, **Ishmakhemedon** in Uzbekistan and **Okeyev** in Kirghisia, have begun to make their mark.

260 Abuladze, Tengiz (1924-   ). Georgian feature director. At State Theatrical Institute, Tblisi 1943-6. Graduated Moscow 1953 (under Yutkevitch). Has made a number of documentaries. Feature films: *Lurdja Magdani* (co-dir: Chkeidze) 56; *Someone Else's Children* (co-dir: Djaparidze) 59; *Grandmother, Iliko, Illarion and Me* 63; *The Prayer* 68.

261 Aimanov, Shaken (1914-   ). Kazakh actor and director with a strong national style: a pioneer of Kazakh cinema. Began acting career 1933. Became director at Kazakh Drama Theatre. First film role 1940. Most important screen performance—title role in *Dzhambul* 1953, about a legendary folk-singer. Films directed: *Poem of Love* (co-dir: Gekkell) 54; *Daughter of the Steppes* 55; *We Live Here* 57; *Our Splendid Doctor* 58; *Crossroad* 63; *Wings of Song* 66; *Land of Our Fathers* 67.

262 Alov, Alexander (1923-   ). Feature director of quick-moving and dramatic action films, in collaboration with Naumov (q.v.). Graduated Moscow

Bogin's THE TWO (with Victoria Fedorova).

1951 (under Savchenko). Began work at Kiev studios as assistant to Savchenko who died while making *Taras Schevchenko*. Alov and Naumov completed it, 1951. Other films in collaboration with Naumov: *Turbulent Youth* 55; *Pavel Korchagin* 57; *The Wind* 59; *Peace to the Newcomer* 61; *The Coin* (TV film) 63; *The Ugly Story* 65.

263   Andreyev, Boris (1915-   ). Strong character actor who has played leading role in many epic films. Graduated Theatrical School, Saratov 1937. Acted in Saratov Theatre 1937-8. Began film career 1939. Most important postwar roles: *Song of Siberia*, *Kuban Cossacks*, *The Fall of Berlin*, *Ilya Murometz*, *The Big Family*, *Poem of the Sea*, *The Flaming Years*, *Cruelty*, *The Cossacks*, *The Enchanted Desna*, *The Optimistic Tragedy*.

264   Atamanov, Lev (1905-   ). A leading animator. Graduate from first Cinema School, 1926, under Kuleshov. Began work as director and animator 1927. Made many cartoon fairy-tales

and legends prewar. Postwar films include: *The Golden Antelope* 54; *The Snowqueen* 57; *The Key* (contemporary satire); *The Bench* 68.

265   Batalov, Alexei (1928-   ). Popular and versatile actor, turned to feature direction in the Sixties. Grad-

Bondarchuk's WAR AND PEACE

uated Moscow Art Theatre School Studios 1950. Soviet Army Theatre 1950-3; Moscow Arts Theatre 1953-6. First film role in 1954. Important parts in: *The Big Family, The Rumiantsev Case, The Cranes Are Flying, My Dear Man, Nine Days in One Year, Mother, Lady with a Little Dog, A Day of Happiness, The Light of a Distant Star, The Living Corpse.* Directed: *The Overcoat* 60; *Three Fat Men* 66.

266 Bogin, Mikhail (1936-   ). Young director who made a big impact with his diploma work, *The Two,* which he shot in Riga. Graduated Moscow 1965. Feature film; *Sozya* 67.

267 Bondarchuk, Sergei (1920-   ). Outstanding actor who emerged as front-rank director in Fifties. Studied at Theatre School, Rostov-on-Don prewar. Stage *début* in a front-line army ensemble during war. Enrolled at Moscow

(under Gerasimov) 1946. First film role in *The Young Guard* while student. Other roles include: *Story of a Real Man, Cavalier of the Gold Star, Taras Shevchenko, Admiral Ushakov, The Ships Storm the Bastions, It Must Not Be For-*

Bondarchuk's WAR AND PEACE

gotten, *The Grasshopper, Othello, Seryozha, The Battle on the River Neretva* (in Yugoslavia), *Cheer Up!* Films directed: *Destiny of a Man* (also acted) 59; *War and Peace* (Pts I-IV: also acted) 64-7; *Waterloo* (in Italy) 69.

268 Brumberg, Valentina (1899-) and **Zenajeda** (1900-). Sisters who are veteran cartoon directors still very active at Soyuzmultfilm Studio. Graduated Fine Art Institute 1925. Made many cartoons and designed film posters before the war. Postwar films include: *Great Troubles* 61; *Three Fat Men* 63; *The Brave Little Tailor* 64; *An Hour until the Meeting* 65; *Golden Stepmother* 66; *The Little Time Machine* 67.

269 Bykov, Rolan (1929-). Actor and feature director. Graduated at Schukin Theatre School, 1951. Moscow Youth Theatre 1958-60. Chief director at Leningrad Youth Theatre. First film role 1955. Often appears in the "Fitil"

series—10-minute films consisting of satirical sketches and news. Important roles in: *It Started like This, I Walk around Moscow, Balzaminov's Marriage, Hallo, It's Me, The Overcoat, Open the Door*

When the Bell Rings, Three Fat Men. Directed: Seven Nursemaids 62; The Lost Summer (co-dir: Orlov) 63; Dr. Ai-Bolit (also acted) 67.

270 Cherkassov, Nicolai (1903-1966). Distinguished actor of stage and screen. Started career as musician and dancer. Film *début* 1927. At Leningrad Academy of Opera and Ballet and Leningrad Theatre Academy until 1933. Then joined Pushkin Theatre, Leningrad. Gained international reputation in Thirties through roles in *Peter the Great, Alexander Nevsky, Baltic Deputy,* etc. Postwar roles include: *Ivan the Terrible, Spring, Pirogov, Alexander Popov, Battle of Stalingrad, Moussorgski, In the Name of Life, Rimsky-Korsakov, Don Quixote, All Is Left to the People.*

271 Chkheidze, Revaz (1926-   ). A leading Georgian director. Studied at Shota Rustaveli Theatre Institute 1943-46 and Moscow 1953 (under Yutkevitch and Romm). Films: *Lurdja Magdani* (co-dir: Abuladze) 55; *Our Courtyard* 56;

Maya from Tshneti 62; A Soldier's Father 65.

272 Chukhrai, Grigori (1921-   ). Director of key importance to cinema of Fifties. Graduated Moscow 1953 (under Yutkevitch and Romm). Asst. dir. to Romm 1953. Films: *The Forty-first* 56; *Ballad of a Soldier* 60; *Clear Skies* 61; *There Lived an Old Man and an Old Woman* 64; *Stalingrad* (full-length doc.) 69.

273 Daneliya, Georgi (1930-   ). Director with lyrical, lightly humorous style. Georgian by birth. Graduated as architect 1955. Worked as architect before joining two-year directors' course at Mosfilm 1958. Linked up with Talankin for diploma work, *There Are also People* 1960 and for first feature, *Seryozha (The Splendid Days)* 1960. Subsequent feature films: *The Way to the Wharf* 62; *I Walk around Moscow* 63; *Thirty-three* 65; *Cheer Up!* 69.

274 Demyanenko, Alexander (1937-   ). Young comedy actor who fre-

Above: Nikolai Cherkassov (at right) in ALL IS LEFT TO THE PEOPLE (directed by Latanson)
Below: Chukhrai's THE FORTY-FIRST (with Izolda Izvitskaya and Oleg Strizhenov)

quently plays awkward, bashful roles. Gave up studying law to join Moscow Arts Theatre Studio School. Played several small film roles during student years. Films include: *Peace to the Newcomer, Grown-up Children, Operation Laughter, Kidnapping—Caucasian Style, State Criminal.*

275   Derbenev, Vadim (1934-   ). Outstanding cameraman and later director at Moldavian studios. Graduated as cameraman Moscow 1957. Shot: *Ataman Kodr, Cradle Song, Man Following the Sun, Horizon.* Directed: *Journey into April* 63; *The Dream Knight* 64; *The Last Month of Autumn* 65.

276   Dolin, Boris (1903-   ). Director of nature study documentaries. Postwar films: *Looking at Wild Animals, Man on the Trail* 50; *Defended by Birds* 54; *The Mischievous Robber* 56; *The Faithful Heart* 58; *The Surprising Hunt* 60; *The Blind Bird* 62; *More Amazing than a Fairy-Tale* 63.

277   Donskoy, Mark (1901-   ). Veteran director with ability to recreate a bygone era. Best-known for film versions of novels by Maxim Gorky, who was his friend. Graduated as solicitor Simferopol, Crimea. Fought in Civil War: taken prisoner by Whites. Wrote book on his experiences. Worked as detective and solicitor in Ukrainian Police. Started film career 1926 as asst. dir. and scriptwriter. Most important early films: *Rainbow* 41; *The Gorky Trilogy* 38-40. Postwar films: *Unconquered* 45; *The Village Schoolteacher* 47; *Alitet Leaves for the Hills* 50; *Mother, Foma Gordeyev* (both from Gorky) 56; *At a High Cost* 58; *How Do You Do, Children?* 62; *A Mother's Heart, A Mother's Devotion* 66; *Chaliapin* 69.

278   Dunsky, Yuli (1922-   ). Scriptwriter; half of the award-winning Frid (q.v.) and Dunsky team. Graduated Moscow, 1957. Scripts include many science-fiction stories and: *The Case of Pit No. 8, As Old as the Century, Seven Nursemaids, There Lived an Old Man and an Old Woman, Love and Tigers, Just One Life* (co-prod. with Norway), *Two Comrades-in-Arms.*

279   Frid, Valeri (1922-   ). Award-winning scriptwriter. Graduated Moscow, 1957, together with his collaborator, Dunsky (q.v.).

280   Gabrilovitch, Sergei (1899-   ). Outstanding scriptwriter. Worked as a pianist for many years in his youth. Then journalist. First film *The Last Night* 1937. Postwar scripts include: *Return of Vassili Bortnikov, The Gadfly, Lesson of Life, Murder on the Rue Dante, Two Captains, The Communist, Stories about Lenin, Resurrection, Lenin in Poland, Sophia Perovskaya, No Ford Through the Fire.*

281   Gaidai,   Leonid (1923-   ). Leading comedy director. Graduated

Donskoy's A MOTHER'S HEART (with Elena Fadeyeva)

Moscow 1955. Films: *The Long Way* (co-dir: Nevzorov) 56; *The Bridegroom from the Other World* 58; *The Dog Barbosse and the Unusual Cross* (short), *The Moonshiners* 61; *The Businessmen* 63; *Operation Laughter* 65; *Kidnapping—Caucasian Style* 67; *The Diamond Arm* 68.

282 Gerasimov, Sergei (1906-   ). Director, actor and leading figure in cinema. Vice-Chairman of Filmworkers' Union. Professor of Acting in drama faculty, Moscow. Chief of Joint Acting and Directing Workshop at Moscow (VGIK). Started as actor in 1925. Graduated Leningrad Institute of Stage Art 1928. Was closely involved with Faculty of Eccentric Actors (FEX). Directed first film 1930. Most important early films: *The Teacher* 39; *Masquerade* 41. Postwar films: *The Young Guard* 48; *Liberated China* (documentary co-prod.

with China) 50; *The Country Doctor* 52; *Nadejda* 55; *And Quiet Flows the Don*

U.S.S.R. 143

Gerasimov's AND QUIET FLOWS THE DON
(with P. Glebov as man, below)

58; *Men and Beasts* 62; *The Journalist* 67.

283 Grebnev, Anatoli (1923-   ). Georgian-born scriptwriter deeply concerned with contemporary themes, notably problems of alienation. Front-line correspondent during war. Graduated as critic, Theatre Institute, Moscow 1949. Drama editor "Soviet Art" (later "Soviet Culture") until 1959. Scripts: *Waiting for Letters, Wild Dog Dingo, Two Sundays, Auntie with Violets, Rain in July, Wake Mukhin Up, Strong in Spirit* (cowriter: Lukin), *Journey to Another City*.

284 Gricius (Gritzius), Jonas (1928-   ). Outstanding Lithuanian cameraman. Graduated Moscow, 1954 (in Moskvin's class). Worked as asst. to Moskvin (q.v.) at Lenfilm for two years (*The Gadfly, Don Quixote, Stories about Lenin*) before returning to Lithuania. Took over camerawork of Kozintsev's *Hamlet* when Moskvin died. Continues close association with Kozintsev. Lithuanian films: *Turkeys, Living Heroes* (third episode), *Footsteps in the Dark,*

The Girl and the Echo, Nobody Wanted to Die, Staircase to the Sky. Leningrad films: *Hamlet* 64; *King Lear* 69.

285 Grigoriev, Roman (1911-   ). Important documentarist. One of the founders of Ukrainian newsreel studios, Kharkhov, 1931. Central Documentary Studios, Moscow, 1933. Led newsreel camera teams at front during war. Wrote several scripts before directing first film *Bulganin* (script by Ehrenburg) 1946. In early Fifties made films about Soviet republics of which *Yakutia* 1952 is considered best. Films include: *Moscow and Muscovites* 56; *Brussels 1958* 58; *People of the Blue Fire* 61; *Pipeline "Friendship"* 64.

286 Grigoriev, Yevgeni (-   ). Significant and controversial scriptwriter of mid-Sixties. Was building worker. Joined scriptwriters' course during search for new talent in factories and work-places. Won State prize with second script (about young street corner loafers). Films: *Our House, Three Days of Victor Chernishov*.

287 Gritsenko, Nicolai (1912-   ). Distinguished actor of stage and screen. Member of Vakhtangov Theatre since graduating at Schukin Theatre School 1940. Important roles in: *The Big Family; Sisters; Man without a Passport, A Gloomy Morning; Anna Karenina* (as Karenin).

288 Heifitz, Yosif (1905-   ). Director with long record of outstanding films. In Sixties gained new reputation for his screen versions of Chekhov stories. Best-known early films: *Baltic Deputy* 1936, *A Member of the Government* 1940 (both with Zarkhi). Postwar films in collaboration with Zarkhi: *Defeat of*

Heifitz's LADY WITH A LITTLE DOG, with Iya Savina and Alexei Batalov

Japan 46; *In the Name of Life* 47; *Precious Grain* 48; *Fires of Baku* 50. Heifitz alone: *Spring in Moscow* 53; *The Big Family* 54; *The Rumiantsev Case* 55; *My Dear Man* 58; *Lady with a Little Dog* 60; *Horizon* 61; *A Day of Happiness* 64; *In the Town of "S"* 66.

289 Ishmukhamedon, Elyar (1942-). Uzbek feature director with fresh, youthful style. Graduated Moscow. Films: *Rendezvous* 63; *Tenderness* 66.

290 Ivanov-Vano, Ivan (1900-). One of the founders of Soviet animated film. Specialises in Russian folk tales. Graduated Fine Arts Institute Moscow, 1923. Most important postwar films: *The Little Hump-backed Horse* 48; *The Brave Hare* 55; *The Left Hander* 64; *How One Peasant Kept Two Generals* 65; *Go to Nowhere* 66; *Legend of a Cruel Giant* 68.

291 Ivashov, Vladimir (1939-). Young actor who won international acclaim for his film *début* in *Ballad of a Soldier*. Graduated Moscow 1963. Subsequent roles include: *The Seven Nurse-*

Kalatozov's THE CRANES ARE FLYING,
with Tatiana Samoilova

maids, Auntie with the Violets, Pechorin's Notes, The Iron Flood.

292 Kalatozov, Mikhail (1903-   ).
Veteran director with romantic style.
Began film career 1923 as projectionist,
cutter and cameraman. First film 1928.
Made key contribution to feature development in Fifties. Most important prewar
film: *Salt for Svanetia* 1930. Postwar
films: *Conspiracy of the Doomed* 50;
Close Friends 54; *The First Echelon* 56;
The Cranes Are Flying 57; *The Letter
That Wasn't Sent* 60; *I Am Cuba* (co-
prod. with Cuba) 62; *The Red Tent* (co-
prod. with Italy) 69.

293 Kalik, Moisei (1927-   ). Feature director with lyrical style. Graduated Moscow 1958 (Yutkevitch's class).
Films: *Youth of Our Fathers* (co-dir:
Ritzarev), *Ataman Kodr* (co-dir: Ulits-
kaya and Ritzarev) 58; *Cradle Song*
59; *Man Following the Sun* 62; *Goodbye,
Boys* 65.

Kalik's MAN FOLLOWING THE SUN
(with Nika Krimnus)

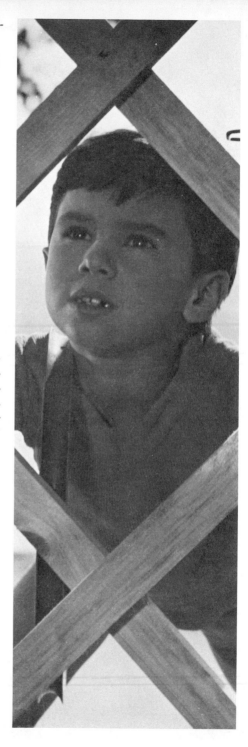

Khutsiev's RAIN IN JULY

294 Karasik, Yuli (1923-   ). Feature director. Graduated Moscow. Films: *Waiting for Letters* 60; *Wild Dog Dingo* 63; *The Man I Love* 66; *The Sixth of July* 68.

295 Karmen, Roman (1906-   ). Distinguished documentarist. Photographer for magazine "Oganjok" 1923. Graduated as cameraman, Moscow 1932. Newsreel cameraman in Spain 1936-39, and in China 1938-9. During war led groups of cameramen in France. Shot several well-known wartime documentaries. Postwar films: *Berlin* 45; *Judgement of the People* (about Nuremburg trials) 47; *Oilworkers of the Caspian Sea* 53; *Vietnam* 54; *How Broad Is Our Country* (first 70 mm Soviet film) 58; *Dawn of India* 59; *The Island of Flame* 61; *A Guest from the Island of Freedom* 63; *The Great Patriotic War* 65; *Death of a Commissar* 66; *Granada, Granada, My Granada* 67.

296 Khitruk, Fedor (1917-   ). Brilliant animator with strong personal style. His experiments have played important part in development of Soviet animation of the Sixties. Graduated at College of Art, 1936 and stayed on for post-graduate work. Went to Soyuzmultfilm as animator, 1938. In army during war. Returned to studio, 1947. Directed first film, 1962. All his films have won international awards. Titles include: *Story of a Crime* 62; *Teddy-Bear* 64; *Boniface's Holiday* 65; *A Man in a Frame* 66; *Othello—67* 67.

297 Khrabrovitsky, Daniil (1923-   ). Scriptwriter, previously journalist and essayist. Turned to direction in mid-

Sixties. In 1968 began work on co-prod. with France, about the resistance movement. Scripts: *The Four, Everything Starts on the Road, Certified Correct, Nine Days in One Year, Clear Skies, Roll-call* (also directed) 65.

298 Khutsiev, Marlen (1925-   ). Born in Georgia. Feature director deeply concerned with contemporary problems. Highly individual approach. Graduated Moscow 1950 (under Savchenko). Caused storm of controversy with *Ilyitch Square* which he revised and renamed. In 1968 began preparing script for film on life of Pushkin. Films: *Spring in Zarechnaya Street* (co-dir: Mironer) 56; *Two Fedors* 58; *I Am Twenty* (Ilyitch Square) 61-63; *Rain in July* 67.

299 Konchalovsky-Mikhalkov, Andrei (1937-   ). Controversial, up-and-coming feature director. Son of poet Sergei Mikhalkov and grandson of artist Pyotr Konchalovsky. Began training at Conservatoire as pianist, but gave it up because he felt he would never be

"good enough." Wrote some TV scripts. Then joined Moscow Film School where he worked closely with Tarkovsky (q.v.). Short features: *The Boy and the Pigeon* 58; *The Skating-Rink and the Violin* (co-dir: Tarkovsky) 59; *Andrei Rublev* 64. Full-length: *The First Teacher* 65; *The Story of Asya Klyachina, Who Loved but Did Not Marry* (Asya's Happiness) 66 (released 69); *A Nest of the Gentry* 69.

300 Kopalin, Ilya (1900-   ). Veteran documentarist. Began film work with Vertov on *Kino Eye*. Made first independent film, 1927. Leader of a camera group during war. Postwar films include: *The Day of the Victorious Country* (co-dir: Setkino) 47; *The Unforgettable Years* 57; *City of Great Destiny* 60; *First Trip to the Stars* 61; *Pages of Immortality* 65.

301 Kozintsev, Grigori (1905-   ). Veteran director and expert on Shakespeare. Professor at Lenfilm Studio Workshop. Studied at Academy of Fine Arts 1919-22. Founder of Factory of Ec-

Konchalovsky-Mikhalkov's
THE FIRST TEACHER

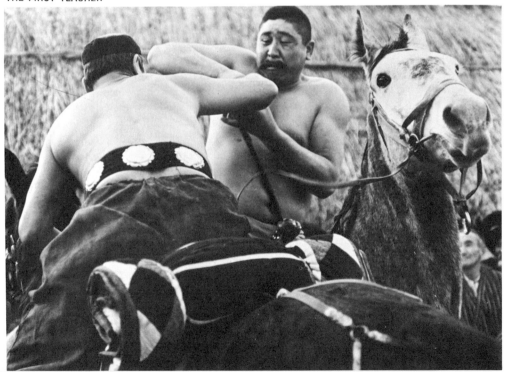

Kozintsev's HAMLET (with Mikhail Nazwanov and Elza Radzin-Szolkonis)

centric Actors (FEX). All prewar films made with Trauberg, including *The Overcoat 26; New Babylon 29;* and *The Maxim Trilogy 32-8.* Postwar films: *Ordinary People* (with Trauberg) 45; *Pirogov 47; Belinsky 51; Don Quixote 57; Hamlet 64; King Lear 69.*

302 Kulidjanov, Lev (1924-   ). Director with strong, realistic style. Chairman of Filmworkers' Union. Graduated Moscow 1954. Films: *Ladies* (co-dir: Oganisyan) 54; *It Started Like This* (co-dir: Segel) 56; *The House I Live In* (co-dir: Segel) 57; *Our Father's House 59; When the Trees Grew Tall 61; The Blue Notebook 63; The Lost Photograph 59; Crime and Punishment 69.*

303 Lanovoi, Vassilli (1934-   ). Outstanding actor. Began film career 1954. Graduated Schukin Theatre

School 1957. Important roles in: *Red Sails; Colleagues, Pavel Korchagin; War and Peace; Anna Karenina* (as Vronsky), *The Sixth of July.*

304 Lavrov, German (1929-   ). Outstanding cameraman. Graduated Moscow 1958. Films include: *Nine Days in One Year, Ordinary Fascism, Rain in July.*

305 Lisakovitch, Viktor (1937-   ). Younger generation documentary and popular science film director, with a modern, lyrical style. Films: *Autumn of Hope 62; Hallo, Nette, His Name Was Fedor, He Must Be Accused 63; Path to Tomorrow, Katyusha, Memory of the People 64; Only One Life, Dreams without End 65; The Road Begins at Mangishlak, Meet Leonid Engibarov, Chronicle without Sensation 66; Memories at Chkalov 67; The Diplomats* (full-length) 68.

306 Makhnach, Leonid (1933-   ). Outstanding documentary director. Graduated Moscow 1957. Films include: *The Towns Change Their Face, Komsomol Celebration* 58; *U.S.S.R.—America, The Greatest Hope of the People* 59; *You Are a Criminal, Oberlander!, Meeting with the Pamir Mountains, Sharik and Shurik, The Most Live of All Living* 60; *Siberian Singing, You and I* 61; *Sun, Rain and Smiles* 62; *A Drop of Poison* 65; *Bravery* 66; *Freedom for You and for Us* 68.

307 Metalnikov, Budimir (1925-   ). Scriptwriter. Enrolled at Moscow after demobilisation from wartime army. Films: *Steep Hills, Our Father's House, Alyoshkina's Love, An Ordinary Story, The Russian Women, House and Master* (also directed) 67; *Tchaikovsky.*

308 Mitta, Alexander (1933-   ). Feature director. Before entering films, studied at Institute of Constructive Engineering and drew cartoons for humour magazine "Krocodil." Graduated Moscow, 1961. Films: *My Friend Kolka*

(co-dir: Saltikov) 61; *Without Fear or Reproach* 63; *Open the Door when the Bell Rings* 66.

309 Monakhov, Vladimir (1922-   ). Distinguished cameraman recently turned director. Graduated Moscow. His work on *Destiny of a Man* gained several awards. Also shot: *The Grasshopper, Shop Window, The Heights, The Optimistic Tragedy.* Directed: *Uninvited Love* 64; *Miracles* 67.

310 Moskvin, Andrei (1901-1961). Distinguished cameraman. In films since early Twenties. Began artistic career in FEX (Factory of Eccentric Actors). Prewar shot many of the Kozintsev and Trauberg films. Died in 1961 while working on *Hamlet*; camerawork was completed by his pupil, Gricius. Postwar films: *Ivan the Terrible, Ordinary People, Pirogov, Belinsky, Don Quixote, Stories about Lenin, The Gadfly, Lady with a Little Dog, Hamlet.*

311 Naumov, Vladimir (1927-   ). Feature director. Enrolled at Moscow

Paradjanov's SHADOWS OF OUR FORGOTTEN ANCESTORS
(with Larissa Kadochnikova and Ivan Nikolaichuk)

immediately after the war. Always worked in collaboration with Alov (q.v.).

312 Okeyev, Tolomush (1935-   ). Promising feature director at Khirghiz studio. Trained at Leningrad Film Institute of Cinema Engineers. Films: *These Are Horses* 65; *Bakai's Pasture* 66; *The Sky of Our Childhood* 67.

313 Olshanski, Yosif (1917-   ). Scriptwriter of many important films: usually works with wife, Nina Rudniva. Graduated in history, philosophy and literature. Script written independently: *The House I Live In.* Scripts in collaboration with Rudniva: *Three Came from the Forest, The First Day of Peace, If This Be*

Love, Heat, Don't Forget—Lugavaya Station, Alexander Hertsen.

314 Oya, Bruno. Tall, handsome, versatile Estonian actor and entertainer. Sings jazz and folk-songs: plays guitar: excels at basket-ball and water-polo. Worked in Poland as singer and film actor. Roles include: *When Love Was a Crime* (Polish), *Wolves' Echoes* (Polish), *Nobody Wanted to Die, The Red Tent.*

315 Papanov, Anatoli (1922-   ). Strong character actor of stage and screen: usually plays "heavies." First "heroic" role in *The Living and the Dead.* Wounded during war. Enrolled at Theatre Institute immediately after war. Graduated 1949. Roles include: *Man*

Following the Sun, Home Trip, Your Own Blood, Cossacks, The Living and the Dead, Complaints Book Please, Our House, Into the Storm, Children of Don Quixote, Beware Automobile, In the Town of S, The Red Tent.

316 Paradjanov, Sergei (1924-). Born in Georgia. Director with highly individual style and deep interest in country legend and village tradition. Studied singing at Tbilisi Conservatoire. Graduated Moscow (Savchenko's class) 1951. Began film career as asst. dir. at Kiev Studios, studied and made four films there. Went to Armenia 1968, to begin work on new film. Films: *Andriesh* (co-dir: Bazelyan) 54; *The First Lad* 58; *Ukrainian Rhapsody* 61; *Shadows of Our Forgotten Ancestors* 64; *Sayat Novar* 69.

317 Pilikhina, Margarita (1926-). Important camerawoman. Graduated Moscow. Films include: *Man from Planet Earth, Foma Gordeyev, Ginger, I Am Twenty, Day Stars, Tchaikovsky.*

318 Polskikh, Galina (-). Popular and attractive young actress.

Graduated Moscow (Gerasimov's class). Roles include: *Wild Dog Dingo, I Walk Round Moscow, There Lived an Old Man and an Old Woman, The Journalist.*

319 Pyriev, Ivan (1901-1968). Distinguished director, famous at one time for his musicals, and later for his screen adaptations of Dostoyevsky. A founder of Film-workers Association. Started working-life as paperboy. Joined army as private in First World War. Graduated at Drama College, Moscow (directors' department). Associated with *avant-garde* theatre in Twenties. First film 1929. Best-known musical *The Rich Bride* 1937. Postwar films: *Song of Siberia* 47; *Kuban Cossacks* 49; *We Are for Peace* (co-dir: Joris Ivens) 51; *Test of Fidelity* 54; *The Idiot* 58; *White Nights* 59; *Our Mutual Friend* 61; *Light of a Distant Star* 65; *Brothers Karamazov* (died before completion) 68.

320 Raizman, Yuli (1903-). Veteran director who has made major contribution to cinema from Twenties to

Raizman's THE COMMUNIST

present day. Began to study literature at Moscow University, but left to start work in cinema as asst. dir. to Protazanov 1924. Prewar films include *The Last Night*, 1936. Postwar features: *The Train Goes East* 47; *Rainis* 49; *Cavalier of the Golden Star* 50; *Lesson of Life* 55; *The Communist* 57; *If This Be Love* 61; *Your Contemporary* 67.

321 Riazanov, Eldar (1927-   ). A leading comedy director who enjoys making fun of bureaucracy. As a boy, wanted to become a sailor, but enrolled at Moscow (in Kozintsev's class). Graduated 1950. Made newsreels and documentaries 1950-55. Then went to Mosfilm. Films: *Voices of Spring* (co-dir:

Gurov) 55; *Carnival Night* 56; *The Girl without an Address* 57; *Man from Nowhere* 61; *Hussar's Ballad* 62; *Complaints Book, Please* 64; *Beware Automobile!* 66; *Zigzag of Fortune* 69.

322 Romm, Mikhail (1901-   ). Veteran director who plays important role in contemporary cinema as filmmaker and teacher. While studying at Sculpture Faculty of Art Institute, became interested in literature and drama, and wrote first scripts. First film (asst. dir.) 1932. Prewar films include: *Boule de Suif* 34; *Lenin in October* 37; *Lenin in 1918* 39. Postwar films: *The Russian Question* 47; *Vladimir Ilyitch Lenin* 49; *Secret Mission* 50; *Admiral Ushakov, The Ships Storm the Bastions* 53; *Murder*

Romm's NINE DAYS IN ONE YEAR: above, with Innokenty Smoktunovsky and
Alexei Batalov, and below, Smoktunovsky with Tatiana Lavrova

Saltikov's THE CHAIRMAN, with Mikhail Ulyanov

on the *Rue Dante* 56; *Nine Days in One Year* 61; *Ordinary Fascism* (full-length doc.) 65.

323 Rostotsky, Stanislav (1922-   ). Feature director with wide range of themes. Went to front straight from school; wounded in battle. After war, began to study at Moscow (in Eisenstein's class). Trainee-director at Mosfilm 1946-50. Returned to film school (in Kozintsev's class) and graduated 1952. Films: *Land and People* 55; *It Happened in Penkova* 57; *May Stars* 59; *In the Seven Winds* 62; *Pechorin's Notes* 67; *Let's Live until Monday* 68.

324 Saltikov, Alexei (1934-   ). Feature director whose film *The Chairman* was one of the turning-points in cinema of the Sixties. Graduated Moscow (in Romm's class) 1961. Films: *Boys from Our Courtyard* (co-dir: Yastrebov) 59; *My Friend Kolka* (co-dir: Mitta) 61; *Beat the Drum* 62; *The Chairman* 65; *The Kingdom of Women* 67; *The Director* 69.

325 Samoilova, Tatiana (1934-). Leading romantic actress: daughter of distinguished stage actor Samoilov. Trained at Vachtangov Theatre in Moscow, and then joined Mayakovsky Theatre. Became internationally famous after her role in *The Cranes Are Flying*. Other parts: *The Mexican, The Cranes Are Flying, The Letter that Wasn't Sent, Alba Regia* (in Hungary), *Anna Karenina*.

326 Samsonov, Samson (1921-). Feature director. Studied Moscow 1949 under Gerasimov (q.v.) and assisted him on *The Young Guard* while a student. Films: *Grasshopper, Shop Window 55; The Fiery Miles 57; As Old as the Century 60; The Optimistic Tragedy 64; The Arena 68.*

327 Sanayev, Vsevolod (1912-). Outstanding character actor: usually plays working-class or peasant parts. Graduated at Theatrical Institute, Moscow. Film *début* 1937. Roles include: *The Return of Vassili Bortnikov, The First Echelon, Song of Koltsov, Five Days—Five Nights, The Optimistic Tragedy, Grown-* up *Children, Your Son and Brother, The Great Ore.*

328 Savelyeva, Lyudmila (1942-). Dancer chosen for role of Natasha in *War and Peace*. Graduate of Kirov Ballet School, Leningrad. This was her first acting role.

329 Savina, Iya (1936-). Distinguished and attractive actress: gained early experience at the Folk Theatre at Moscow University, where she studied journalism. Roles include: *Lady with a Little Dog, The Sinner, Open the Door when the Bell Rings, The Story of Asya Klyachina, Who Loved but Did Not Marry (Asya's Happiness), Anna Karenina.*

330 Schneiderov, Vladimir (1900-). Prize-winning director of nature and popular science films. First film 1925. Postwar films include: *The Beginning of Life, Among the Reeds in the Volga Delta* 50; *A Journey with a Cine Camera* 52; *Charles Darwin* 60; *Under Ancient Desert Skies* 61; *Otto Yulevitch Schmidt* 63; *Across Zangezur* 67.

331 Segel, Yakov (1923-). Feature director. Interested in psychological themes, especially in relation to young people. *Début* in cinema as child actor in Thirties. Graduated Moscow 1954 (Gerasimov's class). Films: *Secret of Beauty* (co-dir: Ordinsky) 55; *It Started like This* (co-dir: Kulidjanov), *The House I Live In* (co-dir: Kulidjanov) 57; *First Day of Peace* 59; *Goodbye Doves* 61; *The Volga Is Flowing* 64; *Wake Mukhin Up!* 65.

332 Shengelaya, Eldar (1933-). Georgian director of fantasies, blending legend with real life. Graduated Moscow, 1958 (Yutkevitch's class). Films: *Legend of the Ice Heart* (co-dir: Sakharov) 57; *A Snow Fairy-Tale* (co-dir: Sakharov) 59; *White Caravan* (co-dir:

Samsonov's THE OPTIMISTIC TRAGEDY (with Margarita Volodina)

Melyava) 64; *He Did Not Want to Kill* 67.

333 Shepitko, Larissa (1939-   ). Gifted woman director with probing style. Graduated Moscow 1963. Began film career as actress. Shot first film in Khirghiz Studio. Films directed: *Heat* 63; *Wings* 66.

334 Shostakovitch, Dmitri (1906-   ). Distinguished composer, closely associated with cinema from the very beginning of his musical career. Pioneered the use of music as integral part of film. Studied at Leningrad Conservatoire. Involved in cinema when invited by Kozintsev and Trauberg to write music for *The New Babylon*. His prewar film scores include music for *Counterplan*, incorporating the famous song "Salute to Life." Many of his operas, notably *Katerina Ismailova* have been filmed. Postwar films include: *Pirogov, The Young Guard, Meeting on the Elbe, The Fall of Berlin, The Unforgettable Year 1919, Belinsky, The Gadfly, The First Echelon, Khovanschina, Five Days and Five Nights, The Condemned of Altona* (in Italy), *Hamlet, Sofia Perovskaya*.

335 Shpalikov, Gennadii (1937-   ). Scriptwriter and playwright concerned with contemporary themes. Graduated Moscow. First stage play produced 1968. Scripts include: *I Am Twenty, I Walk around Moscow, I'm from Childhood, A Long Happy Life* (also directed) 66.

336 Shtraukh, Maxim (1900-   ). Distinguished actor associated with cinema since the Twenties. Played in many of the great prewar films including *Battleship Potemkin* and *Man with a Gun*. Has frequently played the role of Lenin. Postwar films include: *Conspiracy*

of the Doomed, Murder on the Rue Dante, Stories about Lenin, Lenin in Poland.

337 Shukshin, Vassili (1929-   ). Versatile director, author, scriptwriter. Became well-known as actor while student at Moscow (Romm's class). Wrote several novels, short stories and scripts, before turning to direction. Roles include: *Two Fedors, The Golden Train, When the Trees Grew Tall, Alenka, We Are Two, The Journalist*. Films directed: *There Was a Lad* 64; *Your Son and Brother* 66.

338 Skobtseva, Irina (1927-   ). Popular actress. Wife of Bondarchuk (q.v.). Graduate in journalism at Moscow University. Films include: *Othello, Seryozha, White Nights, I Walk around Moscow, Thirty-Three, War and Peace*.

339 Skuibin, Vladimir (1929-62). Very promising director with individual style. Tackled several controversial themes. Died of incurable illness before full flowering of talent. Worked on final

actor of stage and screen. Gained first acting experience during war, when he was a partisan. Rejected as "untalented" by many theatres after the war. Eventually accepted by "Big Theatre" in Leningrad. Later went to Maly Theatre, Moscow. Fabulous stage success as Prince Mishkin in *The Idiot* established him as serious actor. Film roles: *Murder on the Rue Dante, Soldiers, Near to Us, Guest in the Night, The Letter that Wasn't Sent, Storm, The First Day, Nine Days in One Year, Mozart and Salieri, Hamlet, Beware Automobile!, On the Same Planet* (as Lenin), *The Living Corpse, Degree of Risk, Tchaikovsky.*

film while semi-paralysed. Documentary film tribute to him, *Only One Life*, made in 1965. Films: *On the Ruins of the Estate* 56; *Cruelty* 59; *The Miracle-Worker* 60; *The Trial* 63.

340 Smoktunovsky, Innokenty (1925-). Most popular and best-known

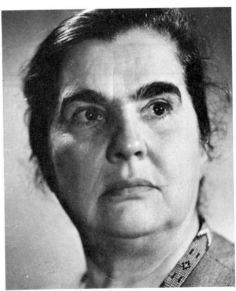

341 Soltntseva, Yulia (1901-). Actress and film director. Widow of Dovzhenko. Worked closely with her husband and since his death has devoted her life to making films based on scripts and other material he left. Studied Moscow University and State Institute of Music and Drama. First film role 1927. Asst. dir. on many of Dovzhenko's prewar films, and co-dir. of *Shors*, 1939. Postwar films: *Michurin* (co-dir.) 48; *Igor*

Bulichov 53; *Unwilling Inspectors* 54; *Poem of the Sea* 58; *The Flaming Years* 60; *The Enchanted Desna* 65; *Unforgettable* 69.

342 Stolper, Alexander (1907-   ). Director of films with strong war themes. Has been journalist and stage director. Started film work as scriptwriter. First film as director 1930. Made several very popular films during war. Postwar films: *Our Heart* 46; *Story of a Real Man* 48; *Far from Moscow* 50; *The Road* 55; *Unrepeatable Spring* 57; *The Difficult Happiness* 58; *The Living and the Dead* 64; *Soldiers Aren't Born* 68.

343 Talankin, Igor (1927-   ). Director with lyrical style. Studied at Glasunov Theatre and Music School, then took two-year directors' course at Mosfilm. Diploma film: *There Are also People* (co-dir: Daneliya) 1960. His first two films were based on works of Vera Panova. Films: *Seryozha* (co-dir: Daneliya) 60; *The Entry* 62; *Day Stars* 68; *Tchaikovsky* (co-prod. with U.S.A.) 69.

344 Tarkovsky, Andrei (1932-   ). Gifted feature director who made a big impact with his first full-length film. Graduated Moscow 1961. Worked closely with Konchalovsky while a student. Assisted Konchalovsky (q.v.) with script for *The First Teacher*. His second feature, *Andrei Rublev* aroused a storm of controversy and its release was postponed. School films: *There Will Be No Leave Today* 59; *The Skating-Rink and the Violin* 60. Feature films: *Ivan's Childhood* 62; *The Passion of Andrew Andrei Rublev* 66, released 69.

345 Tikhonov, Vyacheslav (1928-   ). Versatile actor. Graduated Moscow. Roles include: *The Young Guard*,

It Happened in Penkova, May Stars, Warrant Officer Panin, Two Lives, In the Seven Winds, Optimistic Tragedy, War and Peace (as Prince Andrei), *Let's Live until Monday.*

346 Ulyanov, Mikhail (1927-   ). Dynamic character actor of stage and

screen: has some resemblance to Spencer Tracy. Trained at Schukin Theatre School, attached to the Vaktanga Theatre, where he is now the leading actor. Remarkable lead performance in *The Chairman*. Roles include: *The House I Live In, Volunteers, An Ordinary Story, Baltic Sky, Battle on the Road, Silence, The Chairman, The Living and the Dead, The Brothers Karamazov* (helped to finish after death of director, Pyriev).

347 Urbansky, Yevgeni (1932-1966). Rugged, romantic-looking actor of stage and screen. Trained at actor's school at Moscow Arts Theatre. Stage *début* 1957 at Stanislavsky Theatre. First film role the same year. Killed in car-crash while on location for *The Director*, which was temporarily abandoned. Yekaterina Naroditskaya made film tribute to him 1968. Film roles include: *The Communist, Ballad of a Soldier, Clear Skies, The Letter that Wasn't Sent, The Great Ore*.

348 Urussevsky, Sergei (1908-   ). Leading cameraman who has worked closely with many outstanding directors, particularly with Kalatozov (q.v.). Graduated Institute of Fine Art, Moscow. Also studied photography. Joined film industry 1935 and shot first film 1940. Front-line cameraman during war. Postwar films: *The Land of the Blue Mountains, The Village Schoolteacher, Alitet Leaves for the Hills, Cavalier of the Golden Star, Return of Vassili Bortnikov, The First Echelon, The Forty-First, Lesson of Life, The Cranes Are Flying, The Letter that Wasn't Sent, I Am Cuba*. Directed: *The Trotter's Gait* 69.

349 Vengerov, Vladimir (1920-   ). Director of film versions of classics. Graduated Moscow 1943 (under Eisenstein). First film was a documentary. Feature films: *The Living Corpse* (filmed theatre), *The Forest* 53; *Dirk* (co-dir: Schweitzer) 54; *Two Captains* 56; *The Lights Go On in the City* 58; *Baltic Sky* 61; *Home Trip* 63; *A Factory Town* 65; *The Living Corpse* (free version) 69.

350 Virtinskaya, Anastasia (1944-   ). Outstanding young actress famous as screen Ophelia. Comes from a popular theatrical family (father was a very well-known ballad singer). Took part in few films while student at Schukin Theatre School. Film roles in *Red Sails, The Amphibian Man, Hamlet, War and Peace, Tchaikovsky*.

351 Yarmatov, Kamil (1903-   ). Distinguished Uzbek director. Studied at Workers' Faculty at Moscow 1926. Graduated Moscow 1931. *Début* in cinema as actor 1924. First film directed 1931 (also played leading role). Postwar films: *Road without Sleep* 46; *Alishar Navoi* 47; *Pakhta-Oi* 52; *Rakhmanov's Sisters* 54; *When Roses Bloom*

Opposite: Tarkovsky's IVAN'S CHILDHOOD

Yoseliani's FALLING LEAVES (with Marina Kartzivaeze
—both stills—and Ramaz Gueorgoliani, above)

59; *Poem of Two Hearts* 67; *Horsemen of the Revolution* 68.

352 Yezhov, Valentin (1921-   ). Outstanding scriptwriter. Enrolled at Moscow after being demobbed from army. Graduated 1951. Now teaches in scriptwriting faculty. Collaborated with Solovyev for: *World Champion, The Man from Planet Earth*. Other scripts: *Liana, Ballad of a Soldier, The Volga is Flowing, Thirty-three, Wings* (co-writer: Ryazantseva), *A Nest of the Gentry*.

353 Yoseliani, Otari (1934-   ). Young Georgian director whose first feature, shot in crisp, contemporary, free-ranging style, broke new ground. Shorts: *Water-colour* 58; *Song about Flowers* 59; *April* 61; *Cast Iron* 64. Feature film: *Falling Leaves* 67.

354 Yussov, Vadim (1929-   ). Talented cameraman with individual style. Graduated Moscow 1958. Films include: *The Skating-Rink and the Violin, Ivan's Childhood, I Walk Round Moscow, The Passion of Andrew (Andrei Rublev)*.

355 Yutkevitch, Sergei (1904-   ). Veteran director whose wide range of films includes many based on life of Lenin. Professor at Moscow since 1938. Doctor of Artistic Theory. After studying art at Kiev and Moscow, attended Directors' Studio Course 1923. Early work in theatre and cinema as actor and scenic artist. Helped organise the satirical theatre FEX. Directed first film 1927. Collaborated with Ermler on outstanding early talkie *Counterplan*, 1932; among other prewar films was *Man with a Gun*. Postwar films: *Hallo Moscow!* 45; *The Youth of Our Country* 46; *Three Encounters* (co-dirs: Pudovkin and Ptushko) 48; *Przhevalsky* 51; *The Great Warrior Skanderbeg* (Albanian co-prod.) 53; *Othello* 55; *Yves Montand Sings* (doc. co-dir: Slutsky) 57; *Stories about Lenin* 57; *Meeting with France* (Doc.) 60; *The Bath-house* (partly animated. Co-dir: Karanovitch) 62; *Lenin in Poland* 64; *Theme for a Short Story* 69.

356 Zakariadze, Sergei (1909-   ). Distinguished Georgian actor. Well-

Zalakevicius's NOBODY WANTED TO DIE

known footballer in the Twenties (Georgian Dynamos). Member of Parliament in the Sixties. Began acting 1926. First film role 1934. Has acted in all the important Georgian theatres. Most important postwar roles: *Last Day, First Day, A Soldier's Father, Cheer Up!*

357 Žalakevičius (Zhalakyavichus), Vitautus (1930-   ). Leading Lithuanian director with strong contemporary approach. Graduated Moscow 1956. Films: *It's Not Too Late* (co-dir: Fogelman) 58; *Adam Wants to Be a Man* 59; *Living Heroes* (directed and co-scripted fourth episode. Scripted second episode) 60; *Chronicle of One Day* 63; *Nobody Wanted to Die* 65.

358 Zarkhi, Alexander (1908-   ). Veteran director with strong narrative style. Graduated Leningrad College of Screen Art 1927. First film 1930, and all subsequent films until 1948, co-directed with Heifitz (q.v.). Most important early films: *Baltic Deputy* 36; *A Member of the Government* 40. For postwar films in collaboration: see Heifitz. Films by Zarkhi alone: *Pavlinka* 52; *Nesterka* (filmed theatre) 55; (both in Byelo-Russia). At Mosfilm: *The Heights* 57; *Men on the Bridge* 60; *My Younger Brother* 62; *Anna Karenina* 67.

359 Zguridi, Alexander (1904-   ). Award-winning director of nature films. Postwar films: *White Fang* 46; *Secrets of Nature* 48; *Real Life in the Forest* 50; *In the Icy Ocean* 52; *Story of a Forest Giant* 54; *In the Pacific* 57; *Jungle Track* 59; *In the Steps of Our Ancestors* 60-61; *Magnificent Islands* 65; *Forest Symphony* 67.

Opposite: Yutkevitch's LENIN IN POLAND, with Maxim Shtraukh

YUGOSLAVIA

YUGOSLAVIA

Pop. 20,000,000. A Federation of six republics with a young and rapidly-expanding film industry.

Production:

	Features	Co-product.	Documentaries	Animated
1945	—	—	9	—
1950	4	—	33	—
1955	12	3	82	—
1960	15	1	84	10
1965	19	5	137	11
1967	31	4	127	6

Cinemas:

Prewar—under 400; 1967—1,172.

Studios:

Production Companies in all the larger cities:

Belgrade: Avala film (features), Dunav film (shorts and features), Zastava film (shorts), Filmske novosti (shorts), Kina-klub "Beograd" (features and shorts), FRZ (Filmska radna zajednica) (features).

Novi Sad: Neoplanta (shorts and features).

Zagreb: Jadran film (features), Zagreb film (shorts), Filmski autorski studio (shorts).

Llubljana: Triglav film (features and shorts), Viba film (features and shorts).

Sarajevo: Bosna film (features), Sutjeska film (shorts), Studio film (features).

Titograd: Filmski studio "Titograd" (features and shorts).

Skopje: Vardar film (features and shorts).

Training:

No film school. Film department at Academy of Theatre, Film and Television, Belgrade. Many young film-makers start through the amateur film movement, which is very strong. Some train abroad.

Total Yugoslav production before the Second World War was only about fifty features and some two thousand shorts. First films were shot in 1897 and among interesting early film reportage was some remarkable material about the fall of the Turkish Empire, shot by Milton Manaki in 1905. The activities of the few small production companies that operated 1910-12 ended with the outbreak of the Balkan Wars, followed by the First World War. Among the pioneers and experimentors of the Twenties were Hamilker Boskovic, whose Croatian Film Company produced a dozen features up to its closure in 1923, and Ernest Bosnjak, who shot several features 1922-26 and made the first Yugoslav cartoon film *Watch Out and You'll Find a Million*, before financial and political pressures put an end to his work. Between the wars various organisations with production departments made advertising and educational films, and cameramen—including Sergije Tagatz, Mihailo Ivanjikov, Stevan

Mišković and **Mihailo-Mika Popović**, all of whom helped in the development of post-war cinema—managed to get a number of independently-made features and documentaries on to the screen: **Popović's** *With Faith in God* is considered to be the best prewar feature. But the efforts of these enthusiasts to form production companies failed through lack of financial support.

Because of the sporadic nature of prewar production, the biggest problem that faced the State Film Enterprise when it was set up in 1945 was lack of trained personnel. Well-equipped studios were established in the six republics, but these were no substitute for experience. The first decade was a kind of learning period, in which film-makers had to get to know the basic elements of production—some in the studios, where the experience of the cameramen mentioned above was of great value, and some through training schemes at home and abroad. The first feature was *Slavica* made by Vjekoslav Afrić in 1947.

Early productions concentrated almost entirely on war themes, and although they were in general raw and over-simplified, several, including *Brother Bakonja Brne*, *Equinox* and *The Sun Is Far Away* (Radoš Novaković, 1953) and *Two Peasants* (Žorž Skrigin, 1954) stood out from the rest. By the mid-Fifties, the industry had begun to find its feet and in the following decade many directors, including **Pogačić, Štiglic, Bauer, Hanžeković**, Nikola Tanhofer, Velamir Stojanović, Jože Babić and **Mitrović**, reached out for a wider range of content and technique. Among the best films of this transitional period were *Big and Small, Don't Look Back, Son, Peace Valley, My Own Master, Train Without a Timetable, The Ninth Circle, Captain Leši* and *March to the Drina*.

The first indication of "new cinema" came in 1961, with *Dance in the Rain* and *Where Love Has Gone*. These films heralded a major breakthrough for contemporary style production which has since developed rapidly, with a wide variety of style and content. Significant "new cinema" directors include **Hladnik, Petrović, Makavejev, Djordjević**, Dragoslav Lazić, **Mimica, Klopčić, Pavlović**, Mića Popović and **Kadijević**, and among the films which have been acclaimed abroad are *Switchboard Operator —An Affair of the Heart, Prometheus from the Island of Viševica, I Even Met Some Happy Gypsies, Kaya, I'll Kill You* and the first feature by **Berković**, *Rondo*.

Documentaries: The first documentaries were produced immediately after the war, and this branch of the industry made rapid and impressive strides. At first they were mainly informative, but they gradually developed in style and range. In the Fifties, a group of documentary directors including **Škanata**, Žika Čukulić, **Štrbac, Djordjević**, Sveta Pavlović, **Petrović, Makavejev** and **Zaninović**, developed an approach which was socially committed without being didactic, and earned themselves the collective title, "the Belgrade school." Yugoslav documentary styles, ranging from **Babaja's** satirical stylisation to **Djordjević's** lyricism and **Škanata's** harsh realism have deeply influenced feature production and many of the directors who made their names in the documentary field have since become leading feature directors.

Among the up-and-coming documentary film-makers are Vlatko Filipović, Vefik Hadžismajlović, Midhat Mutapčić and Bakir Tanović.

Animated films: Animation, which is an outstanding feature of Yugoslav film-making, had prewar origins mainly in advertising. Leading exponents in the Thirties were the three Maar brothers, refugees from Nazi Germany. In the early postwar years a number of animated shorts were made at Jadran Film, notably by Walter and Norbert Neugebauer. In 1949, on the initiative of **Hadžić**, a group of newspapermen and cartoonists, mainly from the Zagreb humorous weekly "Kerempuh," made a political satire *The Big Meeting*. Its success led to the creation of a new animation studio, Duga Film (1951-2), and it was here that the modern animation movement was born. **Vukotić's** *How Kiko Was Born* was the first breakaway from the Disney style. Other directors involved in carving out a contemporary, national style were **Marks, Jutriša,** Dovniković, **Kostelac,** Kostanjec, **Grgić, Kirstl** and **Kolar.**

Although Duga Film collapsed through lack of finance, it laid the basis for the famous "Zagreb School." A fully equipped studio was set up within Zagreb Film in 1956. **Vukotić** and **Mimica** emerged as the leading figures, and in the peak year, 1961, **Vukotić's** *The Substitute* won the Hollywood Oscar. The Zagreb School, which won many other international awards, suffered a setback when **Vukotić** and **Mimica** turned to features and some other directors went abroad. But in 1966 a new generation of directors, including Vunak, Bourek, Ante Zaninović, **Dragić** and Štalter, began to emerge and many of them have gained international success.

360   Babaja, Ante (1927-   ). Prize-winning documentary and feature director. Studied economics at Zagreb. Joined film industry 1950. Asst. dir. to Jacques Becker in Paris and to Branko Belan and Krešo Golik. First documen-

tary, *A Day in Rijeka,* 1955, gained many international awards. Other documentaries: *The Mirror* 57; *Misunderstanding* 58; *An Elbow as Such* 61; *Justice* 62; *Can You Hear Me?, The Body* 66. Feature films: *The Emperor's New Clothes* 61; *The Birch Tree* 67.

361   Bašić, Relja (1930-   ). Prominent actor of stage and screen. Graduated Theatre Academy, Zagreb 1956. In 1954, while student, played at Croatian National Theatre, Zagreb. Since then has played in variety of roles ranging from classic to modern. Occasionally directs in theatre. Has appeared in over forty films, including many foreign productions, speaking French, English, German and Italian. Film roles include: *The Blue Seagull, Millions on an Island, Austerlitz, Le Goût de la Violence* (both co-prod. with France), *Rondo, Up the River, The Wife of Husan-Aga, Flammes sur l'Adriatique* (co-prod. with France), *I*

Have Two Mummies and Two Daddies (Too Many Parents), Sunday.

Rooster (advertising film) 65; *Cherchez la Femme* (for TV) 68.

362 Bauer, Branko (1921-   ). Director of socially critical films. Began cinema career as maker of newsreels. Then made five documentaries. Directed feature films for children before beginning his series on adult contemporary themes. Feature films: *The Blue Seagull* 53; *Millions on an Island* 54; *Don't Look Back, Son* 56; *Traces* 57; *The Three Annes* 59; *Martin in the Clouds* 60; *The Supernumerary Girl* 62; *Face to Face* 63; *Nikoletina Bursać* 64; *To Come and Stay* 65; *The Fourth Travelling Companion* 67.

363 Berković, Zvonimir (1928-   ). Director who won international acclaim with his first feature, *Rondo*, 1966. Started career as violinist; was drama critic and stage director before working in films, first as screenwriter, then as director. His screenplay for *Rondo* and his prize-winning script for *H-8* are both based on musical constructions. Other films: *My Flat* (doc.) 63; *Ballad of a*

364 Bulajić, Velko (1928-   ). Director with vivid narrative style. Many of his films depict aspects of national history. Started career as journalist. Graduated as director at Centro Sperimentale, Rome. Made documentaries before turning to features. His documentary *Skopje 1963*, made in 1964, gained many international prizes. Feature films: *Train without a Timetable* 58; *War* 60; *Boom Town* 61; *Kozara* 62; *Skopje 1963* (doc.) 64; *A Glance at the Pupil of the Sun* 66; *Battle on the River Neretva* (spectacle with international cast 69.

365 Djordjević, Puriša (1924-   ). Director with highly personalised poetic style. Best-known for his war trilogy (directed and scripted), 1965-7. Left school at seventeen during war; joined partisan movement; was in concentration camp. Footballer and journalist before starting as newsreel director in 1946. Has directed over fifty documentaries and written ninety scripts for shorts. Feature

Above: Berkovic's RONDO, with Milena Dravic, Relja Basic, and Stevo Zigon. Below: Djordjevic's MORNING

films: *A Child of the Community* 51; *Two Grapes* (co-prod. with Greece) 55; *The Summer Is to Blame for Everything* 62; *The Girl, The Dream, Morning* (war trilogy), 65, 66 and 67; *The First Citizen in a Small Town* 66; *Noon* 68.

366 Dragić, Nedeljko (1936-   ). Cartoon director of the new "Zagreb School" generation. Also talented draughtsman and caricaturist. Studied law at Zagreb. Films: *Elegy* 65; *Tamer of Wild Horses* 67; *Diogenes Perhaps* 68; *Days Are Passing* 69.

367 Dravić, Milena (1940-   ). Very popular and talented young actress. Often teamed with Samardžić (q.v.). Attended ballet school as child. Photo on cover of magazine, after she took part in fashion show, led to first film role. Has played in over thirty films, including: *The Door Stays Open, Boom Town, The Supernumerary Girl, Kozara, Sandcastle, Radopolje, A Man Is Not a Bird, The Girl, Klaxon, Rondo, Before and after the Victory, Morning, The Rest-*

less *Ones, The Smoke, The Wife of Hu-san-Aga, On the Run, Poor Maria, Battle on the River Neretva.*

368 Fehmiu, Bekim (1936-   ). Popular and talented actor of contemporary stage and film, often compared to Brando and Belmondo. First to gain recognition abroad. Graduated in drama at Belgrade. Member of Youth Theatre. Played Ulysses for Italian Television 1968. Film roles in: *Klaxon, The Warm Years, A Time to Love* (pt. II), *Protest, I Even Met Some Happy Gypsies, Don't Mention the Cause of Death, Odysseus* (Italian TV), *The Adventurers* (in Italy).

369 Grgić, Zlatko (1931-   ). Cartoon director of the new "Zagreb school" generation. Studied law. Drew caricatures for magazine "Kerempuh" while student. Worked as animator for films by Vukotić (q.v.), before directing independently. Films include: *Visit from Space, The Fifth One* 64; *The Work of the Devil, The Musical Pig* 65; *Little and Big* 66; *The Shoe Inventor* 67, *Klizi-Puzi, Tolerance* (co-dir: Branko Ranitović) 68.

Above: Dragic's DIOGENES PERHAPS
Below: Grgic's VISIT FROM SPACE

370 Hadžić, Fadil (1922-   ). Feature director, journalist and playwright. Studied at Academy of Fine Arts, Zagreb. Was chief editor of humorous paper "Kerempuh" and while there, organised production of first cartoon. Became manager of first cartoon producing company "Duga Film." Several of his plays have been performed by Croatian National Theatre. Documentaries include: *The Last Gypsy Tent* 58; *The Land of Five Continents* (full-length) 60. Feature films: *Alphabet of Fear* 61; *Did a Good Man Die?* 62; *Battle for Drvar, The Official Position* 64; *The Other Side of the Medal* 65; *A Song for the Dead Miner* 66; *Protest* 67; *Assassination of Crown Prince Ferdinand, Three Hours for Love* 68.

371 Hanžeković, Fedor (1909-   ). Director of key importance in history of national cinema. Studied classical languages in Zagreb and England. Was journalist and literary translator before war. Director and scriptwriter of many documentaries. His films, mainly based on literary themes, reflect regional village life. Feature films: *Brother Bakonja Brne* 52; *Stojan Mutikaša* 54; *My Own Master* 57.

372 Hladnik, Boštjan (1929-   ). Highly significant director concerned with theme of alienation. The first to use an experimental approach. Interested in films since childhood. Wrote and directed amateur film at seventeen. Graduated in directing at Academy of Dramatic Art, Ljubljana; at the same time gained History of Art degree at University and shot several prize-winning amateur shorts. Studied directing in Paris 1957-60. Asst. dir. to Chabrol, de Broca, Duvivier and Siodmak. His experimental documentary *A Fantastic Ballad* (1954)

won many prizes. First two features aroused storm of controversy. Feature films: *Dance in the Rain* 61; *Sandcastle* 62; *Erotikon* 63; *Maibritt* 64; *The Sunny Whirlpool* 68.

373 Jutriša, Vladimir (1922-   ). A leading director of "Zagreb school." Collaborates with Marks (q.v.). Films: *Spring Songs, Criticus* 61; *The White Avenger* 62; *Metamorphosis, A Modern Fable* 64; *The Good-Hearted Ant* 65; *The Fly* 66; *Sisiphus* 67; *Little Siren* 68.

374 Kadijević, Djordje (1933-   ). Up-and-coming director of contemporary style films. Graduated in History of Art, Belgrade University. Was publicist and art critic. Feature films: *The Feast* 67; *The Expedition* (*The Trek*) 68.

375 Klopčič, Matjaž (1934-   ). Feature director and scriptwriter of contemporary style films. Graduated in architecture at Llubljana University. Studied film art and literature in Paris, where he collaborated with Godard and other young directors. Directed several shorts and worked as asst. dir. and art director. Feature films: *On the Run, Paper Planes* 67.

376 Kolar, Boris (1933-   ). A leading cartoon director of "Zagreb school." Films tend towards black humour. Was caricaturist for newspapers and magazines. Gained experience as assistant to Vukotić (q.v.) before directing own films: *A Boy and a Ball* 60; *Boomerang* 62; *Citizen 1M5* 63; *The Monster and You* 64; *Woof! Woof!, The Discoverer* 65; *Obsession* 68; *The Specialist* 69.

377 Kostelac, Nikola (1920-   ). A leading animator who gained first international success for "Zagreb school." Studied architecture before turning to

Above: Kadijevic's THE EXPEDITION, with Slobodan Perovic at centre.
Below: Klopcic's PAPER PLANES (with Snezana Niksic and Polde Bibic)

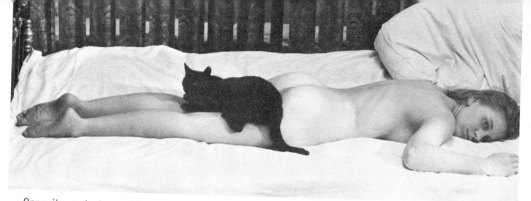

Opposite and above: Makavejev's THE SWITCHBOARD OPERATOR—AN AFFAIR OF THE HEART (with Eva Ras, at left with Slobodan Aligrudic). Below, right: Makavejev's INNOCENCE UNPROTECTED.

cinema. Was assistant to Vukotić (q.v.). Films include: *Meeting in a Dream, Meeting in a Meadow, Opening Night* 57; *Nocturne* 58; *The Boxing Ring* 59.

378 Kristl, Vladimir (1923-   ). Award-winning cartoon director of "Zagreb school." Published many poems. Graduated at Academy of Fine Arts. Worked in Europe and South America as taxi-driver, shepherd, portrait painter and actor 1953-9. Left Yugoslavia again 1963 to direct films in West Germany. Experiments with abstract forms. Films made in Yugoslavia: *La Peau de Chagrin* (co-dir: Ivo Vrbanic) 60; *Don Quixote* 61; *The Earnest Man* (short feature) 62.

379 Makavejev, Dusan (1932-   ). Significant director with contemporary style. Graduated in philosophy at Belgrade University and in film technique at Belgrade Academy. Has written satirical essays and a play for student theatre. Was film critic and journalist. Made several amateur films at Belgrade Cine Club 1952-58. Satirical documentary *The Parade* 1962, aroused violent controversy. Feature films: *A Man Is Not a*

Dramatic Theatre for many years. Films include: *The Last Track, Traces, Train without a Timetable, Siberian Lady Macbeth, Boom Town, Kozara, The Men, The Man from the Photography Department, Radopolje.*

Bird 65; The Switchboard Operator—An Affair of the Heart (or Love Dossier) 67; Innocence Unprotected 68.

381 Marković, Rade (1921-   ). One of the best and most popular actors. Long established on the stage. Has played in over thirty films, including: *Immortal Youth, The Girl, Radopolje, The Peach Thief* (in Bulgaria), *The Other Side of the Medal, The Protégé, The Detour, Three Wishes* (Czech), *The Knife, The Wife of Husan-Aga, The Naked Man, The Tough Ones, Escapes.*

382 Marks, Aleksandar (1922-   ). A leading cartoon director of "Zagreb school." Graduated at Academy of Arts, Zagreb. Works in collaboration with Jutriša (q.v.). They were assistants to Mimica before working as independent team.

383 Mimica, Vatroslav (1923-   ). Important director with probing, con-

380 Marković, Olivera (1923-   ). Popular actress. Began studying History of Art but switched to drama at Belgrade. Was leading lady of Belgrade

Above: Marks's and Jutrisa's THE FLY.
Below: Mimica's MONDAY OR TUESDAY

temporary style, and leading experimental animator of "Zagreb school." National Liberation Army during war. Then journalist and literary critic. Studied medicine at Zagreb but left to join film industry 1949, as manager and art director at Jadran Film. After directing three features, spent nine years as cartoon director: then returned to features. Animated films include: *The Scarecrow 57; The Lonely Man, Happy Ending 58; At the Photographers, The Inspector Goes Home 59; The Egg 60; A Little Chronicle 62; Typhoid Sufferers 63.* Experimental shorts: *The Telephone 62; The Wedding of Mr. Marzipan 63.* Feature films: *In the Storm 52; Mr. Ikl's Jubilee 55; The Man from the Quiet Streets* (scripted but not filmed) *57; Suleaman The Conqueror* (Italian) *61; Prometheus from the Island of Viševica 65; Monday or Tuesday 66; Kaya, I'll Kill You 67.*

in decorative painting at Academy of Applied Arts. Began film career as amateur 1960. Has published film essays, short stories and a novel. Feature films: *Raindrops, Waters, Warriors* (one episode) *62; The Enemy 65; The Return 66; The Rats Wake Up 67; When I'm Dead and White 68.*

384 Mitrović, Žika (1921-   ). Prolific director of popular action films, often with war themes. A key figure in development of Serbian cinema. Shot newsreels while partisan fighter during war. Immediately after war shot *New Victories.* Many other documentaries. Feature films: *The Echelon of Doctor M 55; The Last Track 56; Look for Vanda Kos 57; Miss Stone 59; Captain Leši, Signals over the City 60; The Salonika Terrorists 61; The Reckoning* (Part II of Captain Leši), *The Gun from Nevesinje, 63; March to the Drina 64; Bitter Grass 65; The Knife, Before and after the Victory 66; Dr. Homer's Brother 67; Operation Belgrade, Catala 68.*

385 Pavlović, Živojin (1933-   ). Important director with deep concern for "lower depth" characters. Graduated

386 Perović, Slobodan (1926-   ). Leading character actor with a flair for light comedy. Graduated Belgrade. Films include: *The False Passport, Parson Cira and Parson Spira, Three, The Inspector, The Rats Wake Up, The Expedition (The Trek).*

387 Petković, Aleksandar (1930-   ). Leading cameraman of the younger generation. Began film work as amateur. Has shot over twenty feature films including: *The Enemy, Raindrops, Waters, Warriors, The Return, A Man Is Not a Bird, The Feast, The Switchboard Operator, Wild Shadows, Before the Truth, The Tough Ones, The Expedition (The Trek).*

Two films by Pavlovic: above, THE RATS WAKE UP;
below, WHEN I'M DEAD AND WHITE

Petrovic's I EVEN MET SOME HAPPY GYPSIES, with Bekim Fehmiu at left (and Olivera Vuco at centre)

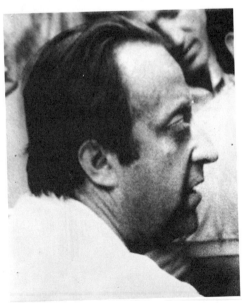

388 Petrović, Aleksandar (1929-). Award-winning director with striking visual style; often concerned with problems of alienation. Studied film technique at Prague: worked in Paris studios: graduated in history at Belgrade University. Was asst. dir. and film critic before making first feature. Now lecturer at Belgrade Academy. Shorts: *Flight above the Marshes, Petar Dobrovic* 57; *The Roads* 58; *War against War* 60; *The Data, Fairs* 64. Feature films: *Where Love Has Gone* 61; *The Days* 63; *Three* 65; *I Even Met Some Happy Gypsies* 67; *It Rains in My Village* 69.

389 Pinter, Tomislav (1926-). Award-winning cameraman. Began film career 1946. Has shot about 150 shorts and feature films including: *A Matter of Facts, Prometheus from the Island of Viševica, Three, Monday or Tuesday, Rondo, I Even Met Some Happy Gyp-*

sies, *The Birch Tree, The Fourth Travelling Companion, The Battle on the River Neretva.*

390 Pogačić, Vladimir (1919-   ). Feature director of key importance to development of national cinema. Director of Jugoslovenska Kinoteka (Film Archive). Studied History of Art in Zagreb. Worked on Radio Zagreb after war. Actor and stage manager at Student Theatre, Zagreb, which he founded. Films include: *Story about a Factory* 48; *The Last Day* 52; *Equinox* 53; *Legends About Anika* 54; *Nikola Tesla* (doc.), *Big and Small* 56; *Saturday Evening* 57; *Alone* 59; *Heaven with No Love* 61; *The Man from the Photography Department* 63.

391 Popović, Mihailo-Mika (1908-   ). Veteran cameraman and director; helped to establish postwar cinema. Began film work after leaving business school in Twenties. Directed outstanding feature film *With Faith in God* 1932. Best postwar documentaries: *New Earth, Typhus Has Destroyed,* both 1946. Shot eight feature films including: *The Sky through the Leaves, The Girl, The Dream, Morning, Noon.*

392 Rakonjac, Kokan (1935-   ). Award-winning feature director. Began making films 1957 as amateur. Has made many TV docs. Feature films: *Raindrops, Waters, Warriors* (one episode) 62; *The Town* (one episode), *The Traitor* 63; *Klaxon* 65; *The Restless Ones* 67; *Wild Shadows, Before the Truth* 68.

393 Samardžić, Ljubiša (1937-   ). Very popular and versatile young actor, often teamed with Milena Dravic (q.v.). Graduated drama department Belgrade. First Yugoslav actor to gain international prize (best actor 1967, Ven-

ice—*Morning*). Other film roles include: *The Supernumerary Girl, Kozara, Sandcastle, The Days, The Inspector, The Girl, The Knife, The Protégé, Do Not Come Back along the Same Road, The Dream, Fighters Go to Paradise, Noon, The Naked Man, Poor Maria, The Battle on the River Neretva, Ebb Tide.*

394 Sekulović, Aleksandar (1918-   ). Veteran cameraman. Shot first film (newsreel) while a partisan fighter in war. Met Tissé among visiting Soviet film team 1945. Went to Soviet Union with him as assistant. Assistant to Zori Skrigin for first postwar film *Slavica*. Director of photography for over twenty films including: *Big and Small, Saturday Evening, Alone, Siberian Lady Macbeth, The Inspector, Kozara, Kapo* (in Italy), *A Time to Love* (pt. I), *Fighters Go to Paradise, When Pigeons Fly.*

395 Škanata, Krsto (1925-   ). Outstanding documentary director; one of the initiators of modern documentary movement. Escaped from p.o.w. camp

Two films by Vukotic: above, A STAIN ON THE CONSCIENCE;
below, THE SEVENTH CONTINENT

during war and joined Italian partisans. In films since 1948. Helped found film industry in Ethiopia 1959-60. Films include: *Under the Shadow of Magic* 55; *Work and Physical Culture, The Great Century* 58; *Where the Law Ends* 64; *The First Case—Man* 65; *The Intruder, I Resign from the World* 66; *Stand Easy, Soldier* 67; *A Vampire's Nostalgia* 68.

396 Slijepčević, Vladan (1930-   ). Documentary and feature director. Frequently deals with controversial social subjects. Studied History of Art. Started work in films as asst. dir. 1949. Wrote several screenplays. Most notable documentary: *Today in a New Town* 1963. Feature films: *Medallion with Three Hearts* 62; *A Matter of Facts* 64; *The Protégé, Where to after the Rain?* 66.

397 Sremec, Rudolf (1909-   ). Director of about fifty shorts. Professor of Philosophy, Zagreb University. Especially noted for films based on material from Slavonia (in Croatia). One of the first directors to tackle important social issues. Films include: *The Sleeping Beauty* 53; *Black Waters* 55; *People on Wheels* 63; *The Soil* 64; *Seasonal Workers* 65; *The Train that Disappeared* 66; *Green Love* 67; *Notes on October* 68.

398 Štiglic, France (1919-   ). Director with lyrical style, often concerned with war themes; in later films turned to comedy. Studied law at Ljubljana. Partisan and journalist during war. Actor in *avant-garde* theatre immediately after war. Started film work in 1945 and made several documentaries including the award-winning *Youth Is at Work* 1946. Feature films: *On His Own Ground* 48; *People of Kajzarje* 52; *The Living Nightmare* 55; *Peace Valley* 56; *The False Passport* 58; *The Ninth Circle* 60; *Ballad of the Trumpet and the Cloud*

61; *That Fine Day* 63; *Don't Cry, Peter* 65; *Amandus* 66.

399 Štrbac, Milenko (1925-   ). Documentary and feature director. Studied law. Began film work as newsreel director 1947. Documentaries: *The Chain Is Broken* 51; *In the Heart of Kosmet* 54; *It Would Have Been Terrible, The Five in the Snow* 58; *Where All the Children Waved to the Passengers* 61; *The Rains of My Country* (full-length) 63. Feature films: *The Travellers from the Vessel "Splendid"* 56;   *The Fifth Class Was also Called* 62; *Out of Step* 67.

400 Tadić, Ljuba (1929-   ). Distinguished actor of theatre, television and cinema. Often plays on Belgrade stage. One of his most successful stage roles was Othello. Graduated Belgrade. Film roles include: *Siberian Lady Macbeth, March to the Drina, The Bitter Part of the River, The Dream, Morning, Out of Step, Wild Shadows, Noon, Before the Truth, Dr. Homer's Brother, The Tough Ones, Escapes*.

401 Vrhovec, Janez (1921-   ). Outstanding actor: film *début* in 1949. Has appeared in over eighty films including: *Boom Town, Raindrops, Waters, Warriors, The Man from the Photography Department, Prometheus from the Island of Viševica, The Restless Ones, A Man Is Not a Bird*.

402 Vukotić, Dušan (1927-   ). Leading animator, founder of "Zagreb school." Studied architecture. Became cartoonist for humorous magazine "Kerempuh." Helped pioneer first cartoons at Duga Film and later at Zagreb Film. Among the first to break away from "Disney" style. Winner of over fifty international awards, including

while still at school. Started career as journalist. In films since 1954. Films include: *Messages* 61; *I Started to Grow Later* 63; *A Tear on the Face* 65; *The Liberators* 67; *An Accordion* 68.

Oscar for *The Substitute (Ersatz)*. Films: *How Kico Was Born* 51; continued as *The Enchanted Castle in Dudinci* 52; Series of thirteen advertising shorts 54-55; *The Disobedient Robot* 56; *Cowboy Jimmy, The Magic Sounds* 57; *Abracadabra, Great Fear, Concerto for Machine Gun, The Cow on the Moon, My Tail's My Ticket* 59; *Piccolo* 60; *The Substitute (Ersatz)* 61; *The Play* 62; *The Seventh Continent* (full-length feature—co-prod. with Czechoslovakia) 66; *A Stain on the Conscience* (combination of cartoon and live action), *Opera Cordis* 68.

403 Zaninović, Stejpan (1926-   ). Documentary director with poetic style. Arrested for left-wing political activities

404 Živojinović, Bata (1933-   ). Very versatile actor. Graduated Belgrade. Played in over forty films including: *Kozara, Radopolje, Three, The Inspector, The Enemy, The Knife, A Glance at the Pupil of the Sun, The Detour, The Feast, Don't Mention the Cause of Death, The Dream, The Birch Tree, I Even Met Some Happy Gypsies, Dr. Homer's Brother, Escapes, Battle on the River Neretva.*

Opposite: Bata Zivojinovic in Petrovic's THREE

INDEX TO
FILM TITLES

INDEX TO FILM TITLES

REFERENCES TO DIRECTORS' BIOGRAPHIES are given in bold type. When a director has no entry number, his name appears in brackets after the title of the film. Original language titles are given only for feature-length fiction films, and these are printed in italic. There are no entry numbers for Albanian films — titles are referred to in the text on pages 9 and 10.

Above the Clouds, **83**

Abracadabra (1959), **402**

Abyss/*Szakadék* (1955), **148**

Accordion, An (1968), **403**

Account of the Party and the Guests— see Party and the Guests, The

Accused, The—see Defendant, The

Aces (1965), **98**

Across Zangezur (1967), **330**

Action J (1963), **102**

Adam's Rib/*Rebro Adamovo* (1956), **18**, 34

Adam Wants to Be a Man/*Adam khochet byt chelovekom* (1959), **357**

Admiral Ushakov/*Admiral Ushakov* (1953), 267, **322**

Ad Urbe Condita (1966), **197**

Adventure (1965), **8**

Adventure in Blue, **241**

Adventure of the Good Soldier Schweik, The (1953), **253**

Adventures of Tom Sawyer, The/*Aventurile lui Tom Sawyer* (1967), 232, **233**

Adventurers, The (L. Gilbert 1969), 368

Adventures (1965), **6**

Adventures of Gerard, The (1968), **212**

Adventures of Werner Holt, The/*Die Abenteuer des Werner Holt* (1964), **107**

Aesop/*Esop* (1969), **35**

Affair of the Heart, An—see Switchboard Operator

After Nine Hundred Days (1953), **103**

Afternoon Full of Adventures, An **135**

After One Year (1962), **104**

Age of Day Dreaming, The/*Álmodozások kora* (1964), 124, **154**

Aimez-vous les Femmes? (J. Leon 1963), 207

Alarm/*Trevoga* (1951), 34, **38**

Alarm in the Circus/*Alarm im Zirkus* (1954), 89, **105**, 106

Alba Regia/*Alba Regia* (1961), 131, **157**, 325

Aldar Kosé/*Aldar Kose*, **261**

Alenka/*Alenka* (B. Barnet 1962), 337

Alexander Hertsen/*Aleksandr Gertsen* (B. Buneyev 1969), 313

Alexander Popov/*Aleksandr Popov* (G. Rappaport and V. Eismont 1949), 270

Alishar Navoi/*Alisher Navoi* (1947), **351**

Alitet Leaves for the Hills/*Alitet ukhodit v gory* (1950), **277**, 348

All Alone/*Singur* (1968), 236, **237**

All Beginnings Are Hard/*Minden kezdet nehéz* (1966), **150**

All Good Citizens/*Všichni dobří rodáci* (1968), **53**

Allies, The (1966), **103**

All Is Left to the People/*Vse ostaetsia lyudyam* (G. Natanson 1963), 270

Allons enfants . . . . pour l'Algérie (1961), **98**

All Our Enemies/*Proti vsem* (1957), **84**

All Quiet on the Eastern Front—see Peace to the Newcomer

All Souls' Day/*Simbata mortilor* (1968), **227**, 228, 245

Alone/*Sam* (1959), **390**, 394

Alphabet of Fear/*Abeceda straha* (1961), **370**

Alyoshkina's Love/*Aleshkina lyubov* (Schukin and Tumanov 1960), 307

Amandus/*Amandus* (1966), **398**

Am I So Bad? (1967), **33**

Among People (1960), **213**

Among the Reeds in the Volga Delta (1950), **330**

Amphibian Man, The/*Chelovek-amfibiya* (S. Kazansky and V. Chebotarev 1962), 350

Anatomy of a Town (1967), **185**

Ancient Coin, The/*Starinata moneta* (1965), 28, **36**

And All Will be Quiet/*Potem nastapi Cisza* (J. Morgenstern 1965), 202

And Quiet Flows the Don/*Tikhii Don* (1958), **282**

Andrei Rublev (1964), **299**

Andrei Rublev (1966)—see The Passion of Andrew

Andriesh/*Andriesh* (1954), **316**

And Then the Guy . . . ./*És akkor a pasas* (1966), **132**, 143, 162

Animals and the Brigands, The (1946), **81**

Anna/*Édes Anna* (1958), 123, **128**, 155, 162

Anna Karenina/*Anna Karenina* (1967), 287, 303, 325, 329, **358**

Anna Szabo/*Szabóné* (1949), 136, **145**, 151, 158

Anna, the Proletarian/*Anna proletárka* (1952), **79**

Another Way of Life/*O něčem jiném* (1963), **47**, 48

Answer to Violence/*Zamach* (1958), 189, 191, 196, 198, **203**, 214

Anton the Musician (1967), **113**

Ape Terror, The (1961), **104**

Apostle, The (1965), **113**

Appassionata/*Taková láska* (1959), **86**

Apple, The (1963), **6, 8**

April (1961), **353**

Aquarium (1954), **140**

Archangel Gabriel and Mrs. Goose, The (1964), **81**

Ardent Heart, The/*Horoucí srdce* (1962), **84**

Arena, The/*Arena* (1968), **326**

Are You among Them? (1954), **177**

Arnold Zweig (1962), **103**

Art of the Young (1949), **201**

Arzt stellt fest, Der (1966), **173**

Ashes/*Popioly* (1965), 196, 202, 211, 216, **217**

Ashes and Diamonds/*Popiól i diament* (1958), 172, 190, **217**, 219

As Long as I Live/*Solange Leben in mir ist* (1965), 108, **114**

As Old as the Century/*Rovesnik veka* (1960), 278, 279, **326**

Assassination of Crown Prince Ferdinand/*Sarajevski atentat* (1968), **370**

Astronauts (1960), **167**

Asya's Happiness—see Story of Asya Klyachina

At a French Fireside/*An französischen Kaminen* (1962), **109**

At a High Cost/*Dorogoi tsenoi* (1958), **277**

Ataman Kodr/*Ataman Kodr* (1958), 275, **293**

At Home in May (1966), **98**

Atlantic Story, An/*Opowieść atlantycka* (1954), **180**

At Midnight/*Éjfélkor* (1957), 131, **150**, 151

Attached Balloon, The/*Privarzaniat balon* (1967), 22, **39**

Attention Hooligans (1955), **177**

At the Age of Love/*La vîrsta dragostei* (1963), **240**, 258

At the Gates of the Earth/La porţile pămîntului (1966), **253**

At the Photographer's (1959), **383**

At Wembley Stadium (1957), **11**

Auntie With Violets/Tetka s filakami (P. Lyubimov 1963), 283, 291

Austerlitz (A. Gance 1960), 361

Autumn/Toamnă (1961), **242**

Autumn in Badacsony (1954), **137**

Autumn of Hope (1962), **305**

Autumn Star/Isten őszi csillaga (1962), 126, **142**, 162

Avenger, The/Mstitel (1959), **79**

Aviation (1966), **113**

Awakening/Przebudzenie (1934), **173**, 180

Awakening/Probuzení (1959), **60**

Axe and the Forest, The, **225**

Bad Luck/Zezowate szczeście (1960), 181, 196, **201**, 214

Bag of Fleas, A (1962), **47**

Bakai's Pasture/Pastbishche Bakaya (1966), **312**

Baker's Emperor, The/Pekařuv císař (1951), **50**, 87

Ballad of a Rooster (1965), **363**

Ballad of a Soldier/Ballada o soldate (1960), **272**, 291, 347, 352

Ballad of the Maestros, The, **226**

Ballad of the Trumpet and the Cloud/Balada o trobenti i oblaku (1961), **398**

Balloons, The (1967), **4**

Baltic Deputy/Deputat Baltiki (1936), 270, **288**, **358**

Baltic Express/Pociąg (1959), 172, **184**, 218

Baltic Sky/Baltiyskoe nebo (1961), 346, **349**

Balzaminov's Marriage/Zhenitba Balzaminova (K. Voinov 1965), 269

Baptism/Keresztelő (1967), **130**, 143

Baptism by Fire/Tűzkeresztség (1951), **125**, 136

Baragan Thistles/Ciulini Bărăganului (1958) **125**, 136

Barefoot and Hatless (1964), **91**

Baron Munchausen/Baron Prášil (1961), 44, 87, **88**

Barrier/Bariera (1966), 187, 189, 198, **212**

Bassari (1960), **182**

Bath-house, The/Banya (1962), **355**

Battle for Drvar/Bitkaza Drvar (1964), **370**

Battle in Peace/Ütközet békében (1951), **132**, 158

Battle of Kolobrzeg (1945), **168**

Battle of Stalingrad/Stalingradskaya bitva (V. Petrov 1949), 270

Battle on the River Neretva/Bitka na Neretvi (1969), 267, **364**, 367, 389, 393, 404

Battle on the Road/Bitva v puti (V. Basov 1961), 346

Battleship Potemkin/Bronenosets Potemkin (S. Eisenstein 1925), 336

Beacon/Leuchtfeuer (1954), **117**

Bear Taken in by the Fox, The (1957), **255**

Beater, The/Naganiacz (1963), 169, **205**, **206**

Beat the Drum/Bei baraban (1962), **324**

Beauty Is with Us (1960), **257**

Beaver Coat, The/Der Biberpelz (1949), **97**

Before and After the Victory/Do pobedata i po nea (1966), 367, **384**

Before God and Man/Isten és ember előtt (1968), **144**

Before the Truth/Pre istine (1968), 380, 387, **392**, 400

Before This Night Is Over/Kým sa skončí táto noc (1965), **78**

Beginning (1964), **8**

Beginning of Life, The (1950), **330**

Be Good Until Death/*Légy jó mindhalá-lig* (1960), 126, **148**, 162

Be Happy, Ann!/*Badi shtastliva Any* (1961), 14, 28, **36**, 352

Béla Bartók (1955), **159**

Bel Ami (L. Daquin 1955), 96

Belinsky/*Belinskii* (1951), **301**, 310, 334

Bells Have Gone to Rome, The/*A harangok Rómába mennek* (1958), 131, **137**, 153

Bench, The (1968), **264**

Benthin Family, The/*Familie Benthin* (1950), 94, **109**, 112

Berlin (1945), **295**

Berlin Romance/*Eine Berliner Romanze* (1956), **105**, 106

Berlin, Schoenhauser Corner/*Berlin Ecke Schönhauser* (1957), **105**, 106

Best Woman in My Life, The/*Nejlepší ženská mého života* (1967), **50**

Best Years, The/*Die besten Jahre* (1965), **115**

Between Heaven and Earth (1957), **98**

Between Two Shores/*Między brzegami* (1962), 165, **194**

Between Two Worlds (1968), **35**

Beware Automobile/*Beregis avtomobilya* (1966), 315, **321**, 340

Beyond Hills and Mountains (1964), **238**

Beyond the Fir Trees/*Dincolo de brazi* (1957), **231**

Beyond the Horizon/*Otvad horizonta* (1960), 12, **38**

Beyond the Railway Gate/*Dincolo de barieră* (1965), **240**, 258

Bicaz, the 563 Level (1959), **234**

Bicycle, The (1955), **207**

Bicycle Race (1954), **168**

Big and Small/*Veliki i mali* (1956), **390**, 394

Big Beat/*Mocne uderzenie* (1966), **203**

Big Family, The/*Bolshaya semya* (1954), 263, 265, 287, **288**

Billiards (1964); **72**

Birch Tree, The/*Breza* (1967), **360**, 389, 404

Bird of Heaven, A/*Égi madár* (1957), **129**, 158

Birds, The (1963), **183**

Birth Certificate/*Świadectwo urodzenia* (1961), **208**, 209, 210

Birth of a Town (1959), **197**

Birth of Menyhért Simon, The/*Simon Menyhért születése* (1954), **163**

Bite to Eat, A/*Sousto* (1960), **69**

Bitter Almonds/*Hořké mandle* (1966), **54**

Bitter Grass/*Gorke trave* (1965), **384**

Bitter Part of the River, The/*Gorki deo reke* (J. Živanović 1965), 400

Black Dolphin Camp (1966), **42**

Black Galleon, The/*Die schwarze Galeere* (1962), **101**, 112

Black River, The/*Chernata reka* (1964), 10, **38**

Black Waters (1955), **397**

Black Wings/*Czarne skrzydla* (1962), **205**, **206**, 211, 216

Blanca (1955), **233**

Blazing Winter/*Răscoala* (1965), **242**, 245, 256

Blind Bird, The (1962), **276**

Blonde in Love, A/*Lásky jedné plavovlásky* (1965), 44, **49**, 70, 71, 73

Blue Notebook, The/*Sinyaya tetrad* (1963), **302**

Blue Pinafore, The (1965), **82**

Blue Room, The (1965), **199**

Blue Seagull, The/*Sinji galeb* (1953), 361, **362**

Blue Stadium, The (1957), **30**

Blum Affair, The/*Affaire Blum* (1948), **97**

Boarding House for Bachelors/*Pension pro svobodné pány* (1967), **60**

Bobe (1965), **164**

Body, The (1966), **360**

Bomb Was Stolen, A/*S-a furat o bombă* (1961), **250, 253**

Bondage/*Kötelék* (1968), **145**

Boniface's Holiday (1965), **296**

Boomerang (1962), **376**

Boom Town/*Uzavreli grad* (1961), **364, 367, 380, 401**

Border Street/*Ulica Graniczna* (1948), **173**

Boring Afternoon, A (1965), 63, **71**

Born 1944 (1965), **183**

Boule de Suif/*Boule de Suif* (1934), **322**

Boxer, The/*Bokser* (J. Dziedzina 1966), **202**

Boxer and Death, The/*Boxér a smrt* (1962), **78**

Boxing (1961), **212**

Boxing Ring, The (1959), **377**

Boyana Master, The (1956), **32**

Boy and a Ball, A (1960), **376**

Boy and the Pigeon, The (1958), **299**

Boy and the Waves, The (1962), **213**

Boy or Girl? (1966), **82**

Boys from Our Courtyard/*Rebyata s nashego dvora* (1959), **324**

Branded—see Alba Regia

Brave Hans, **99**

Brave Hare, The (1955), **290**

Brave Little Taylor, The (1964), **268**

Brave Marco (1955), **6**

Bravery (1966), **306**

Brave Truants, The/*Der tapfere Schulschwänzer* (1967), **104**

Breach, The/*Průlom* (1946), **79**

Breaking the Party (1957), **207**

Bridegroom from the Other World/*Zhenikh s togo sveta* (1958), **281**

Brigade No. 39/*A 39-es dandár* (1959), **144**

Broad Horizons/*Horizonte të hapura* (Albanian 1967-8)

Broken Bridge, The/*Zerwany most* (1962), 165, 169, 198, **203**

Broken Citadel, The/*Citadela sfărîmată* (1956), **259**

Brood Hen and her Golden Chicks, The, **222**

Brother Bakonja Brne/*Bakonja Fra Brne* (1952), **371**

Brothers and Sisters (1963), **102**

Brothers Karamazov, The/*Bratya Karamazovy* (1968), 319, **346**

Brussels 1958 (1958), **285**

Brute, The/*Dúvad* (1959), 126, **128**

Bucharest, the City in Blossom (1955), **257**

Budapest—City of Sports (1967), **127**

Bulganin (1946), **285**

Bulgaria, Land, People, Sun (1966), **33**

Bulgarian Summer (1966), **11**

Bulls of Hidalgo, The (1959), **98**

Businessmen, The/*Delovye lyudi* (1963), **281**

Bus Leaves at 6.20, The/*Autobus odjeżdża 6.20* (1955), **210**

Café from the Past/*Spotkanie w bajce* (1963), 178, 179, 192, **210**

Call My Wife/*Co rekne zena* (J. Mach 1958), 207

Calvary/*Kálvária* (G. Mészáros 1960), 136, 147

Cannonade/*Kanonada* (R. Vabalas and A. Zebriunas 1964), 284

Cantata/*Oldás és kötés* (1963), **137, 143, 153**

Can You Hear Me? (1966), **360**

Capricious Summer—see Indian Summer

Captain Dabac/*Kapitán Dabac* (1959), **41**

Captain Leši/*Kapetan Leši* (1960), **384**

Captain Loy's Dream/*Der Traum des Hauptmann Loy* (1961), **109**, 112

Captain Marten's Treasure/*Skarb kapitana Martensa* (1957), **203**

Captain of Cologne, The/*Der Hauptmann von Köln* (1956), 89, **94**, 108

Captains Do Not Leave the Ship/*Kapiäne bleiben an Bord* (1958), **101**, 110

Captured Squadron/*Pleneno yato* (1962), **19**, 27

Carambol/*Karambol* (1966), 14, **26**

Carbide and Sorrel/*Karbid und Sauerampfer* (1963), **90**, 110

Car Crazy/*Kár a benzinért* (1964), **125**

Career, The/*Kariéra* (1948), **79**

Career, The/*Kariera* (J. Koecher 1955), 181, 188

Careful Little Angel, The (1956), **6**

Carmen (1966), **77**

Carnival Night/*Karnavalnaya noch* (1956), **321**

Carousel of Lowicz, The (1958), **177**

Carriage to Vienna/*Kočár do Vídné* (1966), **57**

Case Is Not Closed, The/*Prípad jeste rekoncí* (1957), **75**

Case of Pilot Maresz, The/*Sprawa pilota Maresza* (1956), **170**

Case of Pit No. 8, The/*Sluchai na shakhte 8* (V. Basov 1957), 278, 279

Cast Iron (1964), **353**

Castles and Cottages/*Schlösser und Katen* (1956), **109**, 111

Catala/*Catala* (1968), **384**

Catherine's Marriage/*Kis Katalin házassága* (1949), **145**, 151, 158

Cat's Word of Honour, A (1963), **72**

Cavalier of the Gold Star/*Kavaler zolotoi zvezdy* (1950), 267, **320**, 348

Ceiling, The (1962), **47**, 55, 66

Certain Major Benedek/*Alázatosan jelentem* (1960), 131, **157**

Certified Correct/*Ispavlennomu verit* (V. Zhilin 1959), 297

Chain, The/*Verigata* (1964), **26**, 34

Chain Is Broken, The (1951), **399**

Chairman, The/*Predsedatel* (1965), **324**, 346

Chaliapin/*Chaliapin* (1969), **277**

Chance Meeting/*První den mého syna* (L. Helge 1964), 73

Changing Clouds/*Változó felhőzet* (1967), **139**

Changing of the Guard (1959), **176**

Chapters about the Human Brain (1966), **153**

Charles Darwin (1960), **330**

Charlie and Co. (1964), **91**

Charming Girl, A/*Un film cu o fată fermecătoare* (1966), **224**, 249, 258

Cheer Up! (1969), 267, **273**, 356

Chequered Bedspread, The/*Die Buntkarierten* (1949), **109**

Cherchez la Femme (1968), **363**

Chess Club/*Klub szachistów* (1967), 192, **194**

Chief of the Souls' Department, The/*Şeful sectorului suflete* (1967), **259**

Child of the Community, A/*Opštinsko dete* (1951), **365**

Children Are Singing, The (1960), **159**

Children of Don Quixote/*Deti Don Kikhota* (E. Karelov), 315

Children's Theatre (1965), **91**

Child's Hands, A (1945), **200**

China—Between Today and Tomorrow (1956), **103**

Chintamans/Čintamani a podvodník (1965), 60

Chit in Danger, 225

Chopin Mazurkas (1949), 200

Chopin Recital at the Duszniki Festival (1947), 200

Chopin's Birth Place (1967), 185

Christened by Fire/Skąpani w ogniu (1963), 203, 216

Christine/Christine (1963), 94

Christmas Dream, A (1945), 88

Christmas Eve/Przedświąteczny wieczór (1966), 172, 214

Christmas Tree (1967), 82

Christmas with Elizabeth/Vánoce s Alžbětou (1968), 57

Chronicle of One Day/Khronika odnogo dnia (1963), 357

Chronicle of Sentiments, A/Hronika na chustvata (1962), 26

Chronicle without Sensation (1966), 305

Circadian Rhythms (1965), 164

Circle, The/Kruh (1959), 75

Circus, The (1954), 176

Circus Is Coming, The (1960), 64

Cities of Chemistry, The, 242

Citizen Brych/Občan Brych (1958), 84

Citizen 1M5 (1963), 376

City of Great Destiny (1960), 300

City of Histros, The (1956), 223

Clear Skies/Chistoe nebo (1961), 272, 297, 347

Close Friends/Vernye druzya (1954), 292

Closely Observed Trains/Ostře sledované vlaky (1966), 45, 66, 68

Close to the Sun/Aproape de soare (1960), 257

Closing Hour, The/Policejní hodina (1960), 84

Clouds Will Roll Away, The/Není stále zamračeno (1950), 53, 57

Coach to Vienna—see Carriage to Vienna

Coal Piles (1962), 185

Code, The/Szyfry (1966), 172, 175, 179, 190, 204

Coffin Shop, The (1966), 80

Coin, The/Moneta (1963), 262, 311

Cold Days/Hideg napok (1966), 142, 143, 155

Colleagues/Kollegi (A. Sakharov 1963), 303

Colonel Wolodyjowski/Pan Wolodyjowski (1969), 177, 196, 198, 202

Colourful China (1957), 137

Colours in Painting (1964), 159

Column, The/Columna (1968), 228, 231, 245, 251

Come and Play, Sir (1965-7), 72

Comedy around a Door Handle/Komedie s klikou (1964), 61

Comic History of Aviation (1958), 43

Commander of the Detachment, The/Komandirat na otriada (1959), 15, 19

Commando 52 (1965), 102

Commissar of Light, The/Komisari i dritës (Albanian 1966)

Communist, The/Kommunist (1957), 280, 320, 347

Compact of Maturity/Cyrograf dojrzałości (1967), 197

Competition (1963), 185

Complaints Book, Please/Daite zhalobnuyu knigu (1964), 315, 321

Composition in Painting (1961), 159

Concert (1961), 154

Concert (1964), 32

Concerto for Machine-gun (1959), 402

Concerto Grosso (1964), 234

Concurrence (1965), 99

Condemned of Altona, The/*I Sequestrati di Altona* (V. De Sica 1962), 334

Condemned Village, The/*Das verurteilte Dorf* (1951), **101**, 112

Confirmation, The/*Die Feststellung* (1958), **105**

Conflicts (1960), **215**

Confrontation, The/*Fényes szelek* (1968), **137**

Congratulation (1965), **113**

Conscience/*Svědomí* (1949), **60**

Conspiracy of the Doomed/*Zagovor obrechennykh* (1950), **292**, 336

Constellation Virgo, The/*Souhvězdí Panny* (1966), **46**, **73**

Contribution/*Kontrybucja* (1966), 169, **197**, 198

Corporal and the Others, The/*A tizedes meg a többiek* (1965), **139**

Cossacks/*Kazaki* (V. Pronin 1961), 263, 315

Counsel for the Prosecution Has the Floor, The/*Prokurator ma glos* (1965), **176**, 198

Council of the Gods/*Der Rat der Gotter* (1950), 96, **109**

Counterplan/*Strechni* (1932), 334, **355**

Counterpoint in White (1964), **257**

Countess Cosel/*Hrabina Cosel* (J. Antczak 1968), 202

Country Doctor, The/*Selskii vrach* (1952), **282**

Courage for Everyday Life/*Každý den odvahu* (1964), 44, 45, 48, 56, 65, 66, **77**

Coward, The/*Zbabělec* (1961), 86

Cowboy Jimmy (1957), **402**

Cow on the Moon, The (1959), **402**

The Cow Who . . . (1968), **8**, **32**

Cradles (1957), **140**

Cradle Song/*Kolybelnaya* (1959), 275, **293**

Cranes Are Flying, The/*Letyat zhuravli* (1957), 265, **292**, 325, 348

Creation, The (1966), **103**

Crew, The/*Zaloga* (J. Fethke 1952), 181

Crime (1964), **160**

Crime and Punishment/*Prestuplenie i nakazanie* (1969), **302**

Crime at Dawn/*Merénylet* (1958), **163**

Crime at the Girls' School/*Zločin v dívčí škole* (1965), **66**, **75**

Crime at the Night Club/*Zlocin v santánu* (1969), **66**

Criticus (1961), **373**, **382**

Cross of Valour, The/*Krzyż walecznych* (1959), 172, **191**, 219

Crossroad/*Perekrestok* (1963), **261**

Crucial Years, The/*Kristove roky* (1967), **52**, 67

Crude Oil (1967), **238**

Cruelty/*Zhestokost* (1959), 263, **339**

Csutak and the Grey Horse/*Csutak és a szürke ló* (1960), **163**

Cul-de-Sac (1966), 187, **207**

Cure for Love, A/*Lekarstwo na milość* (1965), **166**

Curiosity (1966), **113**

Current/*Sodrásban* (1964), 130, **152**

Cybernetic Grandma (1962), **81**

Cybernetics (1964), **153**

Cyclists in Love/*Szerelmes bicik listák* (1965), **123**, 136

Czech Year, The/*Spaliček* (1947), **81**

Dacians, The/*Dacii* (1966), **243**, 245, 251

Daisies/*Sedmikrásky* (1966), **47**, 55, 62, 63

Daisy, The (1965), **6**

Dalibor/*Dalibor* (1956), **61**

Dam, The/*Priehrada* (1950), **41**

Damned Roads, The/*Baza ludzi umarlych* (1958), 198, **206**

Dance in the Rain/*Ples na kiši* (1961), **372**

Dance of the Vampires (1967), 187, **207**

Dancing at Hitler's Headquarters/*Dancing w kwaterze Hitlera* (1968), **166**

Dangerous Freight/*Gefährliche Fracht* (Jung-Alsen 1954), 95

Dani/*Dani* (1957), 147, 156, **157**, 161

Danse Macabre/*A tettes ismeretlen* (1957), 136, **148**

Danube Waves, The/*Valurile Dunării* (1963), 228, **229**, 240, 251, 258

Darclée/*Darclée* (1960), **233**, 245, 252

Darkness/*Temno* (1950), **79**

Darkness in Daytime/*Nappali sötétség* (1963), **128**

Data, The (1964), **388**

Daughter-in-law/*Snaha* (1954), **18**

Daughter of the Steppes/*Doch stepei* (1955), **261**

Dawn above Us/*Nad námi svítá* (1952), **60**

Dawn of India (1959), **295**

Dawn over the Danube (1956), **11**

Dawn over the Homeland/*Utro nad Rodinata* (1951), 13, **18**

Day in Rijeka, A (1955), **360**

Day of Happiness, A/*Den schastya* (1964), 265, **288**

Day of the Victorious Country, The (1947), **300**

Day of Wrath, The/*Harag napja* (1953), 126, **163**

Days, **30**

Days Are Passing (1969), **366**

Days of Matthew, The—see Life of Matthew

Day Stars/*Dnevnye zvezdi* (1968), 317, **343**

Days, The/*Dani* (1963), **388**, 393

Day the Tree Will Bloom, The/*Kde řeky mají slunce* (1961), **61**

Day without Land (1968), **17**

Day without Sun, A (1959), **183**, **213**

Deadlock/*Sikátor* (1966), 124, **149**, 162

Dead Stay Young, The/*Die Toten bleiben jung* (1968), **107**

Death Is Called Engelchen/*Smrt si říká Engelchen* (1963), 56, **58**, **59**, 67

Death of a Commissar (1966), **295**

Death of a Taxi-driver/*Ostatni kurs* (1963), **166**

Death of Joe the Indian, The/*Moartea lui Joe Indianul* (1968), 232, **233**

Death of Mr. Foerster (1963), **66**

Deceitful Gosho (1963), **4**

Deceived Fox, The (1952), **225**

Decline of the Wizards (1965), **182**

Defeat of Japan (1946), **288**, **358**

Defendant, The/*Obžalovaný* (1964), **58**, **59**, 66, 67

Defended by Birds (1954), **276**

Degree of Risk/*Stepen riska* (I. Averbakh 1968), 340

Départ, Le (1967), 187, 189, **212**

Derkovits (1958), **137**, 153

Deserters and Pilgrims/*Zbehovia a pútnici* (1968), **52**

Deserter, The/*Dezerter* (1958), **194**, 214

Deserter, The (1965), **43**

Desire/*Touha* (1958), 44, **53**, 63

Destiny of a Man/*Sudba cheloveka* (1959), **267**, 309

Detour, The/*Diverzanti* (H. Krvavac 1966), 381, 404

Detour, The (1967)—see Side-track

Devil Never Rests, The/*Čert nikdy nespí* (1957), **78**

Devil's Trap, The/*Ďáblova past* (1961), **85**

Devil's Valley, The (1959), **99**

Diagram, The (1966), **215**

Dialogue/*Párbeszéd* (1963), **134**, 136

Dialogue/*Dialog* (1968), **46, 78,** 189, **212**

Diamond Arm, The/*Brilliantovaya ruka* (1968), **281**

Diamonds of the Night/*Démanty noci* (1964), 63, **69**

Diaries of the Peasants (1953), **201**

Did a Good Man Die?/*Da li je umro dobar čovjek?* (1962), **370**

Difficult Happiness, The/*Trudnoe schaste* (1958), **342**

Difficult Love/*Trudna milość* (1953), 169, **208**

Difficult People/*Nehéz emberek* (1964), **142**

Dimensions **241**

Dinosaura (1962), **174**

Diogenes Perhaps (1968), **366**

Diplomats, The (1968), **305**

Direction—Berlin/*Kierunek Berlin* (1969), **203,** 212

Direction Nowa Huta (1951), **201**

Director, The/*Direktor* (1969), **324,** 347

Dirk/*Kortik* (1954), **349**

Discoverer, The (1965), **376**

Discussion, The/*Debatik* (Albanian)

Disobedient Robot (1956), **402**

Distant Journey/*Daleká cesta* (1949), **74**

District of Gaiety, The/*Cartierul Veseliei* (1964), 236, **237**

Dita Saxová/*Dita Saxová* (A. Moskalyk 1968), 63

Diversion—see Side-track

Divided Sky, The/*Der geteilte Himmel* (1964), 89, 118, **122**

Divorce in Budapest (1964), **156**

Documents of Fight (1968), **168**

Dog Barbosse and the Unusual Cross, The (1961), **281**

Doggie and the Four/*Punta a čtyřlístek* (1954), **86**

Dog's Heaven (1967), **82**

Dog's Newsreel, The (1959), **200**

Doll, The/*Lalka* (1968), **175,** 192, 204, 216

Don Gabriel/*Don Gabriel* (1966), 190, **205, 206**

Do Not Come Back along the Same Road/*Po isti poti se ne vračaj* (J. Babić 1966), 393

Don Quixote/*Don Kikhot* (1957), 270, 284, **301,** 310

Don Quixote (1961), **378**

Don't Cry, Peter/*Ne joči Petre* (1965), **398,** 404

Don't Forget Lugovaya Station/*Ne zabud . . . . stantziya Lugovaya* (N. Kurikhin and L. Menaker 1966), 313

Don't Forget My Traudel/*Vergesst mir meine Traudel nicht* (1957), **109**

Don't Irritate the Mouse (1967), **146**

Don't keep Off the Grass/*Füre lépni szabad* (1960), 136, **144,** 147, 161

Don't Look Back, Son/*Ne okreći se, sine* (1956), **362**

Don't Mention the Cause of Death/*Uzrok smrti ne pominjati* (J. Živanović 1967), 219, 368, 404

Don't Take Shelter from the Rain/*Neschovávejte se když prší* (1962), **46,** 48

Door Stays Open, The/*Vrata ostaju otvorena* (F. Čap 1959), 367

Dowry, The/*Wiano* (1963), **197,** 198

Dr. Ai-Bolit/*Aybolit 66* (1967), **269**

Dr. Homer's Brother/*Brat Doktora Homera* (1967), **384, 400,** 404

Drake (1958), **31**

Drawing for Cats (1963), **72**

Dream, The/*San* (1966), **365,** 391, 393, 400, 404

Dream Knight, The/*Rytsar mechty* (1964), **275**

Dreams without End (1965), **305**

Drop of Poison, A (1965), **306**

Drop Too Much, A (1956), **72**

Duel, The (1964), **199**

Duet (1961), **7**

Duet (1964), **215**

Dusks and Dawns (1961), **137**

Dyestuffs (1968), **234**

Dzhambul/*Dzhambul* (E. Dzigan 1953), 261

Earnest Man, The (1962), **378**

Easy-Breezy Seeks the Easy Way (1961), **32**

Ebb Tide/*Oseka* (V. Pavlović 1968), 393

Echelon of Dr. M, The/*Ešalon Dr. M* (1955), **384**, 401

Echo/*Echo* (1964), 208, 209, 219

Echoes on the Shore/*Oshëtimë në bregdet* (Albanian)

Egg, The (1960), **383**

Eighth Day of the Week, The/*Ósmy dzień tygodnia* (1958), 172, **173**, 196, 198

Elbow as Such, An (1961), **360**

Electronicus, **241**

Elegy (1965), **366**

Eleven Years Old (1966), **104**

Emigrant, The (1965), **52**

Emilia Galotti/*Emilia Galotti* (1957), **101**

Emperor and the Nightingale, The (1948), 43, **81**

Emperor's Baker, The/*Císařův pekař* (1951), 43, **50**, 87

Emperor's New Clothes, The/*Carevo novo ruho* (1961), **360**

Empire of the Lazy, The (1961), **255**

Empty Eyes/*Puste ocsy* (1969), **205**, **206**

Enchanted Castle in Dudinci, The (1952), **402**

Enchanted Desna, The/*Zacharovannaya Desna* (1965), 263, **341**

Encounters in the Dark/*Spotkania w mroku* (1960), **180**

Endless Shore, The/*Tărmul n-are sfîrşit* (1962), **254**

End of Agent W4C, The/*Konec Agenta W4C* (V. Vorlicek 1967), 56

End of August at Hotel Ozone/*Konec srpna v hotelu Ozon* (1966), 55, **76**

End of Our World, The/*Koniec naszego swiata* (1964), **180**

End of the Road, The (1958), **197**

End of the Summer, The/*Kraiat na lyatoto* (1967), **19**, 27

Enemy, The/*Sovražnik* (1965), **385**, 387, 404

Energy (1967), **213**

Entry, The/*Vstuplenie* (1962), **343**

Equinox/*Nevjera* (1953), **390**

Erkel/*Erkel* (1952), **139**

Ernst Busch (1967), **98**

Ernst Thalmann, Pt I/*Ernst Thälmann— Sohn seiner Klasse* (1954), **109**, 112

Ernst Thalmann, Pt II/*Ernst Thälmann— Führer seiner Klasse* (1955), **109**, 112

Eroica/*Eroica* (1957), 198, **201**, 214, 219

Erotikon/*Erotikon* (1963), **372**

Ersatz—see Substitute, The

Eruption, The/*Erupţia* (1959), 228, **229**

Escapes/*Bekstva* (R. Novaković 1968), 381, 400, 404

Etcetera (1966), **80**

Eternal Renaissance (1966), **140**

European Champions (1966), **127**

Everyday (1949), **200**

Everyday (1963)/*Ich dzień powszedni* 165, 172, 190, **211**

Everyday Courage—see Courage for Everyday Life

Every Day—Sunday/*Pirosbetűs hétköznapok* (1962), 131, **145**, 151

Every Penny Counts/*Každá koruna dobrá* (1961), **46**

Everything Ends Tonight/*Dnes večer vsechno skončí* (1954), **53**, **57**, 63

Everything for Sale/*Wszystko na sprzedaż* (1968), 189, 192, 202, 216, **217**

Everything Starts on the Road/*Vse nachinaetsya s dorogi* (V. Azarov and N. Dostal 1959), 297

Every Young Man/*Každý mladý muž* (1965), **55**

Eve Wants to Sleep/*Ewa chce spać* (1958), **171**

Evidence (1965), **185**

Examination, The (1952), **119**, **120**

Expedition, The/*Pohod* (1968), **374**, 386, 387

Expelled from Paradise (1967), **6**

Extinguished Flames/*A császár parancsára* (1956), **125**, 126, 151

Eyes of My City, The/*Ochii oraşului meu* (1963), **227**

Eyes of the Sea (1963), **11**

Fable (1964), **4**

Face at the Window/*Tvár v okne* (1963), **78**

Face to Face/*Licem u lice* (1963), **362**

Facing the Audience (1954), **257**

Factory in Germany (1954), **98**

Factory Town, A/*Rabochi posselok* (1965), **349**

Fairs, **387**

Faithful Heart, The (1958), **276**

Fake "Isabella," The/*Hamis Izabella* (I. Bácskai-Lauró 1968), 151

Fall In!/*Nástup* (1952), **84**

Falling Leaves/*Listopad* (1967), **353**

Fall of Berlin, The (1945), **168**

Fall of Berlin, The/*Padenie Berlina* (M. Chiaureli 1949), 263, 334

False Passport, The/*Viza na zloto* (1958), 386, **398**

Family of Man (1966), **213**

Famous 702, The/*Celebrul 702* (1962), **233**, 245, 253

Fanatics, The/*Megszállottak* (1961), **144**, 158

Fantasies, **225**

Fantastic Ballad, A (1954), **372**

Farewell/*Abschied* (1968), **100**, 108, 110

Farewells/*Pożegnania* (1958), **175**, 178, 179, 181

Farewell to a Spy/*Spotkanie ze szpiegem* (1964), **166**

Farewell to the Devil/*Pożegnanie z diablem* (1956), **180**

Far Freedom (1945), **41**

Far from Moscow/*Daleko ot Moskvy* (1950), **342**

Father/*Apa* (1966), 124, 131, 152, **154**, 161

Father's Name/*Imię Ojca* (1969), **213**

Fatia Negra/*Szegény gazdagok* (1959), **125**, 136

Faustus XX/*Faust XX* (1966), **250**

Favourite No. 13/*Lyubimetz 13* (1958), 13, 28, **36**

Fearless Vampire Killers, The—see Dance of the Vampires

Feast, The/*Praznik* (1967), **374**, 387, 404

Feast of Friendship (1967), **91**

Ferryman from Accra, The (1960), **182**

Fêtes Galantes, Les/*Serbările galante* (1965), **259**

Fetters/*Pouta* (1961), **57**

Fever/*Láz* (1957), 126, **132**

Few Steps to the Frontier, A/Pár lépés a határ (1959), **139**, 158

Fiery Miles, The/Ognennye versty (1957), **326**

Fifth Class Was Also Called, The/Prozvan je i Vb (1962), **399**

Fifth Horseman Is Fear, The/. . . . a pátý jezdec je strach (1964), **46**

Fifth One, The (1964), **369**

Fifty-eight Seconds (1964), **133**

Fighters Go to Paradise/Bokseri idu u raj (B. Ćelović 1967), 393, 394

Fig-Leaf/Fügefalevél (1966), 126, **145**

File, The (1966), **174**

Fire! Fire!—see Firemen's Ball, The

Firemen's Ball, The/Hǒří, má panenko (1967), **49**, 70, 71

Fires of Baku/Ogni Baku (1950), **288**, **358**

First Case—Man, The (1965), **395**

First Citizen in a Small Town, The/Prvi gradjanin male varoši (1966), **365**

First Courier, The/Parviat kurier (1968), **36**

First Cry, The/Křik (1963), **54**, 63

First Day, The/Den pervyi (F. Ermler 1959), 340

First Day of Freedom, The/Pierwszy dzień wolności (1964), **173**, 198, 216

First Day of Peace, The/Pervyi den mira (1959), 313, **331**

First Days (1949), **38**

First Days/Pierwsze dni (1951), **210**

First Echelon, The/Pervyi eshelon (1956), **292**, 327, 334, 348

First Lad, The/Pervyi paren (1958), **316**

First Lesson/Parvi urok (1960), 3, 10, 15, 21, 22, **35**

First Rescue Party, The/První parta (1959), **84**

First Shift, The (1962), **185**

First Shock Brigade, The (Albanian)

First Start, The/Pierwszy start (1951), **170**

First Steps, The (1962), **183**

First Teacher, The/Pervyi uchitel (1965), **299**, 344

First Trip to the Stars (1961), **300**

First Years, The/Vitet e para (Albanian)

Five Boys from Barska Street/Piatka z ulicy Barskiej (1953), **173**, 181, 196, 198, 217

Five Bullets/Fünf Patronenhülsen (1960), **90**, 110

Five Days, Five Nights/Pyat dnei—pyat nochei (L. Arnshtam 1961), 327, 334

Five Girls like a Millstone round One's Neck/Pět holek na krku (1967), 48, **77**

Five in the Snow, The (1958), **399**

Five Minute Murder (1966), **146**

Five out of a Million/Pět z miliónů (1959), 45, **46**, 48

Five Seasons (1960), **98**

Flag of Kriwoj Rog/Die Fahne von Kriwoj Rog (1967), **109**

Flaming Years, The/Povest plamennykh let (1960), 263, **341**

Flammes sur l'Adriatique/Plamen nad Jadranom (A. Astruc 1968), 361

Flat, The (1968), **80**

Fledermaus Squadron, The/Geschwader Fledermaus (1958), 96, **97**, 112

Fleischer's Album, (1962), **199**

Flies Hunting/Polowanie na muchy (1969), **217**

Flight above the Marshes (1957), **388**

Flood, The (1947), **168**

Fly, The (1966), **373**, **382**

Fly with Money, A/O muscă cu bani (1954), **250**

Foma Gordeyev/Foma Gordeev (1956), **277**, 317

Footprints (1960), **54**

Footsteps in the Dark/*Shagi v nochi* (R. Vabalas 1963), 284

Forbidden Songs/*Zakazane piosenki* (1947), **170**, 192

Forest, The/*Les* (1953), **349**

Forester's Song (1968), **43**

Forest of the Hanged, The/*Pădurea spînzuraților* (1965), **229**, 232, 251, 252, 258

Forest Symphony (1967), **359**

For Eyes Only/*For Eyes Only (Streng geheim)* (J. Veiczi 1963), 112

Form 9A/*My z deviatej A* (1961), **83**

For the Flourish of the Homeland (1955), **30**

Forty-first, The/*Sorok pervyi* (1956), **272**, 348

Forty-four/*Štyridsatštyri* (1957), **41**

For Whom the Larks Sing/*Akiket a pacsirta elkísér* (1959), **148**, 161

Four, The/*Chetvero* (V. Ordynsky 1957), 297

Four Children in the Flood/*Négyen az árban* (1961), **150**

Four Hundred Cubic Centimetres (1966), 93, **102**, **116**

Four Steps to the Infinite/*La patru paşi de infinit* (1964), **240**, 258

Fourteen Lives Saved/*Életjel* (1954), **128**

Four Thousand Steps to the Sky (1963), **238**

Fourth Travelling Companion, The/*Četvrti suputnik* (1967), **362**, 389

Fox Holes/*Vlčie diery* (1948) **41**

Frame of Mind/*Sposób bycia* (1965), 192, 196, **210**, 212, 218

Free City/*Wolne miasto* (1958), **208**

Freedom for You and for Us (1968), **306**

Freedom, Freedom above All (1960), **98**

Free Peasants (1965), **103**

Fresh Vegetables/*Junges Gemüse* (1956), **114**, 115

Friday the Thirteenth/*V piatok trinásteho* (1953), **41**

Friendship Wins (1951), **103**, **119**, **120**

Friends of Gosho the Elephant, The (1967), **7**

From Blossom Time to Autumn Leaves, **135**

From Hamburg to Stralsund (1949), **119**, **120**

From My Life/*Z mého života* (1955), **61**

From Noon to Dawn/*Déltől hajnalig* (1964), **149**

From One to Eight (1966), **17**

From Tomorrow On (1963), **146**

Full Steam Ahead/*Teljes gőzzel* (1951), 126, **145**

Full Steam Ahead/*Cała naprzód* (S. Lenartowicz 1966), 172

Gadfly, The/*Ovod* (A. Fainzimmer, 1957), 280, 284, 310, 334

Gala Dinner/*Ünnepi vacsora* (1956), **150**

Gala Suit/*Díszmagyar* (1948), **132**

Game, A/*Zabawa* (1960), **195**

Game, The/*Gra* (1969), 178, **184**, 218

Gangsters and Philanthropists/*Gangsterzy i filantropi* (1962), **177**, 178, 196

Garden, The (1967), **80**

Gates to Paradise/*Vrata raja* (1967), 179, **217**

Gaudeamus (1959), **177**

Gaudeamus Igitur (1964), **259**

Generation, A/*Pokolenie* (1954), 172, 181, 191, 196, 198, 207, **217**

Gentle One, The/*Něžná* (1968), **40**

Gentry Skylarking/*Úri Muri* (1949), **125**

George Kastriot—Skanderbeg (Albanian)

Georges Dandin/*Dandin György* (1955), **163**

Geraks, The/*Geratsite* (1958), **18**, 20

Germans, The (1968), **119, 120**

German Story, The (1955), 93, 115, **119, 120**

Gifts Snatched from Nature (1952), **227**

Ginger/*Ryzhik* (I. Frez 1960), 317

Girl, The/*Devojka* (1965), **365**, 367, 381, 391, 393

Girl, The/*Eltávozott nap* (G. Mészáros 1968), 153, 158

Girl and the Echo, The/*Devochka i ekho* (A. Žebriuñas 1964), 284

Girl on the Diving-Board, The/*Das Mädchen auf dem Brett* (1967), **109**

Girl Students—Impressions of a Technical College (1965), **104**

Girl Without an Address, The/*Devushka bez adresa* (1957), **321**

Girl with Three Camels, A/*Dívka s třemi velbloudy* (1967), **61**

Glance at the Pupil of the Sun, A/*Pogled u zjenicu sunca* (1966), **364**, 404

Glass Mountain, The/*Szklana góra* (P. Komorowski 1961), 187

Glass of Beer, A/*Egy pikoló világos* (1955), **145, 151**

Gleiwitz Case, The/*Der Fall Gleiwitz* (1961), **105**, 106, 108, 115, 118

Globke Today (1963), **102**

Gloomy Morning, A/*Khmuroe utro* (G. Roshal 1959), 287

Gniezno Portal, The (1957), **182**

Goalkeeper Lives in Our Street, The/*Brankář bydlí v naši ulici* (Č. Duba 1957), 73

Gold/*Zloto* (1961), **175**, 190

Golden Antelope, The ((1954), **264**

Golden Fern, The/*Zlaté kapradí* (1963), **86**

Golden Fish, The (1951), **81**

Golden Kite, The/*Aranysárkány* (1966), **148**

Golden Rennet, The/*Zlatá reneta* (1965), **84**

Golden Section, The (1962), **159**

Golden Stepmother, The (1966), **268**

Golden Tooth, The/*Zlatniat zab* (1962), 1, **18**, 20

Golden Train/*Zolotoi eshelon* (I. Gurin 1961), 337

Golden Treasure, The (1964), **8**

Goldilocks (1956), **82**

Golgotha/*Golgota* (1966), **231**

Goliath/*Karambol* (1964), 143, **145**

Goodbye, Boys/*Do svidaniya, malchiki* (1965), **293**

Goodbye Doves!/*Proshchaite, golubi!* (1961), **331**

Goodbye to the Past—see Parting

Good Day Mr. H. (1965), **99**

Good-hearted Ant, The (1965), **373, 382**

Good Morning Poland (1969), **173**

Good Soldier Schweik, The (1954), **81**

Good Soldier Schweik, The, Pts I and II/*Dobrý voják Švejk* (1957), **79**

Gorky Trilogy, The/*Trilogiya o Gorkom* (1938-40), **277**

Goto, l'Ile d'Amour, **167**

Go to Nowhere (1966), **290**

Goût de la Violence, Le (R. Hossein 1961), 361

Granada, Granada, My Granada (1967), **295**

Grandmother, Iliko, Illarion and Me/*Ya, babushka, Iliko i Illarion* (1963), **260**

Grandmother's Encyclopaedia (1965), **167**

Grandpa Planted a Beet (1945), **81**

Grasshopper, The/*Poprygunya* (1955), 267, 309, **326**

Great Century, The (1958), **395**

Greatest Hope of the People, The (1959), **306**

Great Fear (1959), **402**

Great Ore, The/*Bolshaya ruda* (V. Ordinsky 1964), 327, 347

Great Patriotic War, The (1965), **295**

Great Troubles (1961), **268**

Great Warrior Skanderbeg/*Velikii voin Albanii Skanderbeg* (1953), **355** and Albania

Green Love (1967), **397**

Green Years/*Zöldár* (1965), **130**

Grimace/*Gyermekbetegségek* (1965), **138**, 152

Gros et le Maigre, Le (1960), 187, **207**

Grotesque Chicken, The (1963), **43**

Grown-up Children/*Vzroslyi deti* (V. Azarov 1961), 274, 327

Guest from the Island of Freedom, A (1963), **295**

Guest in the Night/*Nočnoi gost* (V. Shredel 1957), 340

Guest in the Night, A/*Noční host* (1961), **84**

Gun From Nevesinje/*Nevesinjska puska* (1963), **384**

Gypsies (1962), 130, **152**

Gypsies (1963), **213**

Habitual Spring, A, **243**

Hail Days/*Fagyosszentek* (1962), 126, **150**, 161

Hallo, It's Me/*Zdravstvyi, eto ya* (F. Dovlatyan 1965), **269**

Hallo, Here's Mexico (1967), **127**

Hallo, Nette (1963), **305**

Hallo Moscow!/*Zdravstvai Moskva* (1945), **355**

Hallo, Vera/*Szevasz Vera* (1967), 124, **134**

Hallowe'en/*Zaduszki* (1961), **188**, 216

Hamlet/*Gamlet* (1964), 284, **301**, 310, 334, 340, 350

Hand, The (1965), **81**

Hands Up!/*Rece do góry* (1967), 187, 198, **212**

Hangman, The/*Majster kat* (1965), **41**, 67

Hangmen also Die (F. Lang 1942), 96

Happy End/*Happy End* (1966), **64**

Happy Ending (1958), **383**

Happy Man, The (1961), **31**

Harbour, The (1963), **30**

Hard Summer, A/*Vizivárosi nyár* (1965), **128**

Harlequin and His Lover/*Harlekin és szerelmese* (1966), **129**

Harmony (1965), **113**

Hašek's Exemplary Cinematograph/*Vzorny kinematograf Jaroslava Haška* (1955), **64**, 73, 87

Hats Down! (1960), **31**

Hawks, The/*Neamul Soimăreştilor* (1965), 228, **231**, 245

Healing Water, The/*Büdosviz* (1966), **125**

Heart, The (1964), **185**

Heat/*Znoi* (1963), 313, **333**

Heat, The/*Upal* (1964), 190, **191**, 220

Heaven and Hell/*Pieklo i Niebo* (1965), **208**, 209

Heaven with No Love/*Pukotina raja* (1961), **390**

He Did Not Want to Kill/*On ubivat ne khotel* (1967), **332**

H-8/*H-8* (N. Tanhofer 1958), 363

Heights, The/*Vysota* (1957), 309, **358**

He Lives On (1949), **11**

Helsinki (1962), **77**

He Must Be Accused (1963), **305**

Here and There (1964), **102**

Here Walks Tragedy (1957), **83**

Heroes of Shipka/Geroite na Shipka (S. Vassilev 1955), 13, 20

Hero of Our Time, A—see Pechurin's Notes

Heron—a Reptile Bird?, The (1968), **223**

Herrenpartie (1964), **117**

He, She or It/La Poupée (J. Baratier 1962), 172

He Was My Friend/A fost prietenul meu (1961), **221**, 228, 236, 252

Hic Sunt Leones/Zde jsou lvi (1958), **61**

Hidden Little Houses, **241**

Higher Principle, A/Vyšší princip (1960), 44, **60**

High Wall, The/Vysoká zeď (1964), **57**

Hill of Death—see Kozara

His Majesty's Dates/Mit csinált felséged 3-5-ig? (1964), **144**

His Name Was Fedor (1963), **305**

Historia Naturae (1968), **80**

Histria, Heraclea and Swans (1968), **223**

Hit and Run/Gázolás (1955), **132**

Hobby (1967), **215**

Hold on to Your Hats (1967), **72**

Holiday of Hope (1962), **9**

Holiday on Sylt (1957), 93, 115, **119**, **120**

Holidays (1963), **104**

Home-Castles (1967), **8**

Homecoming—see The Return

Home Trip/Porozhnii reis (1963), 315, **349**

Homo Sapiens (1960), **250**

Honesty and Glory/Becsület és dicsőség (1951), **132**

Honour and Glory/Čest a sláva (1968), **42**

Hope/Naděje (1963), **57**

Hopeless Ones, The—see Round-up, The

Hop-pickers, The/Starci na chmelu 1964), 73, **75**

Hora-Dance, The **223**

Horizon/Gorizont (1961), 275, **288**

Horizon, The (1966), **185**

Horsemen of the Revolution/Vsadniki revolutsii (1968), **351**

Hospital (1962), **199**

Hotel for Strangers/Hotel pro cizince (1966), 65, 66, 77

Hot Line, The/Goraça linia (1965), **180**

Hours of Hope/Godziny nadziei (1956), **210**

Hour until the Meeting, An (1965), **268**

House, The (1958), **167**, **193**

House and Master/Dom i khozyain (1967), **307**

House at the Terminus/Tam na konečné (1957), **58**, **59**

Houseful of Happiness, A/Két emelet boldogság (1960), **134**, 162

House I Live In, The/Dom, v kotorom ya zhivu (1957), **302**, 313, **331**, 346

House of Cards/Kártyavár (G. Hintsch 1968), 143, 147, 162

House on the Wastelands/Dom na pustkowiu (1949), **210**

House on Wheels, A (1966), **4**

House under the Rocks, The/Ház a sziklák alatt (1958), 136, **144**

How Broad Is Our Country (1958), **295**

How Do You Do, Children?/Zdravstvyite deti (1962), **277**

How Grandpa Changed Till Nothing Was Left (1953), **81**

How I Unleashed the Second World War—How I Finished the Second World War/Jak rozpetalem II wojne światowa—jak zakończylem II wojne światowa (1969), **171**

How Kico Was Born (1951), **402**

How One Peasant Kept Two Generals (1965), **290**

How Tales Came to Life (1956), **2**

How to Be Loved/*Jak być kochana* (1962), 172, **175**, 190, 214

Human Folly (1968), **255**

Hundred Days with the Ship "Bulgaria", A (1955), **30**

Hungary Today (1965), **127**

Husband for Susy/*Rangon alul* (1960), **125**

Hussar's Ballad/*Gusarskaya ballada* (1962), **321**

I Am Cuba/*Ya—Kuba* (1962), **292**, 348

I Am on Fire/*Ja gore* (1967), **199**

I Am Twenty/*Mne dvadtsat let* (1961-63), **298**, 317, 335

Icarus XB-I/*Ikarie XB-I* (J. Polák 1963), 55

Ideal (1965), **72**

Identification Marks—None/*Rysopis* (1964), **212**

Idiot, The/*Idiot* (1958), **319**

I Don't Want to Get Married/*Nu vreau să mă însor* (1960), 236, **237**, 246

I Even Met Some Happy Gypsies/*Skupljači perja* (1967), 368, **388**, 389, 404

If/*If* (L. Anderson 1968), 70

If a Thousand Clarinets/*Kdyby tisíc klarinetů* (J. Roháč and V. Svitáček 1964), 44, 66

If There Were No Music (1963), 40, **49**, 70

If This Be Love/*A esli eto lyubov?* (1961), 313, **320**

Igor Bulichov/*Egor Bulychov* (1953), **341**

I Have Two Mummies and Two Daddies/*Imam dvije mame i dva tate* (K. Golik 1968), 361

I, Justice/*Já, spravedlnost* (1967), **46**

Ilya Muromrtz/*Ilya Muromets* (A. Ptushko 1956), 263

Ilyitch Square—see I Am Twenty

I'm Angry for Your Sake (1967), **156**

I'm Five (1967), **32**

I'm from Childhood/*Ya rodom iz detstva* (Turov 1965), 335

Immortality (1959), **137**

Immortals, The—see Dacians, The

Immortal Youth/*Besmrtna mladost* (V. Nanović 1948), 380

I'm NOT Going to Eat (1961), 51

In a Village/*De sfășurarea* (1954), **226**, 228, 229

Incredible Story, An/*Neveroyatna istoria* (1964), 28, **36**

Indian Summer/*Rozmarné léto* (1968), 45, **66**

Innocence Unprotected/*Nevinost bez zaštite* (1968), **379**

Innocent Sorcerers, The/*Niewinni czarodzieje* (1959), 172, 187, 198, 207, 212, **217**

In Our Caves, 31

In Pursuit of Adam/*W pogoni za Adamem* (J. Zarzycki 1969), 214

Inquisitive Letter, The (1961), **82**

In Silence (1965), **185**

Inspector, The/*Inspektor* (M. Djukanović 1965), 386, 393, 394, 404

Inspector and the Night, The/*Inspectorat i noshta* (1963), 14, 15, 22, **35**

Inspector Goes Home, The (1959), **383**

Interior, **241**

International Ballet Competition—Varna (1964), **33**

International Festival in Edinburgh, The (1956), **257**

Interrupted Flight, The/*Przerwany lot* (1964), **170**

In the Club (1963), **183**

In the Country of the Cannibals (1958), **6**

In the Current of Life (Albanian)

In the Flames of the Revolution (Albanian 1967)

In the Foothills of the Pirin Mountain (1958), **30**

In the Heart of Kosmet (1954), **399**

In the Icy Ocean (1952), **359**

In the Name of Life/*Vo imya zhizni* (1947), 270, **288**, **358**

In the Pacific (1957), **359**

In the Pergamon Museum (1962), **91**

In the Seven Winds/*Na semi vetrakh* (1962), **323**, 345

In the Shadow of the Ages, **31**

In the Steps of Our Ancestors (1960-61), **359**

In the Storm/*U oluji* (1952), **383**

In the Town of "S"/*V gorode "S"* (1966), **288**, 315

In the Traces of the Ball (1966), **127**

Intimate Lighting/*Intimní osvětlení* (1965), 70, **71**

Into the Storm/*Idu na grozu* (S. Mikailyan 1965), 315

Intractable Spain (J. and K. Stern 1962), 96

Intransigents, The/*Neprimirimite* (1964), 27, **37**

Intrigue and Love/*Kabale und Liebe* (1959), **101**

Introductory Speech Is By . . . , The (1964), **72**

Intruder, The (1966), **395**

Invention for Destruction, An (1957), **88**

Invincible Love/*Koningskinder* (1962), **90**, 110

Ion Marin's Letter to Scinteia (1949), **235**

I Resign from the World (1966), **395**

Iron Flood, The/*Zheleznyi potok* (E. Dzigan 1967), 291

Iron Flower, The/*Vasvirág* (1957), **134**, 155, 162

I Sing of Peace (1961), **98**

Island of Flame, The (1961), **295**

Island of Roses (1957), **98**

Island of the Mongooses, The (1961), **140**

I Started to Grow Later (1963), **403**

István Szonyi (1959), **140**

I Survived Certain Death/*Přežil jsem svou smrt* (1960), **53**, 63

It Began in Spain (1950), **201**

It Happened in Berlin/*Tatort Berlin* (1957), **107**, 111

It Happened in Penkova/*Delo bylo v Penkove* (1957), **323**, 345

It Happened in the Street/*Tova se sluchi na ulitsata* (1956), 13, 20, **37**

It Happened Yesterday/*Historia współczesna* (1960), **180**, 214

It Is a Long Way Home/*Hosszú az út hazáig* (1960), **145**, 158

It Must Not Be Forgotten/*Ob etom zabyvat nelzya* (L. Lukov 1954), 267

It Rains in My Village/*I dodje propast sveta* (1969), **388**

It's Not Too Late/*Poka .ne. pozdno* (1958), **357**

It's So Simple (1968), **156**

It Started like This/*Eto nachinados tak . . . .* (1956), 269, **302**, **331**

It Would Have Been Terrible (1958), **399**

Ivan's Childhood/*Ivanovo detstvo* (1962), **344**, 354

Ivan Sussasin/*Ivan Sussasin* (1951), **18**

Ivan the Terrible/*Ivan Groznyi* (S. Eisenstein 1945-47), 270, 310

I Walk around Moscow/*Ya shagayu po Moskve* (1963), 269, **273**, 318, 335, 338, 354

I Was Kapo (1963), **182**

I Was Nineteen/*Ich war neunzehn* (1967), 89, 106, **122**

Jack of Spades/*Walet pikowy* (1960), **171**, 190

Jan Hus/*Jan Hus* (1955), **84**

Jánošík/Jánošík (1936), 41, **50**

Janosik (1954), **176**

Jánošík/Jánošík (1962-3), **41**

Jan Žižka/Jan Žižka (1956), **84**

Jazz in Poland (1964), **199**

Jealousy (1963), **6**

Je t'aime, Je t'aime (A. Resnais 1968), 204

Jester's Tale, A/Bláznova kronika (1964), 55, **88**

Jeux des Anges, Les (1964), **167**

Johnny the Musician (1960), **193**

Joke, A (1967), **7**

Joke, The/Žert (1969), **54**

Josef Kilián/Postava k podpírání (1963), 48, **55, 76**

Joseph Haydn (1959), **159**

Journalist, The/Zhurnalist (1967), **282,** 318, 337

Journey in the Cosmos (1966), **8**

Journey into April/Puteshestvie aprely (1963), **275**

Journey to Another City/Puteshestvie v drugoi gorod (S. Mikailyan 1968), 283

Journey to Strange Lands, A (1960), **257**

Journey to Sundevit/Rie Reise nach Sundevit (1966), **92**

Journey to the Primeval Times, A (1955), **88**

Journey with a Cine Camera, A (1952), **330**

Jowita/Jowita (J. Morgenstern 1967), 172, 188, 202

J. S. Bach—Fantasy in G Minor (1963), **80**

Jubilee (1962), **183**

Judgement of the People (1947), **295**

Judge of Zalamea, The/Der Richter von Zalamea (1955), **101,** 108

Jumping Legs, Swinging Wings (1963), **140**

Jungle Track (1959), **359**

Just, The (1969), **185**

Justice (1962), **360**

Just One Life/Vsego odna zhizn (S. Mikailyan 1967-8), 278, 279

Kaiser's Lackey, The/Der Untertan (1951), **117**

Kalin the Eagle/Kalin orelat (B. Borozanov 1950), **12**

Kaloyan/Kaloyan, **5**

Kanal/Kanal (1956), 181, 191, 196, 214, **217,** 219

Kapo/Kapo (G. Pontecorvo 1960), 394

Karl Marx Street (1965), **91**

Karol (1966), **215**

Katerina Ismailova/Katerina Izmaylova (M. Shapiro 1966), 334

Kati and the Wild Cat (1955), **140**

Katya/Katka (1950), **58**

Katyusha (1964), **305**

Kaya, I'll Kill You/Kaja, ubit ću te (1967), **383**

Key, The (1968), **264**

Khovanschina/Khovanshchina (V. Stroyeva 1959), 334

Kid, The/Puştiul (1962), **222**

Kidnapped/Unos (1952), **58,** 59

Kidnapping—Caucasian Style/Kakazskaya plennitza (1967), 274, **281**

King and the General, The/Tsar i general (1966), 10, 22, **24,** 27

Kingdom of Women, The/Babya Tzarstvo (1967), **324**

Kingdom on the Waters, A, **135**

King Lávra (1950), **88**

King Lear/Karol Lir (1969), 284, **301**

King Matt I/Król Maciuś I (1957), **180**

King of Kings/Král Králů (1963), **50**

King of the Beasts (1960), **113**

Kiss, The/Sărutul (1965), **224,** 247

Klaxon/Klakson (1965), 367, 368, **392**

Klizi-puzi (1968), **369**

Knell for the Barefooted/Zvony pre bosých (1965), **40, 67**

Knife, The/Nož (1966), 381, **384**, 393, 404

Knife in the Water/Nóż w wodzie (1961), 187, 189, 196, **207**, 212

Knights of the Teutonic Order/Krzyzacy (1960), **173**, 179, 214, 218

Knight without Armour/Ritsar bez bronya (1966), 13, 21, **25**

Knock-Out/Knock-Out (1967), **242**

Knot in the Handkerchief (1962), **82**

Komsomol Celebration (1958), **306**

Koprivshtitsa, **31**

Kozara/Kozara (1962), **364**, 367, 380, 393, 394, 404

Krakatit/Krakatit (1948), **84**

Kuban Cossacks/Kubanskie Kazaki (1949), 263, **319**

Kuhle Wampe/Kuhle Wampe (1932), **94**, 96

Labyrinth (1962), **193**

Labyrinth of the Heart, The/Labyrint srdce (1961), 44, **60**

Lad and the Fire, The (1962), **257**

Ladies/Damy (1954), **302**

Lady and the Gypsy, The/Fekete szem éjszakája (1958), **139**

Lady-Killer in Trouble/Ozvegy menyasszonyok (1964), **132**

Lady of the Lines, The/Dáma na kolejích (1965), **75**

Lady with a Little Dog/Dama s sobachkoi (1960), 265, **288**, 310, 329

Lake of Fairies, The (1963), **155**

Lame Devil, The/Kulhavy dábel (J. Herz 1967), 68

L'Amour à Vingt Ans (1962), 172, 196, **217**

Lamp, The (1959), **207**

Land/Zemya (1957), **38**

Land, The (1962), **77**

Land and People/Zemlya i lyudi (1955), **323**

Land of Angels, The/Angyaluk földje (1962), **150**, 155, 161

Land of Five Continents, The (1960), **370**

Land of Our Fathers/Zemlya ottsov (1967), **261**

Land of Ours, A/Nasha zemya (1953), 10, 13, **18**, 34

Land of the Blue Mountains, The/Sinegoriya (E. Garin 1945), 348

Lanfieri Colony/Kolonie Lanfieri (1969), **76**

Lanneken Wedding, The/Hochzeit von Länneken, Die (1963), **92**

Larks on a Thread (1969), **66**

Last Battle, The/Kwiecień (1961), 165, **194**

Last But One, The/Az utolsó előtti ember (1963), **144**

Last Day, The/Poslednji dan (1952), **390**

Last Day, First Day/Den poslednii, den pervyi (S. Dolidze 1960), 356

Last Day of Summer, The/Ostatni dzień lata (1958), **188**

Last Goal, The/Két félidő a pokolban (1961), 123, **128**

Last Gypsy Tent, The (1958), **370**

Last Month of Autumn, The/Poslednii mesyats oseni (1965), **275**

Last Night, The/Poslednyaya noch (1936), 280, **320**

Last Night, The/Die letzte Nacht (1961), **107**

Last Night of Childhood, The/Ultima noapte a copilăriei (1966), **257**

Last of the Nabobs, The/Egy magyar nábob—Kárpáthy Zoltán (1966), 126, 143, 151, **163**

Last Rose from Casanova, The/*Posledni růže od Casanovy* (1966), **61**

Last Shot, The/*Posledni výstřel* (1950), **86**

Last Shot, The/*Ostatni strzal* (1958), **210**, 211

Last Stage, The/*Ostatni etap* (1948), **180**

Last Track/*Poslednji kolosek* (1956), 380, **384**

Last Trick of Mr. Schwarzwald and Mr. Edgar, The (1964), **80**

Late Afternoon/*Późne popoludnie* (1964), **211**

Late Season/*Utószezon* (1967), **128**, 136, 147, 161

Laughing Man, The (1966), **102, 116**

Law and the Fist, The/*Prawo i pięść* (1964), **177,** 178, 196

Lawrence's Orchard (1952), **176**

Lazienki Park in Warsaw, The (1959), **182**

Leap, The/*Skok* (1968), **191,** 202

Leave it to Me/*Nechte to na mně* (1955), **49, 50**

Left Hander, The (1964), **290**

Legend, The/*Legenda* (1968), **221,** 228, 244, 256

Legend of a Cruel Giant (1968), **290**

Legend of Love, A/*Legenda o lásce* (1957), 13, **61**

Legend of the Ice Heart/*Legenda o ledyanom serdtse* (1957), **332**

Legends about Anika/*Anikina vremena* (1954), **390**

Legion of the Streets/*Legion ulicy* **173**

Lemonade Joe/*Limonádový Joe* (1964), 43, **64**

Lenin in 1918/*Lenin v 1918 godu* (1939), **322**

Lenin in October/*Lenin v Oktyabre* (1937), **322**

Lenin in Poland/*Lenin v Polshe* (1964), 280, 336, **355**

Lenka and Prim—see Stress of Youth

Lesson, A (1960), **82**

Lesson in History, A/*Urokat na istoriata* (1957), **23**

Lesson of Life/*Urok zhizni* (1955), 280, **320,** 348

Lesson to the Infinite, A, **243**

Let's Live until Monday/*Dozhivem do ponedelnika* (1968), **323,** 345

Letter, The (1962), **215**

Letter From a Kuci Doctor (Albanian)

Letter M (1964), **43**

Letter that Wasn't Sent, The/*Neotpravlennoe pismo* (1960), **292,** 325, 340, 347, 348

Liana/*Lyana* (B. Barnet 1955), 352

Liberated China (1950), **282**

Liberated Land/*Felszabadult föld* (1950), **125,** 158

Liberators, The (1967), **403**

Life after Ninety Minutes (1965), **69, 76,**

Life Begins/*Das Leben beginnt* (1959), **92**

Life in Germany (1965), 119, **120**

Life Is Beautiful, **200**

Life Is Rising from the Ruins (1945), **58**

Life of Matthew, The/*Żywot Mateusza* (1967), 189, **195**

Life Once More/*Życie raz jeszcze* (J. Morgenstern 1964), 169, 198, 219

Life Was the Stake/*Hra o život* (1956), **86**

Light (1962), **141**

Light and Stone (1960), **234**

Lightning Road (1962), **6**

Light of a Distant Star, The/*Svev dalekoi zvesdy* (1965), 265, **319**

Lights and People (1960), **17**

Lights Go On in the City, The/*Gorod zazhigaet ogni* (1958), **349**

Like a Drop in the Sea (1962), **140**

Like a House on Fire—see Firemen's Ball, The

Liliomfi/*Liliomfi* (1954), **144**

Lime (1965), **17**

Lion and the Ditty, The (1962), **72**

Lissy/*Lissy* (1957), 89, **122**

Little and Big (1966), **369**

Little and the Big Happiness, The/*Das kleine und das grosse Glück* (1953), 89, **101**, 121

Little Ann (1958), **6**

Little Bobes/*Malý Bobeš* (J. Valášek 1961), 73

Little Boy and the Charcoal, The, **241**

Little Chronicle, A (1962), **383**

Little Girl, The/*Malkata* (1959), **16**

Little Grey Thing (1962), **6**

Little Hump-Backed Horse, The (1948), **290**

Little Liar/*Fetița mincinoasă* (1953), **250**

Little Prince, The/*Der kleine Prinz* (1966), 110, **122**

Little Siren (1968), **373, 382**

Little Time Machine, The (1967), **268**

Little Train, The (1959), **82**

Little Umbrella, The (1958), **72**

Little Western, The (1960), **174**

Living and the Dead, The/*Zhivye i mertvye* (1964), 315, **342**, 346

Living Corpse, The/*Zhivoi trup* (1953), **349**

Living Corpse, The/*Zhivoi trup* (1969), 265, 340, **349**

Living Heroes/*Zhivye geroi* (1960), 284, **357**

Living Nightmare/*Volča noć* (1955), **398**

Living Stones (1957), **200**

Living Tradition (1960), **103**

Living Traps (1961), **140**

Living Tree (1963), **137**

Local Romance, A/*Žižkovská romance* (1958), 44, **46, 48**

Lodger, The/*Sublokator* (1966), **199**

Lonely Man, The (1958), **383**

Long-Ears (1961), **4**

Longest Night, The/*Nai dalgata nosht* (1967), 3, 10, 14, 22, **24**

Long Happy Life, A/*Dolgaya schastlivaya zhizn* (1966), **335**

Long Live the Republic!/*Ať žije republika!* (1965), **57**

Long Way, The/*Dolgii put* (1956), **281**

Look at This City (1962), **98**

Look for Vanda Kos/*Potraži Vandu Kos* (1957), **384**

Looking at Wild Animals (1950), **276**

Looking Back/*Ohlédnuti* (1969), **65**

Look Out! (1959), **43**

Lord at Alexanderplatz, A/*Ein Lord am Alexanderplatz* (1967), **100**

Lorenz v Lorenz/*Ehesache Lorenz* (1959), **107**, 110

Lost Doll, The (1959), **82**

Lost Generation/*Falak* (1967), 131, 136, **142**, 143

Lost Letter, A/*O scrisoare pierdută* (1956), **235, 258**

Lost Paradise, The/*Elveszett paradicsom* (1962), **144**, 147, 155, 162

Lost Photograph, The/*Poteryannaya fotografiya* (1959), **302**

Lost Summer, The/*Propalo leto* (1963), **269**

Lost Trail, The/*Ztracená stopa* (1956), **57**, 63

Lotna/*Lotna* (1959), 165, 196, 207, **217**

Lot's Wife/*Lots Weib* (1965), **100**, 111

Lottery Swede, The/*Der Lotterieschwede* (1958), **107**, 111

Love and Tigers/*Sevodnya -novyi attraktsion* (N. Kosheverova and A. Dudko 1964), 278, 279

Love at Freezing Point/*Dragoste la 0°* (1964), **253**

Love Dossier—see Switchboard Operator, The

Love Letters (1966), **102**

Love's Confusion/*Verwirrung der Liebe* (1959), **94**

Loves of a Blonde—see Blonde in Love, A

Love Travels by Coach/*Hintónjáró szerelem* (1954), **148**

Lucky Tony/*Szczęściarz Antoni* (1961), **176**

Lucy/*Lucie* (1963), **79**

Lullaby (1948), **82**

Lupeni '29/*Lupeni '29* (1961), 228, **231**

Lurdja Magdani/*Lurdzha Magdany* (1956), **260**, **271**

Machine, The (1961), **215**

Magic Chair, The/*Bűvös Szék* (1952), **132**

Magic Hat, The/*Divotvorný klobouk* (1952), **74**

Magic Hoe, The (1960), **31**

Magician (1962), **200**

Magic Lantern II, The (1960), **58**, **59**

Magic Sounds, The (1957), **402**

Magnificent Islands (1965), **359**

Maibritt/*Maibritt* (1964), **372**

Malicious Adolescent, The/*Adolescentul răutăcios* (1968), 246, **259**

Mammals, The/*Ssaki* (1962), 186, 187, **207**

Man Following the Sun/*Chelovek idet za solntsem* (1962), 275, **293**, 315

Man for Man, A (1966), **33**

Man from Nowhere/*Chelovek niotkuda* (1961), **321**

Man from Planet Earth/*Chelovek s planeta Zemlya* (B. Buneyev 1959), 317, 352

Man from the First Century, The/*Muž z prvního století* (1961), **64**

Man from the Photography Department, The/*Čovek sa fotografije* (1963), 380, **390**, 401

Man from the Quiet Streets/*Čovjek iz mirne ulice* (1957), **383**

Man I Love, The/*Chelovek, kotorogo ya lyublyu* (1966), **294**

Man in a Frame, A (1966), **296**

Man Is Not a Bird, A/*Čovjek nije tica* (1965), 367, **379**, 387, 401

Man on the Track/*Czlowiek na torze* (1957), **201**, 214

Man on the Trail (1950), **276**

Manufactures (1967), **182**

Man under Water (1961), **43**

Manuscript Found in Saragossa, A—see Saragossa Manuscript, The

Man Who Did Not Return, The/*Muž, ktorý sa nevrátil* (1959), **78**

Man Who Had His Hair Cut Short, The/*De Man die Zijn Haar Kort Liet Knippen* (A. Delvaux 1966), 216

Man with a Dog, A/*Muž se psem* (1968), 62

Man with a Gun/*Chelovek s ruzhem* 336, **355**

Man without a Passport/*Chelovek bez pasporta* (A. Bobrousky 1966), 287

Man with the Golden Touch, The/*Az aranyember* (1962), **132**

Marathon/*Maraton* (I. Novak 1967), 44

Marble, The (1963), **82**

March to the Drina/*Marš na Drinu* (1964), **384**, 400

Margaret (1965), **127**

Maria and Napoleon/*Marysia i Napoleon* (1966), **170**, 178, 216

Marienstadt Adventure, The/*Przygoda na Mariensztacie* (1954), **170**

Marked by Darkness (1959), **83**

Markéta Lazarová/*Markéta Lazarová* (1967), **85**

Market of Miracles/*Jarmark cudów* (1966), **177**

Marksmen (1967), **7**

Martin in the Clouds/*Martin u oblacima* (1960), **362**

Martyrs of Love/*Mučedníci lásky* (1966), 62, **69**, 70

Masquerade/*Maskarad* (1941), **282**

Masquerade (1965), **32**

Master Goe **225**

Master Nikifor (1956), **197**

Master of Gymnastics (1967), **127**

Match Box, The (1958), **31**

Matches (1962), **99**

Matrimonial Advice Column/*Poradnik matrymonialny* (1968), **176**, 192

Matrimony in the Shadows/*Ehe im Schatten* (1947), **109**

Matter of Conscience, A/*Kwestia sumienia* (1967), **205, 206**

Matter of Facts, A/*Pravo stanje stvari* (1964), 389, **396**

Mattie, The Goose-boy/*Lúdas Matyi* (K. Nádasdy 1949), 148

Maxim Trilogy, The/*Trilogiya o Maxime* (1932-38), **301**

Maya from Tshneti/*Maia iz Tskhneti* (1962), **271**

Maybowl/*Maibowle* (1959), 111, **114**

May Stars/*Maiskie zvezdy* (1959), **323**, 345

Mazepa/*Mazepa* (1968), **167**

Mazowsze Ensemble, The (1952), **200**

Meanders/*Meandre* (1966), 244, **254**

Me and My Grandfather/*Én és a nagyapám* (1954), **132**

Measure for Measure (1963), **113**

Medallion with Three Hearts/*Medaljon sa tri srca* (1962), **396**

Medical Care (1953), **200**

Medieval **241**

Meeting in a Dream (1957), **377**

Meeting in a Meadow (1957), **377**

Meeting in Warsaw (1955), **168**

Meeting of Friendship (1965), **30**

Meeting on the Elbe/*Vstrecha na Elbe* (G. Alexandrov 1949), 334

Meetings with Warsaw (1965), **197**

Meeting with France (1960), **355**

Meeting with the Pamir Mountains (1960), **306**

Meet Leonid Engibarov (1966), **305**

Member of the Government, A/*Chlen pravitelstva* (1940), **288, 358**

Memories at Chkalov (1967), **305**

Memories of an Actress, The (1957), **257**

Memories of a Rose, The, **243**

Memories of a Strange Night/*Utolsó vacsora* (1961), 151, **163**

Memory of Our Day, The (1963), **69**

Memory of the People (1964), **305**

Men, The/*Muškarci* (M. Djukanović 1962), 380

Men and Banners/*A kőszivű ember fiai* 1965), **163**

Men and Beasts/*Lyudi i zveri* (1962), **282**

Men of the Blue Cross, The (1955), **201**

Men on the Bridge/*Lyudi na mostu* (1960), **358**

Men with Wings/*Leute mit Flügeln* (1960), 89, 95, 118, 121, **122**

Merry Christmas Indeed!/*Ach, du fröhliche* (1962), **114**

Merry-Go-Round/*Körhinta* (1955), **128**, 158, 162

Message (1967), **133**

Messages (1961), **403**

Messenger of Dawn/*Posel úsvitu* (1951), **61**

Metamorphosis (Romanian), **225**

Metamorphosis (Romanian 1968), **238**

Metamorphosis (Yugoslavian), (1964), **373, 382**

Metropolis (F. Lang 1926), 94

Mexican, The/*Meksikanets* (V. Kaplunovsky), 325

Mexico Tomorrow/*Jutro Meksyk* (1965), 172, 179, **211**

Michaela's Morning, **225**

Michael the Brave/*Mihai Viteazul* (1969), **243**, 251

Michurin/*Michurin* (1948), **341**

Mickey Magnate/*Mágnás Miska* (1949), **139**

Midnight Adventure/*Priklyucheni v polunosht* (1964), **18**

Midnight Incident, A (1960), **72**

Midnight Mass/*Polnočná omša* (1962), **60**

Midsummer Day's Smile, A/*Un surîs în plină vară* (1963), **253**

Midsummer Night's dream, A (1959), 43, **81**

Mikoláš Aleš/*Mikoláš Aleš* (1951), **61**

Mikrokosmos (1966), **159**

Millions on an Island/*Milioni na otoku* (1954), 361, **362**

Mill of Luck and Plenty, The/*Moara cu noroc* (1956), 232, **235**, 251

Mimesis (1966), **255**

Minna von Barnhelm/*Minna von Barnhelm* (1962), **101**, 112

Minstrel's Song (1964), **43**

Miracles/*Pro chudesa chelovecheskie* (1967), **309**

Miracle-Worker, The/*Chudotvorets* (1960), **339**

Miraculous Virgin, The/*Panna zázračnica* (1966), **83**

Mirco the Invisible (1958), **31**

Mirror, The (1957), **360**

Mischievous Robber, The (1956), **276**

Mischievous Tutor, The/*Nezbedný bakalář* (1946), **84**

Misfit, The (1951), **82**

Miss Stone/*Miss Stone* (1959), **384**

Mister Dodek/*Pan Dodek* (1969), **168**

Misunderstanding (1958), **360**

Mitrea Cocor/*Mitrea Cocor* (1952), **235**

Modern Fable, A (1964), **382**

Moment of Peace, A/*Augenblick des Friedens* (1965), **188**

Moments in the Forest, **135**

Monday or Tuesday/*Ponedeljak ili utorak* (1966), **383**, 389

Money-maker, The/*Pénzcsináló* (1963), **125**

Mongolia/*Mongolia* (1961), **92**

Monsieur Tête (1958), **193**

Monsieur Verdoux (C. Chaplin 1947), 96

Monster and You, The (1964), **376**

Moon over the River/*Měsíc nad řekou* (1953), **61**

Moonshiners/*Samogonshchiki* (1961), **281**

Moon's Tale, A (1955), **176**

Moon Thieves/*O dwóch takich co ukradli księżyc* (1965), **166**

More Amazing than a Fairy-Tale (1963), **276**

Morning/*Jutro* (1967), **365**, 367, 391, 393, 400

Mornings of a Sensible Youth, The/*Diminețile unui băiat cuminte* (1966), **221**, 228, 244, 246, 256

Mosaic (1962), **160**

Moscow and Muscovites (1956), **285**

Most Live of All Living, The (1960), **306**

Mother/*Mat* (1956), 265, **277**

Mother and Son (1967), **69**

Mother Courage and Her Children/ *Mutter Courage und ihre Kinder* (M. Werkworth 1960), 93, 118

Mother Joan of the Angels/*Matka Joanna od Aniołów* (1961), **184**, 188, 218, 219

Mother's Devotion, A/*Vernost materi* (1966), **277**

Mother's Heart, A/*Serdtse materi* (1966), **277**

Motifs with Stones (1965), **80**

Mountain, The (1964), **213**

Mountains Are Stirring, The/*Lazy sa pohli* (1952), **41**

Mountains on Fire/*Ogniomistrz Kaleń* (1961), 179, **205**, **206**

Mountain Village School (Albanian)

Mouse and the Pencil, The (1958), **4**

Moussorgski/*Mussorgskii* (G. Roshal 1950), 270

Mozart and Salieri/*Motsart i Saleri* (V. Gorikker 1961), 340

Mr. Anatol Seeks a Million/*Pan Anatol szuka miliona*, **210**

Mr. Anatol's Hat/*Kapelusz pana Anatola* (1958), **210**

Mr. Anatol's Inspection/*Inspekcja pana Anatola* (1961), 186, **210**

Mr. Ikl's Jubilee/*Jubilej G. Ikla* (1955), **383**

Mrs. Déry/*Déryné* (L. Kalmár 1951), 161

Mrs. Dulská's Morals/*Morálka paní Dulské* (1958), **60**

Mr. Servadac's Ark (1968), **88**

Much Ado about Nothing/*Viel Lärm um Nichts* (1964), **101**, 108

Muddy Water—*Trübe Wasser* (L. Daquin 1960), 96

Murder—Czech Style/*Vražda po Česku* (1967), **86**

Murderer and the Girl, The/*Zbrodniarz i panna* (J. Nasfeter 1963), 172, 196

Murderer Leaves a Clue, The/*Morderca zostawia ślad* (1967), 172, **211**

Murderers Are among Us, The/*Die Mörder sind unter uns* (1946), **117**

Murder in Lvov (1962), **102**

Murder of Engineer Devil, The/*Vražda Ing. Čerta* (1968), 62

Murder of the Innocents, The (1957), **223**

Murder on the Rue Dante/*Ubiistvo na utilitze Dante* (1956), 280, **322**, 336, 340

Musical Pig, The (1965), **369**

Music and Computer (1965), **153**

Music from Mars/*Hudba z Marsu* (1954), **58**, **59**

Musicians (1960), **183**

Musicians (1963), **99**

My City/*Oraşul meu* (1967), **250**

My Dear Man/*Dorogoi moi chelovek* (1958), 265, **288**

My Flat (1963), **363**

My Friend Kolka/*Drug moi, Kolka* (1961), **308**, **324**

My Friend the Gypsy/*Mùj přitel Fabián* (1953), **86**

My Own Master/*Svoga tjela gospodar* (1957), **371**

Mystery of Blood, The/*Tajemství krve* (1953), 45, **50**

My Tail's My Ticket (1959), **402**

My Way Home/*Így jöttem* (1964), **137**, 153

My Younger Brother/*Moi mladshii brat* (1962), **358**

Nadejda/*Nadezhda* (1955), **282**

Naked among the Wolves/*Nackt unter Wölfen* (1962), **90**, 110

Năică and the Little Fish, **222**

Năică and the Squirrels, **222**

Năică and the Stork, **222**

Năică Leaves for Bucharest, **222**

Nail, The, 226

Naked Man, The/Goli čovik (O. Gluš-čević (1968), 381, 393

Naughty Ball, The (1956), 82

Naughty Bird, The, 135

Naughty Chicken, The (1962), 31

Near to Us/Pyadom s nami (A. Bergunkev (1957), 340

Negrita's Island (1957), 255

Neighbours, The/Sąsiedzi (1969), 211

Nessebur, 31

Nesterka/Nesterka (1955), 358

Nest of the Gentry, A/Dvorianskoye gniezdo (1969), 216, 299, 352

New Art (1950), 200

New Babylon/Novyi Babilon (1929), 301, 334

New Days Will Come/Shte doïdat novi dni (1945), 18

New Earth (1946), 391

New Gilgames/Új Gilgames (1963), 157

New Initiatives (1950), 11

New Joke with Scrap Iron, A, 225

New Victories, 384

New Warriors Shall Arise/Vstanou noví bojovníci (1950), 86

New Year Punchbowl/Silvesterpunsch (1960), 112, 114

New Year's Eve (German) (1963), 91

New Year's Eve (Polish)/Przygoda noworoczna (S. Wohl 1963), 212

N'Fuma (1960), 182

Night, The (1961), 200

Nightingale's Tail, The (1959), 32

Night of Remembrance, A/Celuloza (1953), 184

Night of the Bride, The/Noc nevěsty (1967), 44, 57

Night Train—see Baltic Express

Nikodem Dyzma/Nikodem dyzma (1957), 210

Nikola Tesla (1956), 390

Nikoletina Bursać/Nikoletina Bursać (1964), 362

Nine Chicks (1952), 82

Nine Days in One Year/Devyat dnei odnogo goda (1961), 265, 297, 304, 322, 340

Ninety in the Shade/31 stupňů ve stínu (1964), 86

Ninth Circle, The/Deveti krug (1960), 398

No/Nem (1965), 150, 162

Nobody Gets the Last Laugh/Nikdo se nebude smát (1965), 42, 55, 56, 66

Nobody Wanted To Die/Nikto ne khotel umirat (1965), 284, 314, 357

Nocturne (1958), 377

No. 8 Seiler Street/Seilergasse 8 (1960), 107

No Ford through the Fire/V ogne broda net (G. Panfilov 1968), 280

No Justice on Sunday/Niedziela sprawiedliwości (1965), 169, 203

No Love Please/Tilos a szerelem (1965), 149

No More Divorces/Rozwodów nie bedzie (1963), 172, 214

Noon/Podne (1968), 365, 391, 393, 400

No-One Calling/Nikt nie wola (1960), 190, 191, 219

Noose, The/Pętla (1957), 165, 175, 178, 179

No Place on Earth/Miejsce na ziemi (1960), 208, 209

No Problems in Summer/Nyáron egyszerű (1963), 123

Notes from Portul Rosu (1957), 227

Notes on October (1968), 397

Notes on the History of a Lake (1962), 141

Nuit et Brouillard (A. Resnais 1955), 96

Nun's Night, The—see Night of the Bride, The

Obsession (1961), **81**

Obsession (1968), **376**

Odysseus (F. Rosi 1968), 368

Official Position, The/Službeni položaj (1964), **370**

Oilworkers of the Caspian Sea (1953), **295**

O.K. (1964), **102, 116**

Okudzawa (1967), **182**

Old Czech Legends (1953), 43, **81**

Old Love/Eine alte Liebe (1959), **90,** 110

Old Man Motor-Car/Dědeček automobil (1956), 49, **74**

On a Quiet Evening/V tihata vecher (1960), 14, **25**

On a Sunday Morning (1955), **201**

On a Tightrope/Na laně (I. Novák 1963), 67

Once upon a Time (1957), **167, 193**

One Is Less than One/Einmal ist keinmal (1955), 89, 118, 121, **122**

One Lamp, Many Lamps (1966), **153**

One Morning/Intr-o dimineață (1960), **237**

One of Six Thousand (1966), **185**

One-room Tenants/Wspólny pokój (1959), **175,** 178, 216

One Summer Day Does Not Mean Love/Ein Sommertag macht keine Liebe (1960), **105**

One, Two, Three (1964), **215**

On His Own Ground/Na svoji zemlji (1948), **398**

On Holiday (1950), **37**

Only One Life (1965), **305, 339**

On Miraculous Happenings/O věcech nadpřirozených (1958), **60**

On My Responsibility/Pe răspunderea mea (1956), **226,** 258

On the Eve of the Thirteenth/Noshta sreshtu 13-i (1961), 1, 10, **18**

On the Little Island/Na malkia ostrov (1958), 1, 15, 20, 21, 22, **35**

On the Niemen River/Nad Niemnem, **180**

On the Pavement/Po trotoara (1967), 1, **18**

On the Road (1964), **215**

On the Roofs of Budapest/Pesti háztetők (1961), **142**

On the Ruins of the Estate/Na grafskikh razvalinakh (1956), **339**

On the Run/Zgodba ki je ni (1967), 367, **375**

On the Same Planet/No odnoi planete (I. Olshvanger 1966), 340

On the Threshold (1965), **183**

On the Threshold of Space Travel, **51**

On the Traces of a Lost Film (1968), **223**

On the Will of Man (1959), **11**

Opening Night (1957), **377**

Open the Door When the Bell Rings/Zvonyat, okroite dver (1966), 269, **308,** 329

Opera Cordis (1968), **402**

Operation Belgrade/Operacija Beograd (1968), **384**

Operation Laughter/Operatzia "Y" (1965), 274, **281**

Operation Teutonic Sword (1958), 93, 115, **119, 120**

Optimistic Tragedy, The/Optimisticheskaya tragediya (1964), 263, 309, **326,** 327, 345

Opus Jazz (1963), **199**

Ordinary Fascism (1965), 304, **322**

Ordinary People/Prostye lyudi (1945), **301,** 310

Ordinary Story, An/Prostaya istoriya (Y. Yegorov 1960), 307, 346

Organ, The/*Orgán* (1964), 83

Oriental Carpet, The/*Čintamani a podvodník* (1965), **60**

Orzel/*Orzel* (1958), **170**

Othello/*Otello* (1955), 267, 338, **355**

Othello—67 (1967), **296**

Other Happiness, The/*Drugoto shtastie* (1960), **18**

Other Side of the Medal, The/*Druga strana medalje* (1965), **370**, 381

Otto Yulevitch Schmidt (1963), **330**

Our Courtyard/*Nash dvor* (1956), **271**

Our Daily Bread/*Unser täglich Brot* (1949), **94**, 96

Our Father's House/*Otchii dom* (1959), **302**, 307

Our Foolish Family/*Naše bláznivá rodina* (1969), **57**

Our Heart/*Nashe serdtse* (1946), **342**

Our Holiday (1967), **33**

Our House/*Nash dom* (V. Pronin 1965), 286, 315

Our Kid/*Kolyok* (1959), **157**, 162

Our Lads (1959), **259**

Our Mutual Friend/*Nash obshchii drug* (1961), **319**

Our Oath (1952), **168**

Our People (1963), **238**

Our Red Riding Hood (1960), **43**

Our Soil/*Toka jonë* (Albanian)

Our Splendid Doctor/*Nash milyi doktor* (1958), **261**

Our Village/*In sat la noi* (1951), **235**

Outlaws, The/*Haiducii* (1965), **230**, 245

Out of Step/*U raskoraku* (1967), **399**, 400

Outwitted Fox, The (1957), **6**

Overcoat, The/*Shinel* (1926), **301**

Overcoat, The/*Shinel* (1960), **265**, 269

Ox and the Calf, The (1968), **255**

Ox of Kulm, The/*Der Ochse von Kulm* (1954), **101**

Paddling in a Kayak (1967), **127**

Pages of a Culture's History (1966), **30**

Pages of Bravery (1959), **254**

Pages of Immortality (1965), **300**

Pakhta-Oi/*Pakhta-Oi* (1952), **351**

Palmira (1963), **2**

Pals, **135**

Pals over Mounts and Dales, **135**

Panic on a Train/*Ludzie z pociagu* (1961), 165, **191**

Paper Cockerel, The (1965), **255**

Paper Planes/*Na papirnatih avionih* (1967), **375**

Paprika—see Iron Flower, The

Parade (1960), **32**

Parade, The (1962), **379**

Parade of Disgrace (1966), 9, **17**

Parson Cira and Parson Spira/*Pop Cira i Pop Spira* (S. Jovanovic 1965), 386

Parting/*Rozstanie* (1960), 172, **175**

Party and the Guests, The/*O slavnosti a hostech* (1966), 62, **69**, 77

Passenger/*Pasażerka* (1963), 165, 194, **201**, 212

Passengers Who Are Late/*Spóźnieni przechodnie* (J. Wojciech 1962), 172

Passion (1961), **146**

Passion of Andrew, The/*Strasti po Andreyu* (1966), **344**, 354

Pastor's End/*Farářův konec* (1969), **77**

Path to Tomorrow (1964), **305**

Patria o Muerte (1961), **177**

Paul Dessau (1967), **93**

Paul Street Boys, The/*A Pál utcai fiuk* (1968), **128**, 136

Pavel Korchagin/*Pavel Korchagin* (1957), **262**, 303, **311**

Pavlinka/*Pavlinka* (1952), **358**

Peace Conquers the World (1951), **168**

Peace to the Newcomer/*Mir vkhodyashchemu* (1961), **262**, 274, **311**

Peace Valley/Dolina Miru (1956), **398**

Peach Thief, The/Kradetsat na praskovi (1964), 14, 22, **24**, 29, 381

Pearls of the Deep/Perlicky na dne (1965), **47, 54, 63, 66, 69, 77**

Peau de Chagrin, La (1960), **378**

Pechorin's Notes/Zapiski Pechorina (1967), 291, **323**

Pedestrian, The, **242**

Penguin/Pingwin (1964), 172, **214**

People and Storms (1963), **17**

People from the Empty Area (1957), **183, 213**

People Meet/Mennesker mødes og sød musik opstaar i hjertet (H. Carlsen (1968), 187

People of Dimitrovgrad/Dimitrovgradtsi (1956), 3, **16, 19**

People of Kajzarje/Svet na Kajzarju (1952) **398**

People of the Blue Fire (1961), **285**

People of the Vihorlat Mountains (1956), **83**

People of the Vistula/Ludzie Wisly, **173**

People on the Road (1961), **183**

People on Wheels (1963), **397**

People on Wheels/Lidé z maringotek (1966), **50, 65**

Petar Dobrovic (1957), **388**

Peter and Pavla/Cerny Petr (1963), **49**, 71, 73

Petrica and Somebody Else, **241**

Pharaoh/Faraon (1965), **184**, 188, 219

Photography (1965), **113**

Photo Háber/Foto Háber (1963), 143, 151, 156, **163**

Piccolo (1960), **402**

Pictures from an Exhibition (1963), **32**

Pilgrimage to the Virgin Mary/Procesí k panence (1961), **53, 63**

Pillar of Salt/Sóbálvány (1956), **163**

Pills for Aurelia/Pigulki dla Aurelii (S. Lenartowicz 1958), 211

Pilots in Pyjamas (1968), **102, 116**

Pinching Apples/La mère (1953), **237, 239**

Pipeline "Friendship" (1964), **285**

Piper of Strakonice, The/Strakonický dudák (1955), **79**

Pipes/Dymky (1965), 44, **53**, 56

Pirogov/Pirogov (1947), **270**, 301, 310, 334

Place for the School, A (1963), **182**

Place in the Crowd/Místo v houfu (1964), **46**, 48, **61**, 65

Plastic in the Park (1964), **99**

Play, The (1962), **402**

Plot of Road, A (1968), **234**

Plus Belles Escroqueries du Monde, Les (1963), 196, **207**

Podhale on Fire/Podhale w ogniu (1956), **166**

Poem of Love/Poema lyubvi (1954), **261**

Poem of the Sea/Poema o more (1958), 263, **341**

Poem of Two Hearts/Poema dvukh serdets (1967), **351**

Polarised Light (1960), **164**

Polish Suite (1962), **197**

Poor Man's Joy/Siromashka radost (1958), **18**

Poor Man's Street/Bednata ulitsa (1963), **23**, 29

Poor Maria/Sirota Marija (D. Lazic 1968), 367, 393

Porto Franco/Porto Franco (1961), **226**, 228, 258

Portrait of a Horse (1967), **174**

Portrait of a Man with a Medallion/Portret mezczyzny z medalonem (1959), **194**

Portrait of a Small Town (1961), **213**

Portrait of Cowardice (1968), **234**

Postcards from Zakopane (1960), **177**

Poste Restante (1961), **259**

Potsdam Rebuilds (1946), **103**

Power of Destiny (1968), **43**

Prague Nights/*Pražské noci* (1968), **43, 77**

Prayer, The (1968), **260**

Precious Grain/*Dragotsennye zerna* (1948), **288, 358**

Prelude Eleven/*Preludio 11* (1963), **109**

Presentiment/*Předtucha* (1947), **84**

President's Visit, The/*Odwiedziny prezydenta* (1961), **166**, 216

Prince Bayaya (1950), **81**

Princess and the Pea, The (1959), **99**

Private Gale/*Soukromá vichřice* (1967), **42**

Professor Hannibal/*Hannibál tanár úr* (1956), **128**, 155

Professor Mamlock/*Professor Mamlock* (1961), 89, 95, 118, **122**

Prometheus (1959), **6**

Prometheus from the Island of Viševica/*Prometej sa otoka Viševice* (1965), **383**, 389, 401

Prophet of the Field, The/*Mezei próféta* (1947), **125**

Prosecutor, The/*Prokurorat* (1968), **26**

Protégé, The/*Štićenik* (1966), 381, 393, **396**

Protest/*Protest* (1967), 368, **370**

Proud Bulb, The (1964), **4**

Przhevalsky/*Przhevalskii* (1951), **355**

P.S. to The Laughing Man (1966), **102, 116**

Puppies, The/*Štěnata* (I. Novák 1957), 49

Pyramid, The (1961), **99**

Queue, The (1963), **7**

Quiet Home, A/*Csendes otthon* (1957), **125**

Radiography, **31**

Radopolje/*Radopolje* (S. Janković 1965), 367, 380, 381, 404

Rail, The (1959), **177**

Railway Junction (1961), **183**

Railwayman's Word, A (1953), **201**

Railwaymen (1963), **77**

Rain (1965), **52**

Rainbow/*Raduga* (1941), **277**

Raindrops, Waters, Warriors/*Kapi, vode, ratnici* (1962), **385, 387, 392,** 401

Rain in July/*Yulskii dozhd* (1967), 283, **298**, 304

Rainis/*Rainis* (1949), **320**

Rains of My Country, The (1963), **399**

Rainy July, A/*Deszczowy lipiec* (1958), **170**, 190

Rainy Sunday, A/*Esős Vasárnap* (1962), **139**

Rakhmanov's Sisters/*Sestry Rakhmanovy* (1954), **351**

Rákóczi's Lieutenant/*Rákóczi hadnagya* (1953), **125**

Rape of the Maidens, The/*Răpirea fecioarelor* (1968), **230**, 247

Rascal Snail, The (1951), **176**

Rats Wake Up, The/*Budjenje pacova* (1967), **385, 386**

Real End of the Great War, The/*Prawdziwy koniec wielkiej wojny* (1957), **184**, 196, 218, 219

Real Life in the Forest (1950), **359**

Reason and Emotion (1962), **43**

Reckoning, The/*Obračun* (1963), **384**

Recollections from Childhood/*Amintiri din copilărie* (1964), **222**

Reconstitution, The/*Reconstituirea* (1968), **248**

Recovery/*Genesung* (1955), 89, 95, 121, **122**

Red and Black (1963), **174**

Red and the White, The/Csillagosok, katonák (1967), **137**, 153

Redemption (B. Grezhov 1947), 12

Red Ink/Vörös tinta (1959), **132**

Red-Letter Days/Ünnepnapok (1967), **138**, 152

Red Sails/Alye parusa (A. Ptushko 1961), 303, 350

Red Tent, The/Krasnaya palatka (1969), **292**, 314, 315

Red Whitsun/Olověný chléb (J. Sequens 1954), 44

Reed (1966), **238**

Reflections (1965), **77**

Relatives/Rokonok (1954), **145**, 161

Relay, The/Staféta (1969), **142**

Reliable Man, The (1968), **91**

Rendezvous/Svidanie (1963), **289**

Renaissance (1965), **167**

Report from Kurnesh (Albanian)

Report on the Party and the Guests, A— see Party and the Guests, The

Repulsion (1965), **207**

Requiem for Five Hundred Thousand (1963), **168**

Resection of the Lungs (1961), **51**

Restless Ones, The/Nemirni (1967), 367, **392**, 401

Resurrection/Voskresenie (M. Schveitzer 1960-61), 280

Retarded Life (1960), **51**

Return, The/Povratak (1966), **385**, 387

Return/Zavrachtane (1967), **2**

Return of the Ikons (1965), **2**

Return of the Prodigal Son, The/Návrat ztraceného syna (1966), 44, 56, 66, **77**

Return of Vassili Bortnikov, The/Voz-vrashchenie Visiliya Bortnikova (V. Pudovkin 1953), 280, 327, 348

Return to the Old City (1952), **168**

Return to the Past/Powrót (1960), 169, 192, **203**

Revenge/Pomsta (1968), **43**, **77**

Revenge of the Outlaws, The/Răz-bunarea haiducilor (1968), **230**, 247

Revolt of Toys, The (1947), **82**

Revolutionary Year, The/Revoluční rok 1848 (1949), **61**

Rewarded Feelings (1957), **167**, **193**

Rhapsody in Wood (1960), **225**

Rhythm, **225**

Rhythms (1963), **234**

Rhythms and Images (1966), **227**

Rich Bride, The/Bogataya nevesta (1937), **319**

Right Man, The/A megfelelő ember (1959), **150**

Rimsky-Korsakov/Rimskii-Korsakov (G. Roshal 1953), 270

Risk, The—see Degree of Risk

Road, The/Doroga (1955), **342**

Road, The (1965), **234**

Road Begins at Mangishlak, The (1966), **305**

Roads, The (1958), **388**

Roads (1964), **234**

Road without Sleep/Doroga bez sna (1946), **351**

Roll-Call/Pereklichka (1965), **297**

Roll Call for the Insurgents (1961), **185**

Romance (1965), **72**

Romance for the Bugle—see Romance for Trumpet

Romance for Trumpet/Romance pro křidlovku (1966), **84**

Romeo and Juliet, **225**

Romeo, Juliet and Darkness/Romeo, Julie a tma (1960), **86**

Rondo/Rondo (1958), 195, **199**

Rondo/Rondo (1966), 361, **363**, 367, 389

Room for One/Miejsce dla jednego (1965), 165, **194**, 220

Roots (1963), **234**

Rose, The (1962), **199**

Rosemary's Baby (1968), 187, **207**

Roses for the Prosecutor/Rosen für den Staatsanwalt (1959), **117**

Rosina the Foundling/Rozina Sebranec (1945), **84**

Rotation/Rotation (1949), **117**

Round-Up, The/Szegénylegények (1965), **137**, 143, 153

Rumiantsev Case, The/Delo Rumyantseva (1955), 265, **288**

Russian Miracle, The (1963), 93, 115, **119, 120**

Russian Question/Russkii voproz (1947), **322**

Russian Women, The/Zhenshchiny (P. Lyubimov 1965), 307

Safe Journey, **51**

Sailor's Song/Das Lied der Matrosen (1958), 95, **109**, 111, **114**, 118, 121

Sailors Without a Sea (1958), **83**

Salonika Terrorists, The/Solunski atentatori (1961), **384**

Salt and Sweet (1963), **185**

Salt for Svanetia/Sol Svanetii (1930), **292**

Salto/Salto (1965), 172, 178, **188**, 192

Salt of the Black Country/Sól zlemi czarnej (1969), **191**

Salvation (1959), **186**

Samson/Samson (1961), 165, 216, **217**, 219

Sancta Simplicitas (1968), **250**

Sand and Stone (1967), **185**

Sandcastle/Peščeni grad (1962), **367**, 372, 393

Saragossa Manuscript, The/Rekopis znaleziony w Saragossie (1964), 172, **175**, 178, 179, 190, 204, 216

Saturday Evening/Subotom uveče (1957), **390**, 394

Saturday Night Dance, The/Balul de sîmbătă seara (1968), **253**

Sayat Novar/Sayat Novar (1969), **316**

Scarecrow, The (1957), **383**

Scenes of Battle/Barwy walki (1965), **203**

Scent of Almonds/Dah na bademi (1967), 10, 14, **26**

School, The (1958), **167**

School for Cats (1963), **72**

Schoolmistress, The/Tanitónő (1945), **139**

School of Work, The (1959), **257**

Science Closer to Life (1951), **201**

Science Workers (1966), **11**

Scissors and the Little Boy, The (1965), **32**

Scissors and the Little Girl, The (1966), **32**

Seasonal Workers (1965), **397**

Seasons/Anotimpuri (1963), **257**

Seat, The (1963), **215**

Second Bottle, The (1965), **7**

Second I, The (1964), **7**

Second Track, The/Das zweite Gleis (1962), **107**

Secretary, The (1966), **182**

Secretary, The (1967), **91**

Secret Code, The/Secretul cifrului (1959), **224**, 247

Secret Mission/Sekretnaya missiya (1950), **322**

Secret of Beauty/Sekret krasoty (1955), **331**

Secret of the Golden Shoes, The (1959), **6**

Secrets of Nature (1948), **359**

Secret Supper of the Sedmatsi, The/Tainata vecheria na Sedmatsite (1957), **5**

See You Tomorrow/*Do widzenia do jutra* (J. Morgenstern 1960), 172, 187, 207

Semmelweiss/*Semmelweiss* (1952), **125**

Senta Goes Astray/*Senta auf Abwegen* (1959), **101, 112**

Sentence, The/*Wyrok* (1961), **203**

Sentimental Story, A/*Poveste sentimentală* (1961), 236, **239**, 246, 252

September Love/*Septemberliebe* (1960), **109**

September Nights/*Zářijové noci* (1957), 45, **53**, 63

September 1956 (1961), **168**

September Thoughts (1961), **98**

Septembrists/*Septemvriitsi* (1954), 3, 12, 20, 34, **38**

Seryozha (The Splendid Days)/*Serezha* (1960), 267, **273**, 338, **343**

Seven Arts (1958), **250**

Seventh Continent, The/*Sedmi kontinent* (1966), **402**

Seven from the Rhine (1954), **119, 120**

Seven Nursemaids/*Sem nyanek* (1962), **269**, 278, 279, 291

Shadow, The/*Cień* (1956), **184**, 196, 211

Shadows of Our Forgotten Ancestors/*Teni zabytykh predkov* (1964), **316**

Sharik and Shurik (1960), **306**

Shells Have Never Spoken, The (1962), **227**

Sheriff Teddy/*Sheriff Teddy* (1957), **92**

She-Wolf, The/*Valchitsata* (1965), 15, **35**

Shibil/*Shibil* (1968), 27, **38**

Ship Is Born, A (1961), **197**

Ships Storm the Bastions, The/*Korabli shturmuyut bastiony* (1953), 267, **322**

Shipwrecks/*Wraki* (1957), 172, **205**, **206**, 207

Shiver-Fever, **241**

Shoe Inventor, The (1967), **369**

Shop on the High Street, The/*Obchod na korze* (1965), **58, 59**

Shop on the Main Street—see Shop on the High Street

Shop Window/*Za vitrinoi univermaga* (1955), 309, **326**

Shores and People, **11**

Shors/*Shchors* (1939), **341**

Short History (1956), **250**

Shot in the Head/*Fejlövés* (1968), **123**

Shots on the Stave/*Impuşcături pe portativ* (C. Grigoriu 1967), 236, 249

Show Is On, The/*Cirkus bude* (1954), **64**

Siberian Lady Macbeth/*Sibirska ledi Magbet* (1962), **217**, 380, 394, 400

Siberian Singing (1961), **306**

Sidetrack/*Otklonenie* (1967), 1, 14 **29**

Signals/*Sygnaly* (1959), **203**, 214

Signals over the City/*Signali nad gradom* (1960), **384**

Silence (Romania), **242**

Silence (Bulgaria) (1962), **32**

Silence/*Milczenie* (Poland) (1963), 172, **191**, 220

Silence/*Tishina* (U.S.S.R.) (V. Basov 1964), **346**

Silence and Cry/*Csend és kiáltás* (1968), **137**, 143, 162

Silent Barricade, The/*Němá barikáda* (1949), **84**

Silent Duel/*Duel i heshtur* (Albanian 1967)

Silent Planet, The/*Der schweigende Stern* (1959), 106, **109**, 114, 115, 218

Silent Ruins, **135**

Silesia in Black and Green, **194**

Silver Threads (1961), **140**

Silvery Wind, The/*Stříbrný vítr* (1954), **61**

Simple Love, A/*Fapados szerelem* (1959), **145**

Sin, The (1951), **200**

Singing Makes Life Beautiful/*Dalolva szép az élet* (1950), **139**

Singing Wood (1958), **200**

Sinner, The/*Grezhnitsa* (F. Filippov 1962), 329

Siqueiros (1968), **127**

Sisiphus (1967), **373**, **382**

Sisters, The/*Frona* (1954), **60**

Sisters/*Sestry* (G. Roshal 1957), 287

Six Hundred Years of Bydgoszcz (1946), **168**

Sixth of July, The/*Shestoe Yulya* (1968), **294**, 303

Skating Rink and the Violin, The (1959), **299**, **344**, 354

Sketch, A (1963), **33**

Skid/*Smyk* (1960), **46**

Skopje 1963 (1964), **364**

Sky Begins on the Third Floor, The/*Cerul începe la etajul 3* (1967), **240**

Sky Has No Bars, The/*Cerul n-are gratii* (1962), 228, **240**, 258

Sky Is Our Roof, The/*Kamienne niebo* (1959), 165, **205**, **206**

Skylark/*Pacsirta* (1964), 136, 143, 147, **148**, 161, 162

Sky of Our Childhood, The/*Nebo nashego detstva* (1967), **312**

Sky through the Leaves, The/*Kroz granje nebo* (S. Jankovic 1958), 391

Slavica/*Slavica* (V. Afric 1947), 394

Sledge, The (1955), 156, **157**

Sleeping Beauty, The (1953), **397**

Sleepless Years/*Álmatlan évek* (1959), 136, **145**, 151

Slightly Different World, A (1959), **183**

Slim and the Others/*Chudy i inni* (1966), **186**, 220

Slinger, The/*Práče* (1960), **57**

Smoke, The/*Dim* (S. Kosovalic 1967), 367

Smugglers/*Csempészek* (1958), **145**

Smugglers of Death/*Král Sumavy* (1959), **57**

Snowdrops (1964), **255**

Snow Fairy Tale/*Snezhnaya skazka* (1959), **332**

Snowman, The (1960), **4**

Snowman, The (1966), **82**

Snowqueen, The (1957), **264**

Snow Storm, The (1953), **234**

Soap Bubbles/*Seifenblasen* (1933), **94**

Soil, The (1964), **397**

Soil under Your Feet, The/*Talpalatnyi föld* (1948), **125**, 158

Soldier of Victory, The/*Zolnierz zwyciestwa* (1953), 178, **180**, 181, 192, 198

Soldiers/*Soldaty* (A. Ivanov 1956), 340

Soldiers Aren't Born/*Soldatami ne rozhdayutsya* (1968), **342**

Soldier's Father, A/*Otets soldata* (1965), **271**, 356

Soldiers without Uniform/*Soldati fara uniforma* (1960), **240**, 258

Solvay Dossier, The/*Geheimakten Solvay* (1952), 95, **101**

Someone Else's Children/*Chuzhie deti* (1959), **260**

Something Is Drifting on the Water/*Neco nese voda* (1969), 58, 59, 147

Somewhere in Europe/*Valahol Európában* (G. Radványi 1947), 131, 145

Song about Flowers (1959), **353**

Song about Iron (1963), **140**, 153

Song for Man/*Pessen za choveka* (1954), 3, 9, 13, **25**

Song for the Dead Miner, A/*Konjuh planinom* (1966), **370**

Song of Koltsov/*Pesn o Koltsove* (V. Gerasimov 1960), 327

Song of Siberia/*Skazanie o zemle Sibirskoi* (1947), 263, **319**

Song of the Dove (1960), **113**

Song of the Grey Dove/*Piesen o sivom holubovi* (1961), **40**

Song of the Prairie (1949), **81**

Songs and Dances by the River Mesta (1958), **2**

Songs of Motors (1961), **11**

Songs of the Vistula (1956), **168**

Sophia Perovskaya/*Sofia Perovskaya* (L. Arshtam 1968), 280, 334

Sorcerer's Apprentice, The, **225**

Source, The (1962), **182**

Souvenir from Calvary, A (1958), **177**

Space and Perspective in Painting (1964), **159**

Spartakiade, The (1960), **58, 59**

Special Duty/*Detyre e posacine* (Albanian)

Specialist, The (1969), **376**

Special Marks—None/*Besondere Kennzeichen: keine* (1955), **107**

Splendid Days, The—see Seryozha

Spring/*Vesna* (G. Alexandrov 1947), 270

Spring (1953), **257**

Spring (1966), **7**

Springer and the S.S. Men, The (1946), 43, **81**

Spring in Budapest/*Budapest tavasz* (1955), 131, 136, **145**

Spring in Moscow/*Vesna v Moskve* (1953), **288, 358**

Spring in Zarechnaya Street/*Vesna na Zarechnoi ulitse* (1956), **298**

Spring Songs (1961), **373, 382**

Spring Waters/*Jarní vody* (1968), **61**

Stable in Salvator, A/*Stajnia na Salwatorze* (P. Komorowski 1967), 198, 220

Stain on his Conscience, A/*Mrlja na savjesti* (1968), **402**

Staircase to the Sky/*Lestnitsa v nebo* (R. Vabalas 1966), 284

Stalingrad (1969), **272**

Stamp Collecting (1968), **113**

Stand Easy, Soldier (1967), **395**

Star, The (1965), **4**

Star Goes South, The/*Hvezda jede na jih* (1957), **64**

Star Named Wormwood, A/*Hvezda zvaná Pelynek* (1964), **50**

Stars/*Sterne* (1959), 20, 22, 34, 89, **122**

Stars (1963), **91**

Stars Must Shine (1954), **194, 201**

Stars of Eger, The/*Egri csillagok* (1969), **163**

State Criminal/*Gosudarstvenni prestupnik* (N. Rozantsev 1965), **274**

State Department Store/*Állami Áruház* (1952), **132**

Steel (1950), **103**

Steel (1959), **197**

Steel Made in Bulgaria (1954), **17**

Steel Town, The/*Zoceleni* (1950), **50**

Steep Hills/*Krutye gorki* (N. Rozantzev 1956), 307

Steep Path, The/*Stramnata pateka* (1961), 10, 14, 20, **37**

Steps to the Moon/*Pasi spre luna* (1963), 246, **250**

Stojan Mutikaš (1954), **371**

Stolen Airship, The (1966), **88**

Stolen Frontier, The/*Uloupená branice* (1947), 45, **86**

Stories about Lenin/*Rasskazy o Lenine* (1957), 280, 284, 310, 336, **355**

Stories of That Night/*Geschichten jener Nacht* (1967), **105**

Storm, The/*Vihar* (1952), 126, **128**, 136

Storm/*Fortuna* (1959), (Albanian)

Storm/*Shtorm* (M. Dubson 1959), 340

Story about a Factory/*Prica o fabrici* (1948), **390**

Story about the Road (1958), **213**

Story Books (1963), **2**

Story of a Crime (1962), **296**

Story of a Forest Giant (1954), **359**

Story of a Real Man/Povest o nasto-yashchem cheloveke (1948), 267, **342**

Story of a Second, The (1959), **140**

Story of Asya Klyachina, Who Loved but Did Not Marry, The/Istoriya Asi Kly-achinoi, kotoraya lyubila, da ne vyshla zamukh (1966), **299**, 329

Story of a Young Couple/Roman einer jungen Ehe (1952), **109**, 112

Story of Barnabáš Kos/Prípad Barnabáš Kos (1964), **78**

Story of Little Mook, The/Geschichte vom kleinen Muck, Die (1953), **117**

Story of My Stupidity, The/Butaságom tőrténete (1966), **139**, 151, 246

Story of Poor Hassan, The/Geschichte vom armen Hassan, Die (1958), **105**

Story of the Bass Cello (1949), **81**

Story of the Homeland (1955), **11**

Stoublen Lindens, The/Stublenskite lipi (1960), 3, **5**

Strange Adventure of Herr. Fridolin B/Seltsamen Abenteuer des Herrn Frid-olin B, Die (1948), **117**

Strange Mark of Identity, A/Különös is-mertelőjel (1955), 126, 151, **163**

Stranger, The/Străinul (1964), **233**, 246, 251

Streets Remember, The/Străzile au amin-tiri (1962), **237**

Stress of Youth/Trápení (1961), **57**

Strike, The/Siréna (1947), **79**

Stronger than the Night/Stärker als die Nacht (1954), **94**, 112

Strong in Spirit/Silnye dukhom (V. Georgiev 1967), 283

Structure of Matter, The (1951), **140**

Struggle for Bread (1950), **11**

Struggle for Peace (1950), **11**

Strzelno (1957), **182**

Study about Women, A/Tanulmány a nőkről (1967), **139**, 143, 147, 151

Study of a Working Day (1961), **141**

Substitute, The (1961), **402**

Subterranean, The/Subteranul (1967), **227**

Suicide (1967), **141**, 152

Suit Almost New, The/Ubranie prawie nowe (1964), **176**, 218

Suleiman the Conqueror/Solimano il Conquistare (1961), **383**

Summer Clouds/Bolond április (1957), **128**

Summer Day, A, **194**

Summer Is To Blame for Everything, The/Ljeto je krivo za sve (1962), **365**

Summer on the Baltic (1965), **213**

Summer on the Hill/Nyár a hegyen (1967), **123**

Summer Rain, A/Zápor (1960), 126, **142**, 147

Sun and Shadow/Slantseto i syankata (1962), 15, 21, 22, **35**

Sunday/Nedelja (L. Zaframović 1968), 361

Sunday at Six O'Clock/Duminiča la ora 6 (1965), 244, 246, **248**

Sunday Excursion/Sonntagsfahrer (1963), 95, **105**, 106

Sunday in August, A/Srpnová neděle (1960), **84**

Sunday Romance, A/Bakaruhában (1957), **129**

Sunny Whirlpool/Sončni krik (1968), **372**

Sun, Rain and Smiles (1962), **306**

Sun Rises Once a Day, The/Słońce wschodzi raz na dzień (1969), **186**, 220

Sunshine in a Net/Slnko v sieti (1962), 44, **83**

Supernumerary Girl, The/*Prekobrojna* (1962), **362**, 367, 393

Surfacemen (1957), **130**, 152

Surgery of Mitral Stenosis (1961), **51**

Surprising Hunt, The (1960), **276**

Swan Lake (1965), **31**

Sweet and Bitter/*Édes és keserü* (1966), 147, **157**

Swineherd, The (1957), **82**

Switchboard Operator—An Affair of the Heart/*Ljubavni slučaj ili tragedija službenice P.T.T.* (1967), **379**, 387

Sword and Dice/*Kard és kocka* (1959), **129**, 131, 151, 162

Szszecin—My Town, **194**

Tale about a Beetle, A (1963), **146**

Tale at Ursus, The (1952), **201**

Tale for Everyone, A (1965), **7**

Talent Competition/*Konkurs* (1963), 44, **49**, 70, 71, 73

Tale of the Pine Bough (1960), **6**

Tale on the Twelve Points/*Mese a tizenkét találatról* (1956), **144**, 151

Tales by Čapek/*Čapkovy povídky* (1947), 41, **50**

Tales from the First Republic/*Povídky z první republiky* (1965), 45, **60**, 67

Tales of a Long Journey/*Legenda a vonaton* (1962), **149**

Tamer of Wild Horses (1967), **366**

Taming of the Dragon (1953), **82**

Tana/*Tana* (Albania 1958)

Tango for a Bear/*Tango pre medveďa* (1966), **40**

Tank Brigade, The/*Tanková brigáda* (I. Toman 1955), 48

Tanners, The (1962), **234**

Taras Shevchenko/*Taras Shevchenko* (I. Savchenko 1951), 262, 267, 311

Tchaikovsky/*Chaikovski* (1969), 307, 317, 340, **343**, 350

Teacher, The/*Uchitel* (1939), **282**

Teacher, The (1955), **83**

Tear on the Face, A (1965), **403**

Teddy-Bear (1964), **296**

Teddy Brumm (1958), **113**

Teenager/*Smarkula* (1962), **170**

Telephone, The (1957), **255**

Telephone, The (1962), **383**

Television Fan, The (1961), **43**

Telltales/*Zalobníci* (I. Novák 1960), 73

Tenderness/*Nezhnost* (1966), **289**

Ten Golden Medals (1965), **127**

Ten Thousand Suns/*Tizezer nap* (1967), **141**, 152

Terra, **241**

Testimony of a Table in a Restaurant, The (1963), **227**

Test of Fidelity/*Ispytanie vernosti* (1954), **319**

Test Trip/*Próbaút* (1960), 136, **145**

That Cat/*Až přidje kocour* (1963), 43, 45, **53**, 63, 87

That Christmas/*Tenkrát o vánocích* (1958), **57**

That Czech Song of Ours/*Ta naše písnička Česká* (Z. Podskalsky 1967), 68

That Fine Day/*Tistega lepega dne* (1963), **398**

Théâtre de Monsieur et Madame Kabal, Le, **167**

Theme for a Short Story/*Syuzhet dlya nebolshogo raskaza* (1969), **355**

There Are Also People/*Tozhe lyudi* (1960), **273**, **343**

There Is No Death/*Smart nyama* (1963), **23**, 27, 29

There Lived an Old Man and an Old Woman/*Zhili-byli starik so starukhoi* (1964), **272**, 278, 279, 318

There Was a Lad/*Zhivet takoi paren* (1964), **337**

There Was a Man Roaming (1966), **8**

There Will Be No Leave Today (1959), **344**

These Are Horses/*Eto loshadi* (1965), **312**

They Called Him Amigo/*Sie nannten ihn Amigo* (1958), **92**

They Carve a New Way Forward (Albanian)

They Met in Havana (1961), **177**

They Sang in Sofia (1961), **30**

Thief of San Marengo, The/*Dieb von San Marengo, Der* (1963), **114**

Thirst/*Setea* (1960), 228, **231**, 245, 251

Thirteen Days/*Třinadeset dni* (S. Surchadgiev 1964), 12, 20

13th October, The (1949), **119**

Thirteenth Room, The/*Třináctá komnata* (1969), **84**

Thirty-three/*Tridsat tri* (1965), **273**, 338, 352

This Was My Path—see My Way Home

Thomas Muentzer/*Thomas Müntzer* (1956), **101**, 108

Thorn, The, (1967), **99**

Those Who Are Late/*Spóźnieni przechodnie* (1962), **178**, 179, **192**, 216

Thousand Cranes, A (1968), **17**

Threads of the Rainbow (1968), **17**

Three/*Tri* (1965), 386, **388**, 389, 404

Three, The/*Traja* (1969), **41**

Three Annes, The/*Tři Ane* (1959), **362**

Three Brothers and the Miraculous Spring, The/*Tři bratři a zázračny pramen* (1968), 62

Three Came from the Forest/*Troe vyshli iz lesa* (K. Voinov 1957), 313

Three Daughters/*Tri dcéry* (1967), **83**

Three Days of Victor Chernishov/*Tri dnya Viktora Chernisheva* (M. Ossepyan 1968), 286

Three Encounters/*Tri vstrechi* (1948), **355**

Three Fat Men (1963), 268

Three Fat Men/*Tri tolstyaka* (1966), **265**, 269

Three Heroes, The (1964), **31**

Three Hours for Love/*Tri sata za ljubav* (1968), **370**

Three Nights of a Love/*Egy szerelem három éjszakája* (1967), 143, **150**, 153

Three of Many (1961), **91**

Threepenny Opera, The/*Die Dreigroschenoper* (1962), **117**

Three Romanian Dances, **222**

Three Stars/*Három csillag* (1960), 131, **137**, 151, 162, **163**

Three Starts/*Trzy starty* (1955), **205**, **206**, 207

Three Steps in Life/*Trzy kroki po ziemi* (1965), **177**

Three Stories/*Trzy opowieści* (1953), **205**, **206**, 217

Three Teachers (1962), **33**

Three Wishes/*Tři přání* (1958), **58**, **59**, 381

Three Wishes (1967), **113**

Three Women/*Trzy kobiety* (1956), 198, **208**, 209

Through the Eyes of a Camera (1959), **83**

Thrown-up Stone, The/*Feldobott kő* (1968), **152**

Time Off (1964), **98**

Time Past/*Czas przeszly* (1961), **170**, 178, 198, 219

Time To Love, A/*Vreme ljubavi* (N. Rajić and V. Petrić 1966), 368, 394

Tips for Today (1959), **177**

Tisza—Autumn in Sketches (1963), **130**

Titanic Waltz/*Titanic Vals* (1964), **226**

To and Fro (1962), **130**

Tobacco/*Tyutyun* (1962), 14, **16**, 20, 27

To Come and Stay/*Doci i ostati* (1965), **362**

Today in a New Town (1963), **396**

Today or Tomorrow (1965), **142**

To Distant Shores (1958), **30**

Tolerance (1968), **369**

To Live One's Life (1963), **77**

To Love/*Atalska* (J. Donner 1964), 172

Too Late for Love?/*Godini za lyubov* (1957), 1, 14, **37**

Too Many Parents—see I Have Two Mummies and Two Daddies

To the Sky (1965), **238**

Tough Ones, The/*Delije* (M. Popovic 1968), 381, 387, 400

Tourist, The (1962), **77**

Tourists (1961), **31**

Town, The/*Grad* (1963), **385**, **392**

Towns Change Their Face, The (1958), **306**

Town Will Die Tonight, A/*Dzis w nocy umrze miasto* (1961), 190, 192, **210**, 216

Traces/*Samo ljudi* (1957), **362**, 380

Tracing Back 1907 (1957), **227**

Tracks in the Night/*Spur in die Nacht* (1957), **114**

Train Goes East, The/*Poezd idet na Vostok* (1947), **320**

Train that Disappeared, The (1966), **397**

Train Trip by Degrees, **51**

Train without a Timetble/*Vlak bez voznog reda* (1958), **364**, 380

Traitor, The/*Izdajnik* (1963), **392**

Transit Carlsbad/*Transit Carlsbad* (1966), **46**

Transport from Paradise/*Transport z ráje* (1963), **46**, 48

Trap, The/*Past* (1950), **50**

Travellers from the Vessel "Splendid"/ *Putnici sa Splendida* (1956), **399**

Treasure, The/*Skarb* (1949), **170**

Treasure at Vadul Vechi, The/*Comoara de la Vadul Vechi* (1963), **235**, 248

Treasure of Bird's Island, The (1952), **88**

Trees and People (1962), **77**

Trek, The—see Expedition, The

Trial, The/*Sud* (1963), **339**

Trio (1967), **164**

Trio Angelos/*Trio Angelos* (1963), **40**

Trip, A (1963), **2**

Trotter's Gait, The/*Prashai gulsara* (1969), **348**

Troubled Road/*Nespokoen pat* (1955), **3**, **5**, 10

Truth Cannot Be Hidden/*Húsz évre egymástól* (1962), 126, **129**

Tudor/*Tudor* (1964), **224**, 245, 247

Tunnel, The/*Tunelul* (1966), **240**, 249

Turbulent Town—see Boom Town

Turbulent Years, The—see Flaming Years, The

Turbulent Youth/*Trevozhnaya molodost* (1955), **262**, 311

Turkeys/*Indyuki* (V. Mikalowskus 1958), 284

Twenty Hours/*Húsz óra* (1964), **128**, 136, 147

Two, The, **266**

Two Captains/*Dva kapitana* (1956), 280, **349**

Two Comrades-in-Arms/*Sluzhili dva tovarishcha* (Y. Karelov 1968), 278, 279

Two Confessions/*Két vallomás* (1957), **139**, 162

Two Days—Like the Others/*Mindennap élünk* (1963), **149**

Two Faces of God (1960), **177**

Two Fedors/*Dva Fedora* (1958), **298**, 337

Two Grapes/*Dva zrna grozdja* (1955), **365**

Two Half-Times in Hell—see The Last Goal

Two Lives/Dve zhizni (K. Voinov 1961), 345

Two Men and a Wardrobe (1958), 186, 187, **207**

Two Mothers/Zwei Mütter (1957), **90**, 111

Two Mysterious Men/Dwaj panowie "N" (1962), **171**

Two Neighbours/Doi vecini (1958), **253**, 258

Two Portraits (1965), **142**

Two Sundays/Dva voskresenya (V. Shredel 1963), 283

Two Thousand-year Anniversary of Pécs (1955), **140**

Two Times a Dream/Tabliczka marzenia (1968), **171**

Two Times Two Are Sometimes Five/ Ketszer ketto néha 5 (1954), **150**

Two under the Sky/Dvama pod nebeto (1962), 13, **25**, 29, 34

Two Victories/Dve pobedi (1956), 9, **25**, 28, 34

Two Were Lonely, The/Samotnosc we dwoje (1969), **208**, 209

Typhoid Sufferers (1963), **383**

Typhus Has Destroyed (1946), **391**

Tzar and the General, The see King and the General, The

Ugly Story, An/Skvenei anekdot (1965), **262, 311**

Ukrainian Rhapsody/Ukrainskaya rapsodiya (1961), **316**

Unconquered/Nepokorennye (1945), **277**

Under Ancient Desert Skies (1961), **330**

Under the Blue Cupola (1962), **255**

Under the City/A város alatt (1953), 126, **134**

Under the Phrygian Star/Pod gwiazda frygijska (1954), **184**, 218

Under the Shadow of Magic (1955), **395**

Under the Wing of the Eagle (1963), **223**

Under the Yoke/Pod igoto (1952), **5**, 13, 20

Unfinished Business/Sprawa do zalatwienia (1954), **210**

Unfinished House, The/Casa neterminata (1964), **221**

Unforgettable/Nezabuvaiemoe (1969), **341**

Unforgettable Year 1919, The/Nezabyvaemyi 1919-i god (M. Chiaureli 1951), 334

Unforgettable Years, The (1957), **300**

Unfortunate Bridegroom/Svatba jako remen (1967), 48, **60, 73**

Uninvited Love/Neproshenaya lyubov (1964), **309**

Unknown, The/Nieznany (1965), **194**

Unloved Children (1964), **51**

Unlucky Little Elephant, The (1959), **113**

Unrepeatable Spring/Nepovtorimaya vesna (1957), **342**

Unsent Letter, The—see Letter that Wasn't Sent, The

Until Man Came (1960), **104**

Unwilling Inspectors/Revizory ponevole (1954), **341**

Up the River/Crne ptice (E. Galic 1967), 361

U.S.S.R.—America (1959), **306**

Valerie and the Week of Miracles/Valerie a tyden divu (1968), 62

Valley, The/A volgy (1967), **149**

Valley of Health and Quiet, The (1949), **51**

Valley of the Bees/Údoli vcel (1968), **85**

Valley Resounds, The/*Răsună Valea* (1949), 225, **226**

Vampire's Nostalgia, A (1968), **395**

Vangjush Mio (Albanian)

Variations upon a Theme (1961), **154**

Variety and Poetry Theatre, The (1967), **30**

Various Images (1964), **227**

Vaskata/*Vaskata* (1964), **25**

Vertigo/*Závrat̆* (1962), **57**

Victors, The (Albanian 1968)

Victory over Death/*Ngadhnjim mbi vdekjen* (Albanian)

Vietnam (1954), **295**

Village Mill, The/*Gromada* (1950), **184**

Village of Yastrebino (1965), **33**

Village on the Frontier, The/*Ves v pohraniči* (1948), **60**

Village Schoolteacher, The/*Selskaya uchitelnitsa* (1947), **277**, 348

Villa Negra/*Hattyúdal* (1964), **139**, 147, 158

Violin and the Dream, The/*Housle a sen* (1947), **61**

Virgo/*Zodia Fecioarei* (1966), 236, **237**

Virgo Constellation—see Constellation Virgo, The

Visas for London (1966), **11**

Visit (1963), **160**

Visit at Twilight/*Odwiedziny o zmierzchu* (1966), 179, **210**

Visitez Zakopane (1963), **177**

Visit from Space (1964), **369**

Visit in Hungary, A (1965), **127**

Vivat (1968), **200**

Vladimir Ilyitch Lenin/*Vladimir Ilyich Lenin* (1949), **322**

Voice from Beyond/*Glos z tamtego świata* (1962), 208, 209, 212

Voices of Spring/*Vesennie golosa* (1955), **321**

Volga Is Flowing/*Techet volga* (1964), **331**, 352

Volunteers/*Dobrovoltsy* (Y. Yegorov 1958), 346

Voronet/*Voronet* (1962), **223**

Voula/*Voula* (1965), **16**

Waiting for Godot (1964), **52**

Waiting for Letters/*Zhdite pisem* (1960), 283, **294**

Wait Until I Go to School (1961), **104**

Wake Mukhin Up/*Razbudite Mukhina* (1965), 283, **331**

Walking to Heaven/*Gyalog a mennyországba* (1959), **129**, 143, 162

Walk in the Bieszczady Mountains, A (1958), **213**

Walk in the Clouds, A (1967), **185**

Walk in the Old City, A (1959), **201**

Walkover/*Walkower* (1965), 186, **212**

Walls—see Lost Generation

Wandering/*Bloudění* (1965), 44, **48**, 56, **65**

War, The (1958), **182**

War/*Rat* (1960), **364**

War Against War (1960), **388**

War and Peace/*Voina i mir* (1964-67), **267**, 303, 328, 338, 345, 350

Ward No. 9/*9-es kórterem* (1955), **144**

Warm Years, The/*Tople godine* (D. Lazić 1966), 368

Warning, The/*Varuj!* (1947), **41, 50, 79**

Warrant-Officer Panin/*Michman Panin* (M. Shweitzer 1960), 345

Warsaw Début, The/*Warszawska premiera* (1951), **210**

Warsaw Mermaid, The/*Warszawska Syrena* (1956), **200**

Warsaw 1956 (1956), **168**

Warsaw Suite (1946), **200**

Watch Out for Cars—see Beware Automobile

Water-colour (1958), **353**

Waterloo (1969), **267**

Wawel Concert (1960), **197**

Way Home, The—see My Way Home

Way Up, The (1950), **119, 120**

Way to the Wharf, The/Put k prichalu (1962), **273**

We Are for Peace/My za mir (1951), **319**

We Are Two/Mi—dvoe muzhchin (Y. Lysenko 1963), 337

Wedding of Mr. Marzipan (1963), **383**

Wedding under Supervision—see Unfortunate Bridegroom, The

Week in a Quiet House, A/Týden v tichém domě (1947), **60**

We Live Here/My zdes zhivem (1957), **261**

Well, Young Man?/Hogy állunk, fiatalember? (1963), **150, 155**

We May Eat of the Fruit of the Trees of the Garden/Ovoce rajských stromů jíme (1969), **47, 62**

Western (1965), **113**

Westerplatte/Westerplatte (1967), **208, 219**

West Zone/Nyugati övezet (1954), **163**

We Were Young/A byahme mladi (1961), 9, 10, 12, 22, **39**

What a Night!/Micsoda éjszaka (1958), **150**, 151

What Shall I Be? (1966), **4**

What You Gave Is Life Itself (1963), **140**

When Angels Fall (1959), 186, **207**

When I'm Dead and White/Kad budem mrtav i beo (1968), **385**

When Love Was a Crime/Kiedy miłość była źbrodnia (1967), **210**, 314

When Roses Bloom/Kogda tsvetut rozy (1959), **351**

When Pigeons Fly/Kad golubovi polete (V. Radovanović 1968), 394

When Spring Is Hot/Cînd primăvara e fierbinte (1961), **254**

When the Mist Is Lifting/Viaţa nu iartă (1957), 236, **237, 239**

When the Trees Grew Tall/Kogda derevya byli bolshimi (1961), **302**, 337

Where All the Children Wave to the Passengers (1961), **399**

Where Are You Going? (1966), **164**

Where Do You Go? (1961), **183**

Wherever You Go/Wo Du hingehst (1957), **101**

Where Is the General?/Gozie jest General? (1964), **171**

Where Love Has Gone/Dvoje (1961), **388**

Where the Devil Says Goodnight (1956), **183, 213**

Where the Law Ends (1964), **395**

Where to, after the Rain?/Kula posle kiše? (1966), **396**

White Avenger, The (1962), **373, 382**

White Bus, The (L. Anderson 1966), 70

White Caravan, The/Belyi karavan (1964), **332**

White Dove, The/Holubice (1960), 48, **85**

White Fang (1946), **359**

White Moor/De-aş fi Harap Alb (1965), 246, **250**

White Nights/Belye nochi (1959), **319**, 338

White Room, The/Camera albă (1964), **227**, 245

White Trial, The/Procesul Alb (1965), **239**

Who Can Carry On Longer? (1962), **164**

Whoever May Know/Ktokolwiek wie . . . . (1966), **191**

Who Is Your Friend? (1967), **164**

Why? (1964), **77**

Why Is Mona Lisa Smiling? (1966), **43**

Widow and the Police Officer, The/*Az özvegy és a százados* (G. Palásthy 1968), 161

Wife of Husan-Aga, The/*Hasanaginica* (M. Popović 1967), 361, 367, 381

Wild Beasts/*Dravci* (1948), **86**

Wild Dog Dingo/*Dikaya sobaka Dingo* (1963), 283, **294**, 318

Wild Horses/*Tarpany* (1962), **191**, 220

Wild Shadows/*Divlje senke* (1968), 387, **392**, 400

Wilhelm Pieck—The Life of Our President (1950), 96, **119**

Wind, The/*Veter* (1959), **262**, **311**

Wings/*Krylya* (1966), **333**, 352

Wings of Song/*Krylya pesni* (1966), **261**

Winter Dusk/*Zimowy zmierzch* (S. Lenartowicz 1957), 179, 188

Winter Guests (1968), **223**

Winter in the Delta (1957), **234**

Wish Whatever You Want (1962), **146**

Witches of Salem, The/*Hexen von Salem, Die* (R. Rouleau 1957), 96

With Both Legs in the Sky (1968), **104**

With Faith in God/*S verom u boga* (1932), **391**

With Motorbike and Tent to Tunisia (1961), **98**

With Needle and Thread (1966), **257**

With Our Own Strength (1948), **103**

Without Fear or Reproach/*Bez strakha upreka* (1963), **308**

Without Lies/*Hazugság nelkül* (1945), **132**

With Special Praise (1967), **102**, **116**

Witness, The (1967), **102**, **116**

Wolf Trap/*Vlčí jáma* (1957), 44, **86**

Wolves' Echoes/*Wilcze echa* (1968), **211**, 314

Woman at the Helm/*Asszony a telepen* (1962), **129**, 151

Women Fight for Peace, The (1949), **257**

Women's Fate/*Frauenschicksale* (1952), **94**, 96

Wooden Rosary, The/*Drewniany różaniec* (1965), 165, **205**, **206**

Woodland Pond, A, **135**

Woof! Woof! (1965), **376**

Woolly Tale, The (1964), **82**

Work and Physical Culture (1958), **395**

Work of the Devil, The (1965), **369**

World Champion/*Chempion mira* (V. Gonchukov 1954), 352

Wounded in the Forest/*Ranny w lesie* (J. Nasfeter 1964), 202

Yakutia (1952), **285**

Year in Frank's Life, A (1967), **183**

Year One/*Rok pierwszy* (1960), 165, **194**, 211

Yes/*Igen* (1964), **150**, 155

Yesterday/*Tegnap* (1959), **139**, 147

Yesterday in Fact/*Naprawde wczoraj* (1963), 178, 192, **210**, 216

You (1963), **154**

You and I (1961), **306**

You Are a Criminal—Oberlander! (1960), **306**

You Are Guilty Too/*Partea ta de vină* (1963), 240, **242**, 253, 256

Young Days (1956), **58**, **59**

Young Eagle, The, **135**

Young Guard, The/*Molodaya gvardiya* (1948), 267, **282**, 326, 334, 345

Your Contemporary/*Tvoi sovremennik* (1967), **320**

Your Own Blood/*Rodnaya krov* (M. Yershov 1964), 315

Your Son and Brother/*Vash syn i brat* (1966), 327, **337**

Youth (1960), **58**, **59**

Youthful Years/*Mladá léta* (1952), **61**

Youth Is at Work (1946), **398**

Youth of Chopin, The/*Mlodość Chopina* (1952), **173**

Youth of Our Country, The/*Molodost nashei strany* (1946), **355**

Youth of Our Fathers/*Yunost nashikh otsov* (1958), **293**

Youth without Old Age/*Tinereţe fără bătrînete* (1968), **222, 247**

Yves Montand Sings (1957), **355**

Yvette's Millions/*Millionen der Yvette, Die* (1956), **101**

Zeppelin and Love, The (1947), **43**

Zigzag of Fortune/*Zig-zag udachi nezabuvaemoe* (1969), **321**

Zozya/*Zosya* (1967), 196, **266**